Studying and working in Spain

A student guide

Michael T. Newton
and Graham J. Shields

Manchester University Press
Manchester and New York

Distributed exclusively in the USA by Palgrave

Published by Manchester University Press
Oxford Road, Manchester M13 9NR, UK
and Room 400, 175 Fifth Avenue, New York, NY 10010, USA
www.manchesteruniversitypress.co.uk

Distributed exclusively in the USA by
Palgrave, 175 Fifth Avenue, New York, NY 10010, USA

Distributed exclusively in Canada by
UBC Press, University of British Columbia, 2029 West Mall,
Vancouver, BC, Canada V6T 1Z2

British Library Cataloguing-in-Publication Data
A catalogue record for this book is available from the British Library

Library of Congress Cataloging-in-Publication Data applied for

ISBN 0 7190 5472 9 *hardback*
0 7190 5473 7 *paperback*

First published 2001

10 09 08 07 06 05 04 03 02 01 10 9 8 7 6 5 4 3 2 1

Typeset in Ehrhardt and News Gothic
by Koinonia Ltd, Manchester
Printed in Great Britain
by Biddles Ltd, Guildford and King's Lynn

Studying and working in Spain

MANCHESTER
UNIVERSITY PRESS

Contents

Symbols

*	denotes a university run by the Catholic Church
**	denotes a private university
***	denotes a shared main campus
SC	indicates a 'satellite campus'

List of figures

Part 1

Part 2

Acknowledgements

Grateful thanks are due to the following who have given us invaluable help in our search for accurate information and data on various aspects of our subject:

Jesús Alonso Regalado, Senate Library, Madrid; Mayte Azorín, formerly Head Librarian, Instituto Cervantes, London; Peter Bakica, formerly Chief Executive, International House, Madrid; Maimie Balfour, Information Specialist, University of Northumbria; Inma Carmona Membrive, teacher of English, Córdoba; Mari-Ángeles Conejo Fort, lecturer in English, University of Málaga; Davina Dwyer, Overseas Placement Officer, University of Northumbria; Paul Garbutt, teacher of English, Barcelona; Gabriel Lozano Gutiérrez, EURES Officer, Madrid; Julio Montero, formerly of Fujitsu (computing division), Madrid; María de la Concepción Navarro López, Ministry of Education, Madrid; Antonio Pelegrín Griñán, teacher of English, Murcia; Mari-Carmen Pino, Student Services, University of Málaga; Alfonso Rizo Rodríguez, Head of English, University of Jaén; Javier Sanz, teacher of English, Zaragoza; Ellie Wilson, work placement student, Queen Elizabeth High School, Hexham.

We would also like to thank all those people, in the Spanish university system and other institutions, who have responded so helpfully to our persistent enquiries and filled in questionnaires.

Acronyms and abbreviations

(a) Acronyms

(i) Laws

LAU Ley de Autonomía Universitaria (1978)
LGE Ley General de Educación (1970)
LODE Ley Orgánica del Derecho a la Educación (1984)
LOGSE Ley de Ordenación General del Sistema Educativo (1990)
LRU Ley de Reforma Universitaria (1983)

(ii) Institutions

AGCAS Association of Graduate Careers Advisory Services
AIESEC Association International des Étudiants en Sciences Économiques et Commerciales
CBIET Central Bureau for International Education and Training
CCIVS Co-ordinating Committee for International Voluntary Service
CCOO Comisiones Obreras
CIEE Council on International Educational Exchange
CILT Centre for Information on Language Teaching
CiU Convergencia i Unió
COIE Centro de Orientación e Información del Empleo OR Centro de Orientación e Información al Estudiante
DSS Department of Social Security
EC European Community
EHT Escuela de Hostelería y Turismo
EOI Escuela Oficial de Idiomas
ETA Euskadi ta Askatasuna
ETT Empresas de Trabajo Temporal
EU European Union
EURES European Employment Services

FECEI Federación de Colegios de Enseñanza del Inglés
FRES Federation of Recruitment and Employment Services
IADE Instituto de Administración de Empresas
IASTE International Association for the Exchange of Students for Technical Experience
IB Instituto de Bachillerato
ICADE Instituto Católico de Administración de la Empresa
ICAI Instituto Católico de Artes e Industrias
ICE Instituto de Ciencias de la Educación
IES Instituto de Enseñanza Secundaria
IESE Instituto de Estudios Superiores de la Empresa
INEM Instituto Nacional de Empleo
INJUVE Instituto Nacional de la Juventud
INSALUD Instituto Nacional de la Salud
INSS Instituto Nacional de la Seguridad Social
LEA Local Education Authority
MEC Ministerio de Educación, Cultura y Deporte
NATO North Atlantic Treaty Organization
OJE Overseas Jobs Express
PNV Partido Nacionalista Vasco
PP Partido Popular
PSOE Partido Socialista Obrero Español
REC Recruitment and Employment Confederation
RENFE Red Nacional de los Ferrocarriles Españoles
RSA Royal Society of Arts
SAL Sociedad Anónima Laboral
SNS Sistema Nacional de Salud
SOPP Servicio de Orientación y Planificación Profesional
TIVE Turismo e Intercambio de Jóvenes y Estudiantes
UCD Unión de Centro Democrático
UCLES University of Cambridge Local Examinations Syndicate
UNED Universidad Nacional de Educación a Distancia
UNESCO United Nations Educational, Social and Cultural Organisation
VSO Voluntary Service Overseas

(iii) Other

CAP Curso de Aptitud Pedagógica
COU Curso de Orientación Universitaria
CV Curriculum Vitae
DELE Diploma de Español como Lengua Extranjera
EGB Educación General Básica
ESO Educación Secundaria Obligatoria
FE Further Education
FP Formación Profesional

GAP Gap Activity Projects
HE Higher Education
HND Higher National Diploma
IRPF Impuesto sobre la Renta de las Personas Físicas
ISIC International Student Identification Card
IVA Impuesto sobre el Valor Añadido
MBA Master in Business Administration
NIE Número de Identificación de Extranjero
PAAU Pruebas de Aptitud para el Acceso a la Universidad
TEFL Teaching English as a Foreign Language
TEFLA Teaching English as a Foreign Language to Adults
TESOL Teaching English to Speakers of Other Languages

(b) Abbreviations

Avda Avenida (Avenue)
C/ Calle (Street)
Ctra Carretera (Road)
dcha derecha (right)
DG Dirección General (Directorate General)
esq. corner
izda izquierda (left)
N/A not applicable
N/K not known
S.A. sociedad anónima
S.L. sociedad limitada
s/n sin número (no number)

those readers wishing to delve further into aspects of contemporary Spain, such as its political system, its education system and its economy, as well as other publications which look at aspects of studying and working in Spain.

The guide is intended basically for five groups of people. First, it is targeted at university students of modern languages (including Spanish) wishing to pursue similar studies alongside their counterparts in Spain who are studying either traditional academic degrees in the philology[2] of their chosen language(s) or more practical courses in translating and interpreting. Second, it aims to be of help to university students of other disciplines who wish to combine study of those subjects in a Spanish university with the opportunity to enhance their knowledge of and skills in spoken and written Spanish. Third, it hopes to be of use to independent students who wish either to transfer to Spain to do a full-time university course or to follow part-time a course of study in Spanish or any other subject. Fourth, it aspires to provide some advice and guidance regarding possible sources of employment for students and others looking for part- or full-time work in Spain. Finally, it aims to be of interest and use to academic staff and all those responsible for selecting and establishing contacts and partnerships with universities and employment agencies in Spain.

NB While postgraduate students will undoubtedly find much general information and advice that is useful to them in this volume, it should be realised that it is primarily intended for undergraduates. Those wishing to pursue postgraduate studies in Spain should consult their placement tutor and/or the European or International Office at their home university or college.

2 In practice, in Spain, departments of *filología* teach languages (including linguistics) and their related literatures.

Part 1
Background information

1.1
Spain yesterday and today

Spain today is a radically different country from that of only thirty years ago. Gone is the economic backwardness, the social stagnation, the political instability and the intractable divisions and conflicts that for centuries characterised the country and culminated in the savage civil war of 1936–39. In its place is a modern, industrial economy, a dynamic, free society, now released from the shackles of traditionalism, and a stable democratic state under the enlightened monarchy of Juan Carlos I. Spain is now a democracy where, for the first time in the history of the country, political parties can alternate in power without fear of army intervention.

Since the death in 1975 of one of Europe's most durable modern dictators, General Francisco Franco, the restoration of the Bourbon monarchy and the re-establishment of democracy in 1977 (with the country's first free elections since 1936), Spain has come a long way. However, it is difficult to appreciate that little over a quarter of a century ago the country was still in the grip of an iron autocracy in which political parties and trade unions were banned, there were no free elections and the regions of Spain had no say in the running of their own affairs (the Basque, Catalan and Galician languages were officially banned). Furthermore, until relatively recently, the media were shackled by the authoritarian state machine, and military courts tried not only terrorists of the extreme Basque nationalist group ETA, but many so-called political offenders who dared to speak out against the regime. Only in 1975 were Spanish women freed from the pernicious *permiso marital* whereby a married woman officially needed the permission of her husband before she could open a bank account, take a job, start a business or even undertake a journey of any length away from home.

However, by the mid-1970s it was basically only in the political domain that Spain remained frozen in an anachronistic system, left behind the rest of western Europe. Economically, following a World Bank report and the Stabilisation Plan of 1959, the country had experienced radical change as a new team of more pragmatic economic ministers steered Spain away from the dogmatic autarchy policy of the 1940s and 1950s, and opened up the economy to foreign trade, tourism and investment. Such was the success of this new policy that, in less than twenty years, Spain was transformed from an agricultural economy to one based on industry and services, and, during the so-called economic miracle of the 1960s, the country's economic growth rate, which at times reached seven per cent, was second only to that of Japan. The rapidly expanding tourist industry played a major role in Spain's growing prosperity. Economic change inevitably brought in its wake sweeping changes in Spanish society. Spaniards became predominantly town and city dwellers, the standard of living for many improved considerably and, in both attitudes and aspirations, many Spanish people, especially the young, were becoming much more recognisably European. Symptomatic of this change was the more relaxed attitude of the young towards peer relationships and their increasing indifference to the dictates of a once all-powerful Catholic Church. Once political freedoms were restored, the pace of change gathered momentum, particularly under the Socialist administrations of the former Prime Minister, Felipe González, who held power between 1982 and 1996. During this period, in response to increasing pressures from this more European society, the government enacted a wide range of progressive legislation designed to modernise the country, including the decentralisation of government, an abortion law and numerous laws to update and restructure the education system, to which a high priority was attached.

Spain's leaders were also determined to bring the country once and for all out of its traditional isolation from world affairs and to restore its international prestige. Following the restoration of democracy, Spain joined the Council of Europe (1977), NATO (1982) and the EC (1986), now the European Union (EU). In 1992 Madrid was designated the Cultural Capital of Europe and, in the same year, Seville and Barcelona hosted respectively the World Expo and the Olympic Games. In 1996 Granada's Sierra Nevada ski resort hosted the World Skiing Championships and in 1999 Seville was the chosen venue for the World Athletics Championships. Moreover, in stark contrast to the former years of isolation and ostracism, Spaniards of talent and energy have played key roles in European and international institutions. Two Spaniards, Enrique Barón and José-María Gil-Robles have held the prestigious position of president of the European Parliament, and Javier Solana, now the EU's top spokesperson/envoy on foreign and defence affairs was, until July 1999, Secretary-General of NATO. For many years, Federico Mayor was Secretary-General of UNESCO. In the world of sport, where once no one had heard of any Spanish competitors, a number of energetic and talented Spaniards have, in recent years, made their mark in their chosen field, to the point where they are household names, in some cases even in the UK. Names that immediately spring to mind in this context are: Luis Enrique and Raúl (from the world of football), Severiano Ballesteros, José-María Olazábal and Sergio García (from golf), Carlos Sainz (the rally driver) and Arantxa Sánchez-Vicario, Conchita Martínez and Carlos Moya (who have reached the top rankings in international tennis).

However, it must be said that, for all the commendable improvements that have taken place, Spain is still a country beset with problems. The terrorism perpetrated by ETA is still capable of inflicting indiscriminate destruction on life and property; the relaxation of the former police state has brought dramatic rises in crime rates and citizen insecurity; in spite of recent improvements, Spain has the highest rates of unemployment in the EU in a country where benefit levels are still below the European average; and there are still many pockets of both rural and urban poverty untouched by the changes of recent decades. As successive governments of both left and right continue to apply almost Thatcherite economic policies, the gap between rich and poor seems to grow ever wider.

Nevertheless, any impartial assessment of Spain's development over the last thirty years or so must conclude that, in general, the balance sheet has been positive. One thing at least is indisputable: the Spanish people of today have left behind the deep divisions and antagonisms of the past and seem to be working together in a spirit of tolerance and co-operation to build an open, free and stable Spain which is participating as an active and enthusiastic member of the EU.

1.2
Spanish regions

Figure 1.1 Autonomous communities of Spain

One of the major changes brought about by Spain's new leaders in the late 1970s, and enshrined in the 1978 constitution, was the creation of a new regional structure for the political and administrative organisation of the country. The period 1979–83 saw the establishment of seventeen autonomous communities, each endowed with its own president/chief executive, parliament, government, civil service and regional court of justice. The parliaments of these self-governing regions are elected every four years by direct universal suffrage in a manner which reflects exactly the system which operates at national level for the election of Spain's lower (and senior) legislative chamber, the Congress of Deputies (*Congreso de los Diputados*).

While the system established still falls short of a federal one, these regional authorities have assumed considerable powers of legislation and executive responsibility for their own affairs. This is particularly so in the case of the 'big four' regions, Andalusia, the Basque Country (*Euskadi*), Catalonia (*Catalunya*) and Galicia, which from the outset were granted a greater degree of autonomy than that conceded to other regions. In the case of the last three, their historic regional languages *euskera, catalán* and *gallego*, are now co-official with Castilian Spanish in those regions. Regional elections act as an additional barometer of political opinion, as well as, in the case of the Basque Country and Catalonia, a means of institutionalising strong nationalist opinion.

Since the first regional elections held in Catalonia in 1980, the nationalist *Convergencia i Unió* (*CiU*) has enjoyed continuous power, and in the Basque Country the nationalist *Partido Nacionalista Vasco* (*PNV*) enjoyed exclusive power from 1980 to 1986 after which it became part of a coalition, either with the socialist *Partido Socialista Obrero Español* (*PSOE*) (1986-98) or with other nationalist groups (since 1998). In Galicia, however, the Conservative *Partido Popular* (*PP*) has enjoyed almost continuous exclusive power while the PSOE has remained unchallenged in Andalusia.

This regional structure has important implications for education since responsibility for all aspects of education has now been devolved to the autonomous communities. This includes higher education, which in practice in Spain means the universities. Each regional goverment has a ministry of education (*consejería de educación*) which, in the case of multi-provincial communities, is represented in each of the component provinces. For example, the regional government of Andalusia, the *Junta de Andalucía*, includes the *Consejería de Educación y Ciencia* which has offices or *delegaciones* in the eight provinces of the region, each of which now contains at least one university. While the *Junta* (like other regional governments) retains direct control over the universities, responsibility for primary and secondary education has been partially devolved to the provincial offices.

Although the running of education has been devolved to regional goverments, the basic structure of education remains essentially the same all over Spain. Thus, academics wishing to set up exchanges with institutions there need not fear that there will be wide-ranging differences, as in Germany, between the different regions of the country. They will, however, need to be aware that in certain regions, notably Catalonia, there is a strong emphasis on the use of the regional language in educational establishments. Staff and students should check in advance to ensure that their chosen lecture programme is delivered in Castilian (*castellano*), the Spanish language most likely to have been studied beforehand in the UK.

1.3
Spanish education system

1.3.1 **Before and after the Spanish Constitution of 1978**

The Spanish Constitution, approved in Parliament and by a national referendum in 1978, marks a watershed in the development of education in Spain. Prior to this time, and in particular during the regime of General Franco, it is fair to say that education was not accorded a very high priority. Whilst it is also true that, even at the time of writing (2001), Spain still lags behind many EU countries in terms of percentage of GDP spent on education, considerable progress has been made to bring the country into line with best practice elsewhere.

Article 27 of the Constitution refers specifically to education. It establishes the right of all to an education that will be guaranteed and based 'on respect for the democratic principles of coexistence and fundamental rights and freedoms' and stipulates that 'basic education' is to be compulsory and free of charge. Teachers, parents and even pupils, where appropriate, are given a say in the control and management of all publicly-funded schools and colleges. Parents are guaranteed the right for their children to receive a religious and moral education in line with their own convictions and children are no longer, as before (when Catholicism was the official religion in Spain), to undergo compulsory instruction at school in the Catholic faith. These and other changes to school education were to be enshrined, six years later, in the Right to Education Act (1.3.3). With regard to higher education, clause 10 of article 27 recognises the autonomy of the universities, though leaves it to subsequent legislation to spell out what this would imply. This is examined in sections 1.4.2 and 1.4.3.

1.3.2 **General Education Act (*Ley General de Educación/LGE*) 1970**

Until the early 1980s, the Spanish education system had remained virtually unchanged since the General Education Act of 1970. This Act had, at least in theory, marked a major milestone in Spanish educational history, freeing it for the first time from the stranglehold of traditionalism imposed by the Catholic Church and Franco's only legal political organisation, the quasi-Fascist National Movement. Changes in Spanish society during the late 1950s and the 1960s, notably in the direction of its economic development and consequently modified employment structure, needed urgently to be complemented by radical reforms in the education system of a country that was rapidly industralising. Thus the basic intention of this legislation, following a long period when education at all levels was a privilege for the lucky few, was to expand provision, particularly for the extended primary school sector (see below), providing mass education for the first time. Other specific provisions included the introduction of some state-controlled nursery schools, the reorganisation of primary and secondary education and, within these sectors, the modernisation of methods of teaching and assessment (for example, bringing in continuous assessment to replace regular end-of-year examinations). Another major aim, in practice of limited success, was to expand and improve vocational education, long neglected in Spain.

The 1970 law proposed a fundamental structural shake-up. Primary education, known as 'basic general education' (*educación general básica/EGB*) and provided in mainly state-run *colegios nacionales*, was to cover the 6–14 age-group (previously it had catered for those aged 6–10), while secondary education, known as middle-school education (*enseñanzas medias*), was to comprise a choice between an academic and a vocational or technical route. The former led to the *bachillerato*, a grammar school type of education provided in either state-run *institutos nacionales* or in private *colegios*.[1] Most pupils successfully completing the *bachillerato* were expected to aspire to a university education; this was a three-year course leading to an A-level equivalent examination in a wide range of subjects. The *bachillerato* did not, however, provide a selection process for university; those wishing to enter university had to follow a one-year pre-university year known as the *Curso de Orientación Universitaria* (*COU*). Subsequently, since the mid-1970s, pupils have also had to take a special university selection examination known popularly as *selectividad*.

1 Many private *Colegios* in fact cater for pupils from the beginning of primary school to the end of secondary and may even include a nursery section.

The alternative form of secondary education consisted of a two-stage vocational route provided normally in *centros de formación profesional*, both state-run and private. Level 1 of *formación profesional* (*FP*) was a three-year course leading to an intermediate qualification in a specific trade or profession; students wishing to acquire a more advanced level qualification could proceed to Level 2. Subsequently, a one-year bridging course provided an alternative route to higher education. Because of an ingrained bias among the parents and employers in particular against vocational education, this route has always been much less popular than the academic route. The hope is, however, that under the new education law (*LOGSE*) (see below), this will be possible in the future (see Figure 1.2).

1.3.3 **Right to Education Act (*Ley Orgánica del Derecho a la Educación/LODE*) 1984**

The next major change in education had to wait until 1984 when the then Socialist government, against considerable opposition from the combined might of the right and the Catholic Church, introduced its Right to Education Act, known popularly by its Spanish acronym, *LODE*. Reduced to its simplest form, the aim of this Act was to induce as many private schools as possible (at that time the majority among primary schools, mainly owned by the Church and religious orders) to submit themselves to public control, via governing bodies known as *consejos escolares* (schools' councils), in exchange for state (in practice, now regional) funding of such schools. Under such arrangements, education has to be free of charge and centres are no longer allowed to practise selection. Moreover, the composition of the *consejos* (which have the power to appoint and dismiss head teachers and other staff), was designed to ensure a much wider participation of the public in the management of such schools, with owners constituting no more than 20 per cent of elected members and teachers, parents and (in some cases) pupils making up no less than 40 per cent. While certain concessions were eventually made to allow ex-private schools to retain their own ethos (*ideario*), basically the government got its way and henceforth a new generation of schools, the *colegios concertados* (maintained schools) came into being.

1.3.4 General Organisation of the Education System Act (*Ley de Ordenación General del Sistema Educativo/LOGSE*) 1990

Despite the positive changes introduced by the LODE, the latter did not include major structural changes, which were long overdue (particularly at the secondary level but with obvious implications for the primary stage). These came with the *LOGSE*, which, following the now generally accepted European model, establishes a cut-off point for primary education at the age of 12 and provides a common programme of secondary education for all 12–16 year olds. The latter is known as *educación secundaria obligatoria* (*ESO*) – compulsory secondary education. After talking about it for many years and paying lip service to the idea, the Spanish Ministry of Education (*Ministerio de Educación/MEC*) eventually raised the school leaving age from 14 to 16. *ESO* comprises two cycles of two years' provision, the first of which consists of a wide range of subjects (*asignaturas*), including a compulsory foreign language, usually English. The second stage, however – a real innovation of the Act – includes a significant vocational element for all pupils, the idea being to overcome past prejudice against vocational subjects and to encourage gifted students to follow the vocational path in future.

The Act also devised a completely new-look *bachillerato* which, in addition to compulsory core subjects such as physical education, history, Castilian language and a foreign language, offers pupils a choice between four options or *especialidades*: (i) humanities and social sciences; (ii) natural and health sciences; (iii) the arts; and (iv) technology. This programme looks like a compromise between the UK system (with its narrow A-level specialisation) and the previous wide-ranging Spanish course. The pre-university year course, the *COU*, has been eliminated (in reality incorporated into the *bachillerato*). However, the university entrance examination remains, with the somewhat indigestible title *pruebas de aptitud para el acceso a la universidad* (*PAAU*).This continues to be administered by the universities themselves.

It should also be noted that at the base of this fundamental restructuring of Spanish education was a firm commitment on the part of the Socialist government of the day to an expansion of nursery education (*educación infantil*) for the 0–6 age group. In this aspiration, unlike others (see below), the *MEC* can be proud of the fact that virtually all the 4–6 age group now attend a nursery school, much of this provision having been supplied in recent years by the new regional authorities. There is also a good deal of steam, not as yet discouraged by the PP government elected in 1996, behind the initiative to achieve the same goal for all three-year-old children.

The *LOGSE* was theoretically supposed to be implemented gradually over the ten-year period from 1990 to 2000. At the time of writing (2001), however, the prospects of the process being completed by the original deadline are virtually nil and several changes to both content and timing have already had to be made in response to complaints and requests from the teachers themselves. None the less, Spanish primary and secondary education are, albeit slowly, coming to the end of what has been a long (and often far from trouble-free) period of transition, as the old system has been phased out and the new one gradually introduced. One major problem has been the need to equip the expanded secondary schools with the extra classrooms needed to accommodate the additional secondary-level pupils. In general, the former *institutos de bachillerato* cater for the 14–16 age group (as well as those aged 16–18), while existing primary schools cover the needs of 12- and 13-year olds. Over time, new secondary schools, known as *institutos de enseñanza secundaria* (*IES*), will replace the former *institutos.* Naturally, this problem, plus the need for staff retraining, has involved considerable extra expenditure. It now looks as if the new scheme will not be fully operational before the year 2002 at the earliest (see Figure 1.3).

1.4 Higher education in Spain

Prior to 1970, Spanish higher education, overwhelmingly in the hands of the state, was characterised, like much of the rest of the system, by severe deficiences both of quality and resourcing. This had much to do with the low priority which Franco himself – always highly suspicious of intellectuals – attached to the sector, as with the narrow-minded traditional attitudes promoted by successive ministers of education who showed little interest either in modernising the range and content of courses or in fighting for much-needed resources. Long-delayed action was taken only when, from the late 1960s, the dictator's more open-minded 'technocratic' ministers urged on him the need for reform in the interests of the economy. The fact that between 1962 and 1969 the number of university enrolments rose from some 60,000 to 150,000 must also have concentrated the minds of the authorities. Indeed, there existed a lamentable situation in which, by 1970, Spain had one of the highest ratios in western Europe of students per head of population and, proportionally, one of the lowest numbers of universities (no more than twenty, including four private institutions).

1.4.1 Universities and the General Education Act 1970

A major aspiration of this Act, which recognised the educational needs of a newly industrialised and rapidly developing society, was to expand opportunities in higher education. Subsequently, the authorities set about creating new universities and expanding existing ones with the establishment of university colleges (*colegios universitarios*) and university schools (*escuelas universitaras*) in provinces which had no institutions of higher education. These provided first-cycle higher education courses lasting three years. The so-called 'autonomous' universities, as well as the early polytechnic universities, were born at this time (late 1960s and early 1970s) (see 1.4.4). This was also the period when all forms of higher education, from diploma up to doctorate level, were integrated into a single university system. A significant step was taken in the direction of the democratisation of universities with the decision to replace the system of government-appointed university vice-chancellors (*rectores*) by one of election by all members of the teaching staff (*claustro*) for a limited four-year term.

In theory, the 1970 Act envisaged the progressive granting of some powers to universities to run their own internal affairs; a *patronato* (board of trustees), endowed with some decision-making authority, was to be set up in each university. In practice this, plus several other changes recommended in the Act, was never implemented – partly because of ingrained traditionalism (especially among the professors or *catedráticos*) and partly because of the severe political unrest which had characterised Spanish universities in the late 1960s and which continued almost unabated until Franco's death in 1975. Such unrest had often given the regime an excuse to water down the proposed reforms.

1.4.2 **University Autonomy Act (*Ley de Autonomía Universitaria/LAU*) 1978**

After the return of democracy to Spain, a conscious effort was made to give a higher priority to education. Following the general election of 1977, there was a prolonged period of consultation between the new centrist government of the *Unión de Centro Democrático* (*UCD*) and the universities, which culminated in the submission of a bill to Parliament in November 1978. The draft law, known by its Spanish acronym, *LAU*, contained measures to give universities more autonomy, while retaining some of the weaknesses of the old system, such as the powers of the *catedráticos*. However, for almost five years, it proved impossible to reach a consensus on the final content of the bill. Ironically, the advent of democracy in public life seemed to serve only to politicise arguments over education and hinder progress towards reform. One example of this was the impasse reached over the idea of placing the universities under the control of regional governments. This proposal was supported by much of the left plus Basque and Catalan nationalists, but strongly opposed by the right and other traditionalist pressure groups. In the end, time ran out for the bill, which was never approved by Parliament,

Figure 1.2 Structure of education from 1970

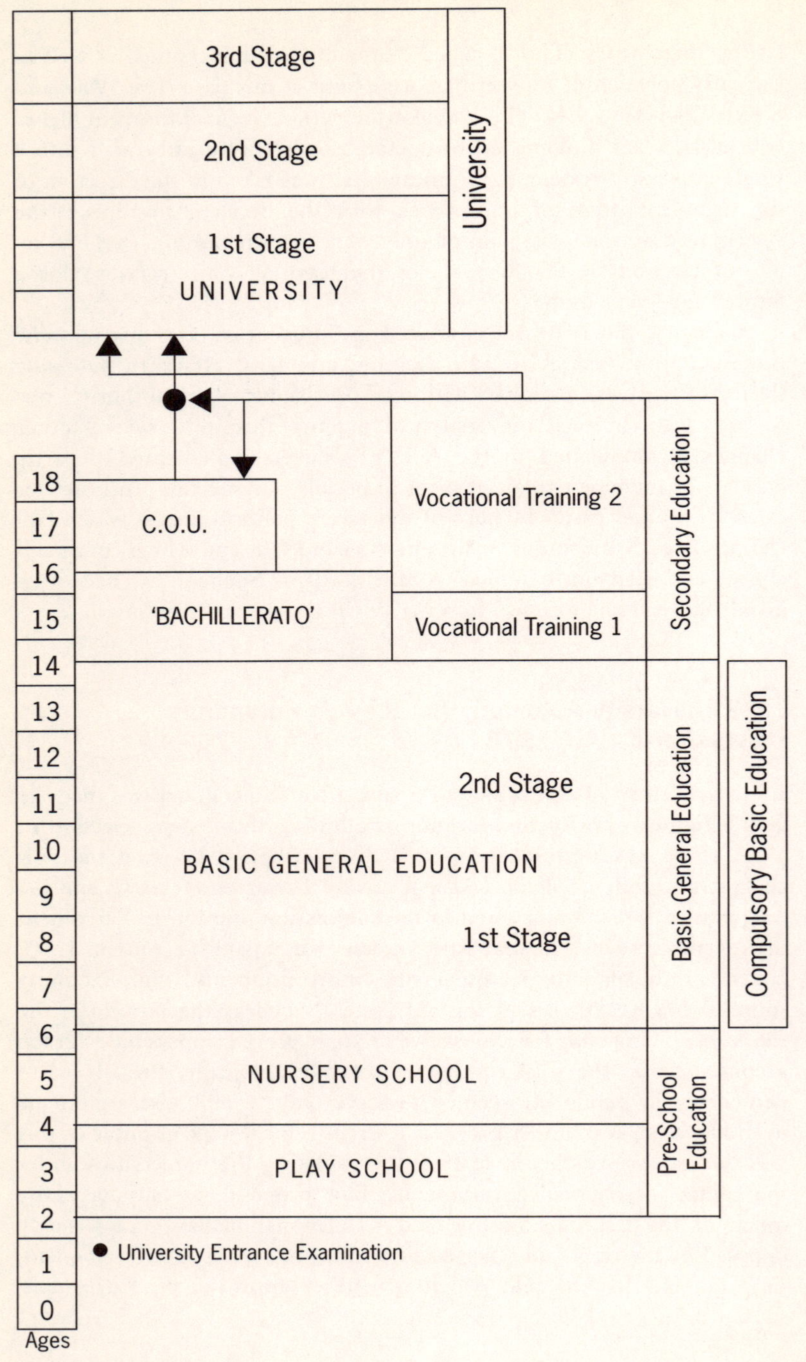

Figure 1.3 Structure of education from 1990

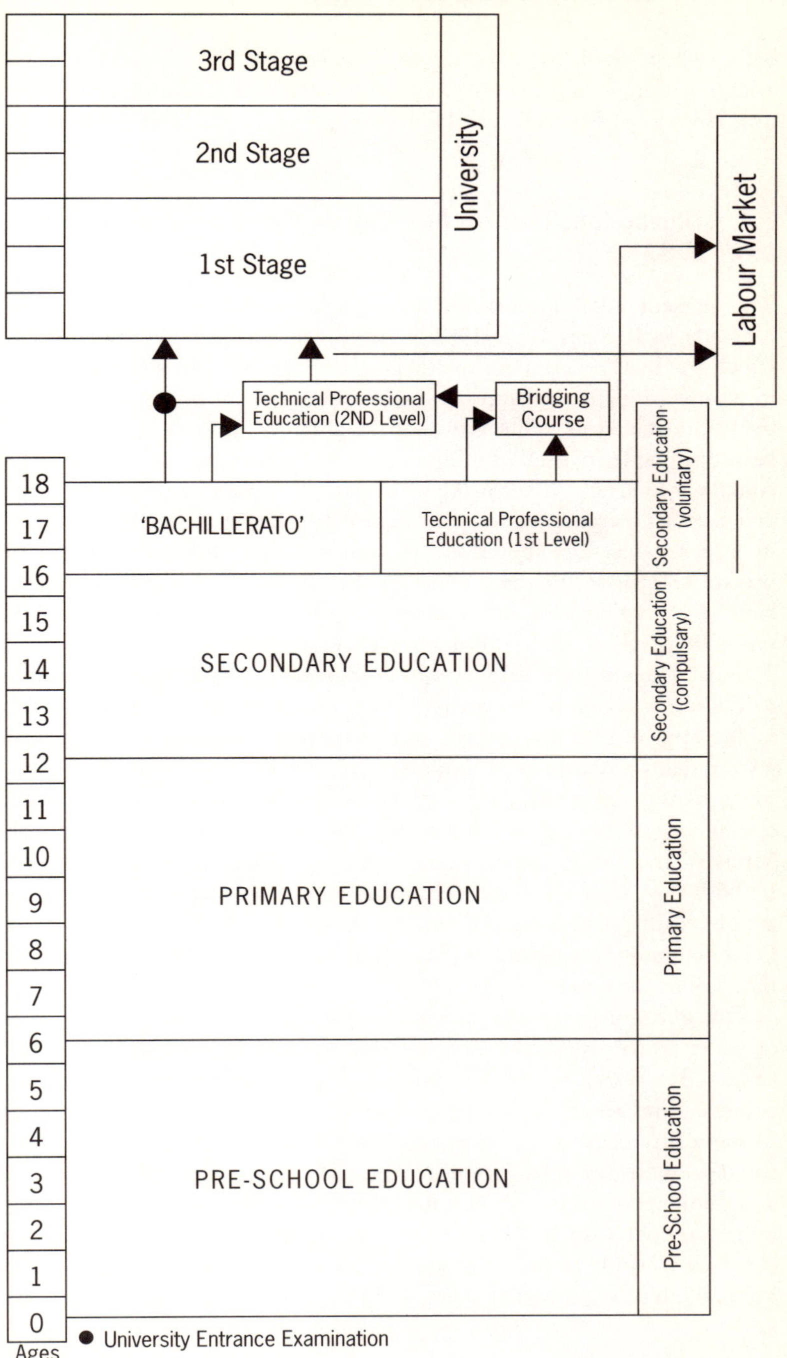

before a new (Socialist) government was elected in 1982. The latter, with a huge parliamentary majority, had no difficulty in pushing through its own law which, ironically, contained many features of the ill-fated *LAU*.

1.4.3 **Universities Reform Act (*Ley de Reforma Universitaria/ LRU*) 1983**

The present legal foundation for higher education in Spain is the Universities Reform Act of 1983, known by its Spanish acronym *LRU* to which the new government of Felipe González was strongly committed in its determination to improve higher education in Spain and bring it up to the standards of its European neighbours. This Act specifies the basic principle of self-administration or autonomy for universities contained in article 27 of the Constitution. For example, institutions are given considerable freedom with regard to such areas as their budget, internal organisation, appointments, course design and partnerships with private enterprise. In the context of the latter, the Act created a new kind of governing body or social council, the *consejo social*, composed of representatives of both the academic community and local civic and political organisations. While central government, through the *Ministerio de Educación, Cultura y Deporte* (*MEC*), retains important powers, such as the approval of new degree titles and inspection, the new regional governments were given an important role in the funding and management of the universities (as well as all schools) in their autonomous communities. The co-ordination of the whole system between the Ministry and the regional *consejerías* was now the responsibility of the Universities' Council (*Consejo de Universidades*) made up of experts appointed by parliament, representatives of the central government and the autonomous communities, as well as the vice-chancellors (*rectores*) of the various universities.

One of the major consequences of the 1983 law has been the creation of more universities (the number has more than tripled in the last twenty-five years) and the provision of many more degree and diploma courses. Until relatively recently, a Spanish student's choice was restricted to some fifty courses but, over the last fifteen years or so, that number has been increased considerably (to over 150 in the year 2000) and more are coming on-stream all the time. Furthermore, students now have more freedom than in the past in terms of the number of options and electives available to them, in addition to their core subjects (see 1.4.8). Increasingly, too, in recent years, as in the UK, programmes have been reorganised on the basis of credit systems as the process of unitisation or modularisation has gatherered momentum in Spanish universities. Likwise, the academic year in most institutions has been divided into two four-month 'semesters' known as *cuatrimestres*.

1.4.4 **Types of institution**

The first point to stress is that, whatever names may be used, there is a single unified system of higher education in Spain. All institutions are either universities in their own right or, as in the case of university colleges, belong to a university. Over time, universities have evolved with the following designations:

(i) *Universidad* (University)
(ii) *Universidad Autónoma* ('Autonomous' University)
(iii) *Universidad Politénica* (Polytechnic University)

Apart from the name, there is very little difference, if any, between the *universidades* and the *universidades autónomas*. The polytechnic universities, however, tend to concentrate on advanced technical subjects, including engineering, and have a high concentration of higher technical schools (see below). Both the autonomous and polytechnic universities have been founded during the last thirty-two years and are small in number. The former are located in Barcelona and Madrid and the latter in Barcelona (Polytechnic of Catalonia), Cartagena (founded as recently as 1998), Madrid and Valencia.

The major sub-divisions of Spanish universities are as follows:

(i) *Facultades*[2] (Faculties)
(ii) *Colegios Universitarios* (University Colleges)
(iii) *Escuelas Técnicas Superiores* (Higher Technical Schools)
(iv) *Escuelas Universitarias* (University Schools) (see 1.4.7).

1.4.5 **Public and private universities**

At the time of writing (2000), Spain has sixty-seven universities, including seventeen which are privately run. The latter can be categorised into those run by the Catholic Church (six) and those run by private foundations

2 Some universities have abandoned the traditional faculty structure and are now divided into *Departamentos* (Departments).

(eleven), most of which have been last decade, following parliamentary approval in the early 1990s of a law legalising the establishment of private universities. Partly as a reaction to the increasing demand for higher education in the country and partly as a reflection of the enthusiasm of the regional authorities to exercise their new right to found and manage universities, no less than twenty-seven of these have been founded since 1990.

The total figure of sixty-seven includes Spain's Open University (*Universidad Nacional de Educación a Distancia/UNED*) which was founded in 1972 with its central offices in Madrid and its equivalent in Catalonia, the *Universidad Oberta de Catalunya* (*UOC*), which opened in Barcelona as recently as 1995. The *UNED* (the term by which this institution is best known) is part of the public sector but, unlike all other public universities, is still controlled by the *Ministerio* in Madrid. The *UOC*, on the other hand, belongs to a private foundation. Also worthy of a separate mention, since they do not function as conventional universities, are the three so-called 'international universities' which specialise, on the one hand, in one-off conferences and refresher courses for academics from Spain and abroad, and, on the other, in summer courses for both home and foreign students. These are the long-established *Universidad Internacional de Menéndez Pelayo,* located in Santander and founded in 1932, the *Universidad Internacional de Andalucía,* founded in 1994 with campuses in Baeza (in the province of Jaén) and La Rábida (in the province of Huelva), and the *Universidad Internacional de Cataluña* founded in Barcelona in 1997. Of these the first two are public and the last private institutions.

In the academic year 1998-99 no less than 1,482,445 students were enrolled in the public universities and 96,347 in the private ones, giving a total of 1,578,792. By far the largest university in Spain, with 110,934 students is the *Universidad Complutense de Madrid* followed by the *Universidad de Sevilla* with 75,948 – although it should be mentioned that technically the *UNED*, with 134,428 enrolments in the same year, caters for the most students.

Size, however, is not everything, though it may, to some extent, reflect a university's popularity. Prestige is sometimes attached to age, as in the Oxbridge tradition. The oldest universities in Spain are: the *Universidad de Salamanca,* founded in 1218, the *Universidad de Valladolid* (1346), the *Universidad de Barcelona* (1430) and the *Universidad de Zaragoza* (1474). The newest public universities, created in the last decade, are the *Universidad Politécnica de Cartagena* (founded in 1998), the *Universidad Pablo Olavide de Sevilla* (founded in 1997), the *Universidad Miguel Hernández de Elche* and the *Universidad Rey Juan Carlos de Madrid* (both founded in 1996). A number of the new universities created in the 1990s were originally university colleges, often founded in the 1970s and dependent on well-established universities within the region. Such were the cases of the *Universidad de Jaén* and the *Universidad de Almería*, previously both part of the *Universidad de Granada*, and the *Universidad de Huelva*, formerly attached to the *Universidad de Sevilla*.

New universities in the private sector, both religious and secular in nature, also mushroomed during the 1990s. A little-known law allowing the Catholic Church to continue to found new universities was invoked to create the *Universidad Católica 'Santa Teresa de Jesús' de Avila* and the *Universidad Católica 'San Antonio' de Murcia*, both approved in 1998 by the appropriate regional authorities, the *Junta de Castilla y León* and the *Región de Murcia*. Of the new secular foundations, which account for the bulk of the expansion in this sector, the most recent is the *Universidad Camilo José Cela*, founded in 1998 and named after Spain's best known living novelist. No less than four were founded in the fertile year of 1997: the *Universidad Internacional de Cataluña*, the *Universidad de Mondragón* (in the Vizcaya province of the Basque country), the *Universidad Internacional SEK de Segovia* and the *Universidad de Vich* in Catalonia.

It is somewhat ironic that the impetus for the creation of the new private universities, founded with the intention of providing competition for those in the public sector, came with the later Socialist administrations of Felipe González in the early 1990s. Perhaps not surprisingly, this process has been encouraged by the Conservative government of José María Aznar since its election in 1996. From the point of view of students (and their parents), the main advantage of these institutions is that they have far fewer students than most public universities and offer (generally) good quality education, based on high quality facilities and healthy staff–student ratios. Their main disadvantage is that their enrolment (*matrícula*) and tuition fees (*tasas académicas*) are invariably higher than those in the public sector.

Perhaps not surprisingly, however, in view of the speed at which these developments have appeared to take place, the creation of some new universities has not been without controversy. A case in point was the *Universidad Miguel Hernández de Elche* which was eventually established in 1996 by a decree of the government of the autonomous community of Valencia, the *Generalitat*. The core of this new university were the faculties of medicine and statistics of the *Universidad de Alicante* located on the satellite campus of Elche. The proposal was opposed not only by the university authorities in Alicante but by virtually the whole body of

Spain's *rectores* who argued that the new university, apart from being damaging to Alicante, was not academically viable. At stake really was the question of who has the ultimate say over the creation and control of new universities, the central government via the *Consejo de Universidades* (where the *rectores* have an important voice on the academic committee) or the regional authorities. To the chagrin of the vice-chancellors, the then minister of education, Esperanza Aguirre, ruled that ultimate authority lay with the regional government of Valencia, the *Generalitat de Valencia.*

1.4.6 **Location of institutions**

Until the quite recent move to release the pressure on some of Spain's overcrowded campuses, universities were normally located solely in provincial capitals and by no means in all of them. In most cases, these bear the same name as their province and take the name of that province (Figure 1.4). For example, the *Universidad de Granada* is situated in Granada city, the capital of the province of Granada, while the *Universidad de Salamanca* is situated in the city of Salamanca, the capital of the province of the same name.

However, in several cases a university has campuses in several provinces of the same region or autonomous community; these usually take the form of university colleges, higher technical schools or university schools (1.4.7.1). The *Universidad de Zaragoza,* for example, has campuses in all three provinces of the region of Aragón: Huesca, Teruel and Zaragoza itself.

A further feature of the Spanish university scene is that, in large cities like Barcelona and Madrid, different universities actually share campuses. Thus, in the national capital, for example, the *Universidad Politécnica de Madrid* shares the 'Complutense' campus with the *Universidad Complutense de Madrid,* while the public *Universidad Autónoma de Madrid* does likewise with the private *Universidad Pontificia de Comillas* at Cantoblanco. Another feature of the system is that satellite campuses of different 'parent' universities can coexist in the same provincial capital; for example, both the *Universidad Complutense de Madrid* and the *Universidad Autónoma de Madrid* have outposts in Segovia, significantly in a different autonomous community. Another example of a university having a campus outside its own region is the *Universidad de Alcalá de Henares* (in the region of Madrid) with an outpost in Guadalajara (located in Castilla-La Mancha). While such situations can and sometimes do lead to administrative and financial problems, it is encouraging to see that, in

Figure 1.4 Location of Spanish universities

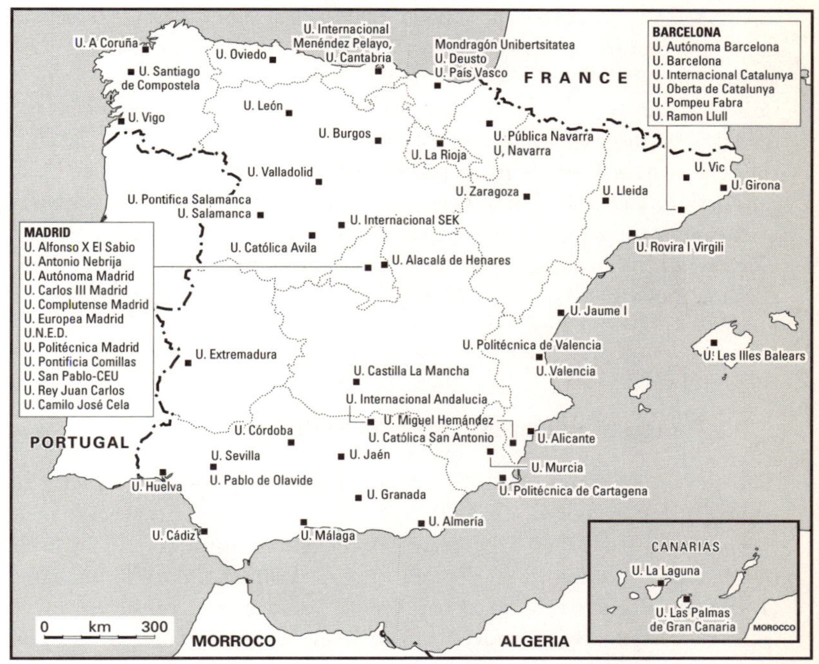

this case, common sense has prevailed – Guadalajara campus belonged to Alcalá long before the new regional arrangements were set in place and, in fact, is geographically quite close to the parent university.

A number of universities, mainly of recent foundation, have adopted the name of the autonomous community where they are located; examples of these are the *Universidad de Cantabria* (in Santander), the *Universidad de Extremadura* (in Badajoz and Cáceres), the *Universidad de Castilla-La Mancha* (with campuses in four provincial capitals), the *Universidad del País Vasco* (with main campuses in Bilbao, San Sebastián and Vitoria) and the *Universidad de La Rioja* (in Logroño).

In a limited number of cases, notably in the private sector, universities have satellite colleges in quite distant cities. The Opus Dei[3]-dominated *Universidad de Navarra,* for example, has campuses in Barcelona, Madrid and San Sebastián, the first two accommodating centres of the prestigious business school, the *Instituto de Estudios Superiores de la Empresa* (*IESE*). Another case is the *Universidad San Pablo-CEU*, whose main facilities are in Madrid but which has campuses in places as diverse as Barcelona, Elche, Seville, Valencia and Valladolid. This university is rather unique in the sense that the educational trust that owns and manages it, the *Fundación San Pablo,* finances a whole network of educational centres from primary schools up to university level. The *SEK* foundation, based in Segovia, is part of an even more complex web of institutions: in addition to linked colleges in Spain (for example, La Coruña and Valencia), there are associated universities and colleges abroad, including Quito in Ecuador, Santiago in Chile, Budapest in Hungary and even Reading in the UK.

1.4.7 **Range of university courses in Spain**

The provision of university education is divided into three cycles or *ciclos*: (i) first cycle (*primer ciclo*), leading to a diploma; (ii) second cycle (*segundo ciclo*), leading to a degree or licienciate; and (iii) third cycle (*tercer ciclo*), leading to a doctorate (*doctorado*). As already indicated (1.4.3), in recent years there has been a rapid expansion of approved courses, particularly at undergraduate level, including short, three-year

3 This lay Catholic organisation was founded in 1928 by the Aragonese priest Monseñor Escrivá de Balaguer with the aim of promoting traditional Catholic values in all walks of professional life. In the 1960s, many of its members rose to occupy influential positions, for example, within the Cabinet, in business and commerce, in education and in publishing.

Figure 1.5 Basic structure of higher education in Spain

Centres (Centros)	*Courses (Carreras)*	*Awards (Titulos)*
Facultades Colegios Universitarios	Licenciaturas	Licenciado/a
Escuelas Técnicas Superiores	Ingeniería Arquitectura	Ingeniero/a Arquitecto/a
Escuela Universitaria	Ingeniería Técnica Arquitectura Técnica Diplomatura Formación del Profesorado	Ingeniero/a Técnica Arquitecto/a Técnica Diplomado/a Maestro/a

diploma courses (*carreras de ciclo corto*) and longer degree courses (*carreras de ciclo largo*) lasting four or five years. Most standard degree courses are composed of a *primer ciclo* of two years followed by a *segundo ciclo* of two more years – although the current tendency is to move back to what, only ten years ago, was the traditional pattern in Spain of five years, comprising a first cycle of three years followed by a second cycle of two. For students wishing to transfer after the first cycle to a different (but compatible) degree programme, most universities offer at least some 'second cycle only' (*sólo segundo ciclo*) courses (see Appendix I).

1.4.7.1 Undergraduate courses

These are delivered largely in three types of university institutions:

(i) The faculties (*facultades*) and university colleges (*colegios universitarios*) offer a wide range of standard degree courses. Courses in faculties tend to last either four or five years; in the university colleges, courses may last four or five years (covering two cycles) or three if only the first cycle is offered. The one exception to this is medicine, where courses invariably last six years. The university colleges consist of one or more faculties and are often satellite institutions located in a different province from the parent university (see 1.4.6). The most populated faculties are law and economics/ business studies which in 1998-99, including public and private universities, together accounted for nearly 340,000 students, almost 23 per cent of the total student body.

(ii) The higher technical schools (*escuelas técnicas superiores/ETS*) offer high level qualifications which are the equivalent of degrees in subjects like agriculture, architecture and various forms of engineering. These courses normally last five years. Many of these schools are located in the polytechnic universities. The *Universidad Politécnica de Madrid* had 47,649 enrolments in its higher technical schools in 1998-99 and the *Universidad Politécnica de Catalunya* 36,949. As with the university colleges, a number of these institutions constitute satellite campuses and are located in a different town or province from the parent university.

(iii) The university schools (*escuelas universitarias*) offer three-year diploma courses in a very wide range of subjects, including business studies, information science, librarianship, nursing, optics, and teacher training (primary education). Students completing some of these courses may aspire, via a bridging course, to higher level study in a faculty, university college or higher technical school. A large number of these are located in provinces other than that of the parent university and some are even found in towns other than provincial capitals. One example of this is the *Escuela Universitaria de Enfermería,* which specialises in nursing, in Ronda, in the province of Málaga.

In addition to the three categories of centre described above, a number of universities are endowed with institutes (*institutos*) some of which are free-standing and some of which have been attached to exisiting faculties. Some universities have no institutes at all, while others are endowed with a large number. The *Universidad Complutense de Madrid,* for example, has no less than twenty-seven. One of the best known of these is the *Instituto Católico de Administración de Empresas* (*ICADE*), a prestigious business school located within the *Universidad Pontificia de Comillas* in Madrid. This groups together the faculties of economics/ business and law. The staff of a high percentage of institutes are involved in advanced research and many do only a limited amount of teaching. Most universities are endowed with an Institute of Education (*Instituto de Ciencias de la Educación/ICE*), which, among other things, runs the equivalent of the UK PGCE courses for graduates aspiring to teach in secondary schools (see 1.4.7.2).

Appendix I provides a complete list of the undergraduate degree and diploma courses currently available throughout Spain. It can be safely assumed that the *carreras de ciclo largo* are offered in the faculties, university colleges and higher technical schools, while the university schools are limited to the teaching of *carreras de ciclo corto*. It is also a safe assumption that postgraduate courses and supervision of doctoral research is carried on only in faculties, colleges and higher technical schools.

1.4.7.2 Postgraduate courses

Though currently undergoing review, teacher training in Spain is currently divided into two kinds of provision. Undergraduates aspiring to teach in secondary education must follow a short three- or four-month postgraduate course in the *Instituto de Ciencias de la Educación* (*ICE*). This course is popularly known as the *CAP*, the acronym for *curso de aptitud pedagógica* – course in teaching proficiency. Some students in fact follow the *CAP* while they are completing the final year of their degree. Those intending to teach in primary education must follow a three-year diploma course, equivalent to a British B.Ed. at a university school. This course is known as *formación del profesorado* or, occasionally, by its former title *magisterio*.

The wide range of postgraduate study that is enjoyed in the UK is not available in Spain. MA or M.Phil. courses really have no equivalent in Spain – although some universities now offer part-time Masters courses for working professionals (e.g. in the tourist industry) and private business schools like *ICADE* offer quite prestigious (and expensive) Masters or MBAs. In fact, as yet, none of these intermediate qualifications have official status comparable to diplomas, licenciates and doctorates (see 1.4.9).

1.4.8 **Composition of undergraduate courses**

The continuing role of the *MEC* in Madrid is reflected in the fact that every diploma and degree course in the country contains a number of common core subjects (*asignaturas troncales*) which may account for up to 30 per cent of the overall course programme or *plan de estudios*. These compulsory subjects are set by the *Consejo de Universidades* and panels of subject experts drawn from various universities. These subjects should not be confused with the *asignaturas obligatorias*; the latter are also compulsory subjects, accounting for approximately 40 per cent of the curriculum, but are set by each university offering that particular diploma or degree. The individual universities also have control over lists of options (*asignaturas optativas*) relating to each programme of studies; these may account for a further 20 per cent of the whole programme.[4] In addition, students have a free choice from a list of institution-wide electives (*asignaturas de libre configuración*) offered by each university and

4 The percentage for *troncales*, *obligatorias* and *optativas* can vary quite widely depending on the institution and course concerned. Normally the aggregate percentage for the first two of these is 70.

accounting for 10 per cent of the whole. (In fact, this is the only one of the above percentages that is rigidly fixed; there is also a compulsory requirement that the subject or subjects taken must be from another course of study.) As in the UK and other countries, each individual subject has a credit rating.

1.4.9 **Qualifications**

Most degree courses in Spain last for four or five years and lead to the award of a *licenciatura,* equivalent to a UK BA or B.Sc. etc. The holder of this degree is entitled to be known as a *licenciado* (male) or *licienciada* (female). Successful architecture and engineering students are awarded the title of *arquitecto/a* and *ingeniero/a* respectively.

Most diploma courses, normally offered in the university schools, last three years and lead to the award of a *diplomatura,* roughly equivalent to a UK HND. The holder of this award is entitled to be known as a *diplomado* (male) or *diplomada* (female). However, in technical subjects, such as architecture and the various branches of engineering (which in fact constitute the majority of courses available), the award made is that of *arquitecto/a técnico/a* or *ingeniero/a técnico/a.* Qualified primary school teachers also have a different title: they are known as *maestros* or *maestras* (see Appendix I).

In terms of prestige, there is little doubt that students would prefer to be awarded a *licenciatura* or become a fully qualified *arquitecto* or *ingeniero.* However, graduate unemployment, particularly in the arts and humanities fields, has become a very serious problem in Spain in recent years. Thus, from the strict employment point of view, there is much to be said for the achievement of a lower level, but more practical, qualification such as *ingeniero técnico*, where the prospects of obtaining work are often better.

One thing that UK students will discover from conversations with their Spanish counterparts is that progression from one year to the next is more fluid than in Britain. It is not unusual, for example, for say third-year students to be studying subjects from the second year during their third year, and in general there is no limit to the number of times candidates can resit examinations. In fact, quite a high percentage of students do not complete courses within the standard time limits of three years for diplomas and four or five years for degrees. This naturally has many financial and social implications for both the students concerned and their families.

1.4.10 Current issues in higher education

In spite of all the changes, and many undoubted improvements, which Spanish higher education has undergone during the last twenty years or so, there is little doubt that many of the problems which beset the system in the past have not been eradicated. The lack of adequate resourcing still lies at the heart of the matter; among the countries of the EU, Spain remains at the lower end of the league in terms of the percentage of GDP devoted to education and specifically to higher education. As before, the situation is exacerbated by the question of overcrowding (*masificación*), only partially resolved by the creation of new universities and the releasing of pressure on some of the most crowded campuses, such as the *Complutense de Madrid* and the *Universidad de Barcelona*. Thus, with the exception of most of the private universities, staff–student ratios continue to be some of the worst in Europe – with all that this implies for the fostering of good relationships between the tutors and those in their charge. Eventually, the falling birth rate, whose effects are already being positively felt in primary and secondary education, will have some impact on the situation. However, until either a much more rigid selection system is introduced (always fiercely resisted in the past) or until a massive injection of additional human resources (i.e. teaching staff) is approved by government, it is difficult to see how this deep-rooted problem can be overcome.

If one of the worst features of the old structure was its overpowering centralisation, there is little doubt that the devolution of control over universities to the regional tier of government will undoubtedly have gone some way to breathing new life into the system. Although in the final analysis, funding comes from central government (since that is by far the main source of financing for the autonomous communities), there is some hope that public–private partnerships at the regional level may lead to new funds being generated for the 'local' institutions of higher education. Unfortunately, however – as we have seen in the controversy which surrounded the creation of the *Universidad Miguel Hernández de Elche* – this devolution has not always gone smoothly and vested interests of all kinds still militate against its full implementation. In any case, the reserve powers of the *MEC* are still considerable and more substantial, ironically, than those retained by central government in a country like the UK where the process of regional decentralisation has barely begun.

1.5
Courses in Spanish for foreign students

Whether part time or full time, students wishing to study in Spain are likely to require some tuition in Spanish language. Part-time students may well wish to limit their experience, either in a gap year or during a summer vacation, to the learning of Spanish, while full-time students, perhaps as part of their compulsory year studying and/or working in the country, will see tuition in Spanish as an essential part of their academic experience. The latter may even need to present a certificate in language attainment to their tutors on return to their home country.

While certain universities, in addition to the long-established specialist in this field, the *Universidad Internacional de Menéndez Pelayo* in Santander, have been providing intensive courses during the summer months for many years, there has been no generalised university tradition in Spain, as in France, of offering all-year-round Spanish courses to foreign students as part of a national commitment to promoting the language and culture of Spain. Over the last two or three decades there has certainly been a steady increase in the number of universities offering both summer and all-year courses in response to increasing demand from abroad. However, due to the already well-established position of independent language schools in many cities and towns, including well-known chains like Berlitz, Inlingua and International House, the university authorities felt for many years that they were under no obligation to include Spanish language tuition as a regular part of their academic programme. After all, until the mid/late-1980s, the numbers of foreign (and certainly UK) undergraduates spending a term or longer in Spain was low, being mainly confined to students of modern languages who often, in any case, had an A-level or equivalent qualification in the language.

Over the last fifteen years or so, however, there have been significant changes, for reasons largely related to the European Union. First, the

European Commission decided to launch various ambitious programmes geared to promoting greater student (and indeed staff) mobility within the Union. This led to the establishment of schemes such as Erasmus, Lingua and Comett, now replaced by Socrates and Leonardo, which gave financial incentives to encourage exchanges not merely between students of languages but of a wide range of other disciplines. Second, and in response to this initiative, universities in member countries (and in particularly the UK, which had lagged behind in this respect) reshaped many of their non-language undergraduate courses to include the compulsory study of a European language, allied to an obligatory study and/or work placement (usually in a student's third year) in the relevant country. Hence the sudden growth in the numbers of students of business studies, engineering and health studies, for example, attending Spanish and other universities of the EU. Third, following Spain's entry into the EC in 1986, university authorities and academics wasted no time in taking advantage of the new opportunities available and in seeking links with educational institutions in other member countries. Up to this time, it had been virtually impossible for Spanish students of languages to afford to study in the relevant countries. Prior to 1986, while increasing numbers of British students of Spanish, for example (including many from the expanding polytechnic sector), were heading for a semester in Spain, very few of their Spanish counterparts were able to come to the UK.

Now, the whole situation has changed quite dramatically. Not only are increasing numbers of British students (both language and non-language) spending substantial periods in Spain, but vastly increased numbers of their Spanish counterparts (and indeed exchange partners) have been arriving here. On both sides, greater efforts have been made to provide 'back-up' language courses to cater for this new generation of Euro-students. Spanish educational authorities have had to reassess their traditional provision in line with the requirements of students from other European countries. In general, special efforts have been made to provide for those students participating in officially-supported exchanges like Socrates.

UK students wishing to study Spanish language (and culture) in their host university/town may have one or more of the following options:

(i) An open course, standard or intensive, provided by the university itself all year round or for a semester, usually offering from beginners to advanced level;
(ii) An open summer course, usually an intensive month-long course and offering courses from beginners to advanced level;

(iii) An intensive limited access course specially designed for Socrates/ Erasmus students from various countries and scheduled for the first month or so of the year or semester;

(iv) An intensive limited access course specially designed to suit the requirements of students from one particular linked institution. Such a course (not so common) is likely to form a part of reciprocal institutional arrangements. It may include a part devoted to 'Spanish language for special purposes', e.g. Spanish for engineers or Spanish for nurses;

(v) In the host city or town, it is quite possible that there will be one or more Spanish language schools offering a range of courses throughout the year similar to those described in (i) and (ii). More often than not, options in Spanish culture are included, along with excursions and visits to local sites of historical and cultural interest;

(vi) Some of the major cities are endowed with an Official Language School (*Escuela Oficial de Idiomas/ EOI*) designed mainly for Spanish students. These schools are not part of any university but are run by the government (through the *Ministerio de Educación, Cultura y Deporte/ MEC*) and offer a wide range of language courses at all levels. Many courses run in the evenings.

Students must pay fees in the case of (v) and (vi) and may pay in the cases of (i) and (ii) if they are not participating in an official exchange with a linked university. Specially designed courses described in (iii) and (iv) are not normally subject to fees as they are likely to have been subsidised by grants from the EU.

Students who require or wish to secure a qualification in Spanish officially recognised by the *MEC* should make enquiries about the existence of a *DELE* course. These letters stand for the *Diploma de español como lengua extranjera* (Diploma in Spanish as a foreign language) which is awarded by the *Instituto Cervantes*, the prestigious body set up in Spain in 1986, with branches all over the world (including the UK – see addresses in Appendix II) to spread and promote knowledge of Spanish language and culture. This diploma is offered at three levels – initial, basic and advanced. Examinations take place in designated centres twice a year; they test all language skills, as well as grammar and vocabulary.

Information on Spanish language and culture courses is published periodically by *MEC* in a very comprehensive book entitled *Cursos de Lengua y Cultura para Extranjeros*. This covers courses provided by both official institutions (mainly the universities but also the EOI language schools) and a whole range of private organisations. A useful document entitled *Language Courses in Spain* is published by Canning House. This also covers official and private institutions but is less comprehensive (for addresses, see Appendix II).

1.6
Working in Spain: an overview

It is becoming increasingly common for British school-leavers to take a year out to work abroad between the end of their sixth-form studies and their entry into higher education. University admissions tutors will look positively on a constructive year out and often highlight the extra maturity the experience brings to students. The process of finding employment (paid or voluntary) has become less daunting over the years through the use of agencies specifically set up to help students intercalating a year between school and university (for example, GAP, VSO, CIEE). These organisations assist you to find a work placement in Spain but opportunities and procedures do vary from one organisation to another. For example, you will need to pay a fee to register with GAP and you need to ensure that you are fully aware of other expenses, such as travel, insurance and medical cover, that you may be expected to find. There is also a limited number of places available each year and a reasonable command of the language will usually be necessary. The voluntary nature of the work does not mean that you receive no financial remuneration, as you will be given accommodation and full board as well as a pocket money allowance.

At the undergraduate level, the creation of the European Union and the development of the Erasmus student exchange schemes and Lingua project (especially for language learning) are the most important parts of the EU's Socrates programme to help students move freely between member states. These initiatives have stimulated a great deal of interest among students in the idea of spending part of their degree programme abroad, and UK and Spanish universities and companies have set up exchanges to cover a wide range of subjects and work placements.

The benefits of these placements are many, including: an active and positive attitude through work; increasing self-confidence and future employability; cultivating a sense of independence; expanding your knowledge and horizons; and earning money to help with your future years at university. At university a period of residence abroad, either studying at another European university, undertaking work placements or a mixture of both, is often (for example, on language degree courses) a required element of the course. These schemes have many advantages, for it usually means that the placements have been tried and tested, and that university tutors will have personal contacts in the partner university or company. Some university departments offer the work placements as part of the degree package and will offer to provide (or at least help to provide) a job, usually for between three and nine months. It is vital that you ascertain at the outset whether the work placement is a compulsory or optional part of the course and also whether a job will be found for you or whether you will be expected to make your own arrangements. Similarly, you need to determine whether the employment is paid or unpaid, as this will have an obvious bearing on your financial situation and your eligibility for certain benefits. In many cases students can request a year out to work abroad even when this is not part of the course. Naturally, this has to be agreed by the teaching department and you need to ask yourself why you want to take a year out of your studies and carefully assess the pros and cons of following this route. For those looking to work only part of the year, seasonal and vacation opportunities do exist as well as opportunities to assist in an academic environment (for example, in Spanish schools). More details can be found in sections 2.5.2.4 and 2.5.2.6.

As already mentioned, the benefits of working abroad are many. Most students are attracted by the idea of an overseas location, but that in itself will not make a job interesting or your placement rewarding. You will need to adapt to new customs and and traditions, and often adjusting to a different environment and culture can be traumatic and stressful. There are students who will recount tales of the boredom and loneliness which they experienced, particularly when they have not had the company of other British students around. This is where careful planning, a positive attitude and a determination to learn Spanish can help offset these negative feelings and hopefully ensure that they are nothing more than initial, fleeting emotions. It is important to emphasise here that the ability to speak some Spanish (Castilian) will greatly enhance your chances of finding gainful employment. Otherwise, it may be possible to get by with English alone in casual employment at the coastal or island holiday resorts.

Despite the fact that Spain has the highest (albeit now falling) unemployment rate in the EU, with a youth unemployment level well above the national rate, the demand for foreign labour remains relatively high, particularly in English-language teaching and the tourist industry, where knowledge of English and/or another language is a strong asset. Nevertheless, competition for casual jobs (for example, fruit-picking) can be fierce and this is one of the reasons why it is so important that you make thorough investigations and preparations when beginning your search for employment in Spain. You should be prepared to use all available resources, including: university links; friends; family; media; information centres; employment agencies; and professional associations. It is also worth noting that access to employment may depend on the possession of certain qualifications or skills. A level of linguistic ability or experience may be a prerequisite for some jobs. As an EU citizen, you will have access to any labour activity in Spain, either as a salaried or self-employed worker. You do not have to apply for a work permit (see 2.5.4 and you have the same rights as Spanish workers as regards salary, working conditions, access to housing, vocational training, social security and trade union affiliation.

Language students in particular have traditionally spent their second or third year studying and working abroad, often supplementing their income by teaching English. Increasingly, however, there are opportunities for all students to work in a variety of fields, including work in banks and industrial companies. These work opportunities have often arisen due to the establishment and growth of British subsidiary companies in Spain, and it is worth investigating the location of multinational businesses and British subsidiaries when you decide or are told where you are going to be located in Spain. Generally speaking, most of the work opportunities revolve around Spain's two major cities, Madrid and Barcelona, the hub of business and finance. In addition, a number of other university cities and towns can offer opportunities for teaching English, and the coastal resorts and islands provide a range of possibilities in the field of hospitality and tourism. Seasonal jobs in fruit-picking and harvesting are far less common than in, for example, Greece, as there is an excess of cheap immigrant labour from North Africa and landless Spanish workers from Andalusia to pick the massive crops of oranges, olives, grapes and strawberries.

All these are simply some examples of the type of work available. A fuller description of the wide and varied range of employment opportunities in Spain is given in section 2.5, together with advice on making an application and collecting the required documentation.

Part 2
Practical advice

2.1
Student experience in Spain

2.1.1 **Academic aspects**

2.1.1.1 Access

The process by which you gain admission to a Spanish university depends entirely on your personal situation and intentions. The following guidelines cover applicants in three different situations: (i) undergraduates at a British university; (ii) independent part-time students (based in the UK); and (iii) independent full-time students (seeking to move to Spain).

(i) UK undergraduates

The likelihood is that you are a full-time undergraduate at a UK university and that, as a compulsory part of your course, you are expected to spend a term, semester or academic year in Spain either studying full-time at a university or combining part-time university studies with part-time work. This being the case, it is almost certain that, whether you come from a department of modern languages/Spanish or from any other department, your placement tutor will have made arrangements for securing a place for you (and probably a number of your fellow students) by liaising directly with her/his opposite number in the Spanish university concerned. It is also more than likely these days that these arrangements will form part of an official institutional agreement between your university and the Spanish institution concerned and that this agreement is sponsored by the EU under a Socrates/Erasmus or Leonardo scheme. If you are in this situation, you will not only have no worries about admission but you are likely to receive at least some grant support under one of the EU funds listed above – although it is possible that you may not receive monies due to you before you depart for Spain.

If you are a full-time student on a course in a UK university and are intending to spend time studying in Spain but are expected to make your own arrangerments about study there, much of the advice given below in (ii) may well be more relevant to you.

(ii) Independent part-time students

If you are not attached to a UK university but wish to pursue a programme of study that interests you at a Spanish university, much will depend on the university concerned, since in this sphere Spanish institutions of higher education, as in other areas (see 1.4.3), enjoy considerable autonomy. However, on the whole, you are likely to find that the university at which you have chosen to study has made some arrangements for what it may well refer to as *alumnos visitantes* or 'visiting students'. Provided that you choose a subject for which there is not a limit to the number of new students (*alumnos de nuevo ingreso*), you should not have any problems. The normal procedure here is to write to the dean (*decano*) of the faculty or director of the college/school concerned (in Spanish, if possible, of course!) explaining which subject or subjects you wish to study. In this letter, it is very important to indicate whether or not you are expecting to receive either a certificate of attendance and/or achievement. This is of vital interest to you since, if you require some sort of certificate, you may be required to pay the full tuition fee (*tasa académica*) for the subject, while simple attendance (*asistencia*) at classes will probably mean a substantial discount. You should send your letter to the secretary's office (*secretaría*) of the faculty or college/school concerned.[1]

You likewise come into this category if you wish to study Spanish on one of the special courses for foreign students offered by your chosen university. However, formalities in this case are rather more straightforward – except, of course, that you will have to pay the full amount of the fee. You simply ask for the appropriate application form (*impreso de solicitud*) to be sent to you – contact the *secretaría* by phone, fax or email – and return the form with the required remittance. These days, this can be done simply by quoting your credit card number; otherwise send a banker's order.

(iii) Independent full-time students

If you have A-levels or other qualifications comparable to the Spanish *bachillerato* (see 1.3.4) and wish to study full time for a diploma or degree in a Spanish university (perhaps because your family has moved to

1 It should be stressed that a visiting student cannot aspire, under any circumstances, to obtain any official award or qualification as a result of these studies.

Spain), there are two major steps which you must take prior to making a formal application to the university concerned. In the first place, you must write to the *Ministerio de Educación, Cultura y Deporte* (*MEC*) in Madrid (address in Appendix II) requesting recognition (*convalidación*) of your qualifications, which, of course, you must send (photocopies will do) with your application. Once this has been achieved – and it may take several weeks – you should apply to Spain's Open University, *UNED* (see 1.4.5 and 3.28.9) for permission to take the university entrance examination, the *PAAU* (see 1.3.4). It is likely that, if you prefer it, you will be able to take these examinations in the *UNED* centre in London. Needless to say, if you already hold a degree of a UK university (or indeed if you have embarked at some stage on university studies), you are exempted from taking the *PAAU*. However, your qualifications must still be approved by the *MEC*.

Once you have cleared these two hurdles, you should apply to your chosen university in exactly the same way as a Spanish national. This involves acquiring the all-important pre-registration application form (*solicitud de preinscripción*) which should be filled in with the utmost care and returned direct to the university concerned. (An example for universities in Andalusia is given in Appendix III.) Filling in this complicated form will certainly be a test of your patience, as well as your Spanish. In addition to filling in the form, you are required to send photocopies of numerous documents, including: your passport, your university entrance qualification card (*tarjeta de selectividad*) and/or your UK diploma/degree certificate, and your *convalidación* documents from the *Ministerio*.

2.1.1.2 Academic year

The semester system is not traditional in Spain but in recent years has been increasingly adopted – although, as in the UK, semesters have tended to be grafted on to the pre-existing terms which still survive. The autumn term tends to start rather later than in the UK, never earlier than the first week in October and sometimes later. Teaching for the year tends to come to an end in mid or late May, and June is devoted to examinations. Where a semester system applies, first semester examinations take place in late January/early February and those for the second semester in June. While the summer vacation is very long (at least three months), the Christmas and Easter vacations are quite short: the Christmas break lasts no more than two weeks (though must include 6 January, which is a public holiday) and Easter may stretch to little more than Holy Week (*Semana Santa*) itself. On the other hand, Spain's numerous national and local fiestas (plus *puentes* – additional linking days taken unofficially), as well as fiestas associated even with particular faculties or schools, ensure that, at least in this respect, Spanish lecturers and students are not hard done by!

2.1.1.3 Academic timetable

The academic day is a very variable feast in Spain and can change from one university to another and, within one institution, from one teaching centre to another. Some institutions operate a two-shift system (day and evening) partly to accommodate the needs of working students (both young and old) and partly to take some of the pressure off severely overcrowded teaching accommodation. Where a one-shift system operates, classes are normally held from 9.00 am till 2.00 pm (for day students) and from 4.00 pm till 9.00 pm (for evening students). This allows for the long break for lunch, which many Spaniards (including students) take at home. As in this country, lectures last for one hour (but do not start necessarily on the hour) – though sadly it has to be recognised that quite often they do not start on time.

One thing relating to examinations that you will perhaps consider rather unusual, and which happens in certain cases, is that a lecturer will decide with his class of students on what day and at what time an examination will take place.

2.1.1.4 Contact with Spanish staff

A major feature that will usually strike you as a student in Spain is the size of most classes and the virtually complete absence of small-group teaching, even in subjects like modern languages. The two main exceptions are: (i) the private universities (see 1.4.5) and (ii) the special courses in Spanish for foreign students. (In the case of the latter, many organisers pride themselves on offering classes with a maximum of 10–15 students, way below the Spanish average.) For many years, Spanish universities have been subject to severe *masificación*, a problem to which one possible answer (since attempts to tighten up the rather liberal system of access have failed) seems to be the falling birth rate. This is one of the reasons why you will find the Spanish education system rather impersonal and the staff somewhat remote compared with your likely experience in the UK. This impression is reinforced by the fact that in Spain the UK system of personal tutorials is usually conspicuous by its absence, and in general there is very rarely a course leader to whom you can readily turn for academic guidance. Individual lecturers indicate on their doors the hours, usually no more than two or three per week, when they are available for consultation (*horas de consulta*). Outside these hours, unless they can be 'button-holed' at the end of a class, it is assumed that they are not available.

All this can be very bewildering to you at first. Hence the vital importance of the personal contact (hopefully) made by the placement tutor at your home university with her/his counterpart in Spain prior to your arrival in Spain. This person will, in many cases, be the Socrates or Leonardo co-ordinator appointed by a department for a particular programme or set of programmes, often involving the UK and other European institutions. If the UK co-ordinator has been in direct personal contact with her/his opposite number in Spain and, if the arrangement is intended, as indeed it should, to be a fully reciprocal exchange, you may well receive cordial and helpful treatment. In some cases, contacts have been known to go out of their way, in both an academic and social sense, to help UK students. However, the norm is that Spanish staff, even the most willing, are less available than most of their British counterparts, so you must learn at an early stage to become more independent and, as soon as possible, to befriend as many Spanish students as possible.

2.1.2 **Social aspects: contact with Spanish students**

Although Spanish people generally, and students in particular, are renowned for being open and friendly, making contact (and, even more importantly, keeping a contact) is not as easy as might be thought. Since the majority of Spanish students attend their local university (at the most 20 per cent attend a university outside their home province/region) and continue to live at home, there has traditionally been no need for universities to develop the wide range of social and cultural activities that are characteristic of most UK universities. For the majority of Spanish students, university is just an extension of their school life and they continue to have largely the same friends as before. In the main, their social life is centred not on the university, as is largely the case in the UK, but on the bars and cafeterias which they have probably already been frequenting for several years. The one place where you will be able to meet Spanish students is the faculty bar (*bar de la facultad*), but only during the normal academic day. Hence, it is vital to make use of the (often long) breaks between lectures when the bar is teaming with students. It may indeed sometimes be the place where you can track down staff who, interestingly, do not usually have separate facilities as in the UK. It is also vital that you should find out as soon as possible which areas of the town concerned tend to be frequented by the students and which are their favoured haunts.

2.1.3 **Socrates/Leonardo students**

In recent years, Spanish universities, encouraged by a favourable attitude in Brussels to the Spanish bids for EU funding, have shown increasing enthusiasm for establishing Socrates or Leonardo links with their counterparts in other countries of Europe, notably France, Germany and the UK. Many are now involved in link-ups involving several partner institutions in different EU countries. A major benefit of participation in such a scheme is that you may qualify for some extra funding from the appropriate EU fund. Another advantage for the UK student contemplating studying in Spain is that an increasing number of Spanish universities are now providing 'top-up' programmes of Spanish language, often at the beginning of each academic year (see 1.5). Needless to say, learning the language in its 'natural' environment has many advantages. However, the downside of this development is that, where EU-sponsored agreements do not exist, as a foreign student in such institutions you will almost certainly be excluded from such arrangements and may, to some extent, find yourself generally neglected. Increasingly, Socrates and Leonardo students are going to get priority.

2.2
Advance preparations (what to do before you go)

2.2.1 **Selection of university/course: sources of information**

If you are a full-time undergraduate at a UK university, the chances are that you will have little say in the university which you will be attending during your placement in Spain. Certainly, you will not have a totally free choice from all of Spain's sixty-seven universities! At most, your tutors may allow you some choice between the half dozen or so with which your home university is likely to have links, but this will depend very much on the nature of the course you are following and on what (hopefully similar) programmes are available in Spain. However, this restricted choice is not something that should worry you, since you can be pretty certain that your placement tutor will have spent a lot of time and energy prior to your departure building up the most suitable links for your particular course. Indeed, in most cases now, it is likely that such links will have been built up and consolidated over a number of years and that exchanges have been running smoothly to the benefit of all concerned.

If, however, you are an independent student as described in 2.1.1.1 (ii and iii), clearly you will have to reach a decision by yourself. Staff in your former school or staff in the Spanish department at your local university or further education college may be able to give you advice and perhaps recommend certain universities. It is even possible that you have some friends or relations living in Spain, either British or Spanish, who could offer some help. Another consideration might be whether your town has a twinning arrangement with a town in Spain (see town information concerned in Part 3). However, in the final analysis, the choice is yours – and you should take every step to ensure that it is an informed one. So, apart from making use of some possible personal contacts either here or in Spain, what can you do to obtain information about universities and the courses on offer? One obvious suggestion is that you should turn to Part 3 of this guide and study the university sections which give such information. Alternatively, or additionally, you can look at the select bibliography and undertake further reading on the subject of Spanish universities. Moreover, you may wish to contact the relevant body/organisation as listed under 'Useful addresses' in Appendix II). Whatever your sources, prior to making your decision, you should send away to those universities (to the *oficina/servicio de información* in most cases) which interest you and request that they send you as much information as possible on (i) the university in general and (ii) the courses in which you are particularly interested.

Assuming that you have a completely open mind about where you would like to go, the factors which you should take into account when selecting a centre should include the following (not necessarily in this order):

(i) The general geographical location and climate (if you intend to be in Spain in the summer and cannot take the heat, you should probably select a university in the north).
(ii) The language spoken in the region (while lectures at a particular university may be delivered in Castilian, you may find that in certain areas it is not the language of everyday speech, thus limiting your opportunities on the social front).
(iii) The size of the university (you may prefer a small, private university and class sizes may be more what you are used to in the UK. On the other hand, larger universities may mean a better student atmosphere – the Spanish word is *ambiente* – in the city or town concerned).
(iv) The size and nature of the town (only you will know what kind of place you like to live or spend substantial time in – and remember that you are likely to be there for quite a while!).
(v) The appropriateness of the course to your needs (however, if you are a full-time undergraduate student, don't expect it to mirror exactly your course in the UK; in certain respects it may turn out better than here and in other respects worse).
(vi) The availability of various key student services, including accommodation service, health centre, general library, computer facilities, sports centre, etc. (however, do not expect these, in most cases, to match up to what you have been used to in the UK).

2.2.2 **Useful first contacts**

Once you have decided which Spanish university you wish to attend (and, where appropriate, have taken the correct steps to secure a place), your next move is to build up on the information which you have hopefully already collected on the town and university concerned. Apart from continuing to read as much as you can, one possibility is to make contact with people who have already studied there. In this category, if you are a full-time undergraduate, three groups spring to mind: (i) those students from your university who are currently there; (ii) those students, likely to be in the final year of their degree, who have been there in the recent past; and (iii) any Spanish exchange students from the relevant university in Spain. All these should be regarded as potentially your most fruitful and most up-to-date sources of information. With regard to the last two groups, they are close to hand and it may well be that your tutor is, in any case, planning to arrange a meeting between your future university cohort and the final year students and the relevant exchange students in your midst. There are many ways in which contacts made in this way will help you prepare yourself for your visit to Spain. You will learn more about the town concerned and the university, and you may well gain vital assistance and/or practical tips with regard to such essential matters as accommodation, places to meet Spanish students, the best places to shop, the best way to get to your destination, etc.

2.2.3 **Accommodation: preliminary enquiries**

As a full-time undergraduate who is participating in a well-established exchange with a partner university in Spain, there is really no reason why you should not be able to glean a good deal of information before you depart from the UK. In a small number of cases it is possible that your placement tutor will have made arrangements with colleagues at the Spanish university, in which case the likelihood is that you will have been found a place in a hall of residence (*colegio mayor*) either on the campus or in the centre of town. At the very least, it is likely that your tutor will be organising meetings for participating students and general advice on accommodation will be given. If accommodation is not arranged for you in advance, one of the best things you can to is to make contact with the groups of students mentioned in 2.2.2 (ii and iii). Otherwise, a sensible step is to find out the addresses of the UK students from your university already in the centre concerned (your department or faculty office is almost certain to have them) and contact them by letter or phone in Spain. It may well be that a group which is renting a flat for half the year would appreciate being able to nominate successor tenants for the second half of the year.

2.2.4 **Insurance and health matters**

2.2.4.1 Form E111

Since Spain and the UK are both members of the EU, citizens of both countries theoretically enjoy the benefits of a reciprocal state system of health cover. However, this scheme only applies to both accident and emergency treatment. In order to ensure that you can take advantage of this system, you should make sure that you take with you Form E111, which can be obtained from the Post Office. You should fill in the form on the spot and make sure that it is stamped by the person responsible. In theory, this form has no fixed time limit but the UK Department of Health is now advising travellers to Spain that it is better to renew the form on an annual basis, since experience has shown that, in some cases, doctors/hospitals there have not been happy to accept forms that appear to be out of date. In any case, if you use the form while in Spain, you should apply for a replacement on your return to the UK.

You qualify for Form E111 if you are a national of the UK or other EU country or if you are classified as a stateless person or refugee, but it is stressed on the form that 'your E111 will no longer be valid if you go to live outside the UK'. Other useful information on eligibility is given on page 32 of the booklet entitled *Health Advice for Travellers* which contains the E111 form. This booklet also contains a wealth of general advice on health matters for people travelling abroad.

While in Spain, you should keep the E111 in a safe place, along with your passport and other documents. On pages 48–9, clear instructions are given about what to do should you need treatment while in Spain. Above all, it is stressed that medical treatment will only be provided under the EU Regulations by doctors practising under the Spanish health-care system. You should be aware that there may not be a health scheme doctor close to where you are staying, so you may have to travel some distance to his surgery (*consultorio*), to the health centre (*centro sanitario*) or the outpatients' hospital (*ambulatorio*). Make sure too that you seek treatment during surgery hours or by special arrangement. The above booklet stresses, should you need hospitalisation, this will only be provided free of charge 'in a public ward at a public hospital'. In all cases, emergency or otherwise, you must tell the doctor or hospital staff concerned that you have a Form E111 and wish to be treated under the reciprocal scheme. You are advised that each time you need treatment, you should show the original of the E111 to the doctor or hospital staff concerned and that you should only hand over a photocopy. This advice is given in case you need to use the scheme again while you are in the country.

On page 49 of the booklet, it is stressed that if you fail to hand over an E111 'you will be charged as a private patient and are unlikely to get your money back. Under the strict terms of the Spanish Health Service, refunds of private patient charges are extremely rare and are only considered if that treatment is given in a clear life or death situation'. In any case, you should be aware that, under the state health-care scheme, even Spanish nationals must pay up to 40 per cent of medicines prescribed by a doctor and this will also apply to you. Medicines are obtainable at the chemist's or pharmacy (*farmacia*).

It is worth devoting a little time to reading the E111 booklet, since it contains much valuable information to people intending to spend time abroad. While you are in Spain, if you have any queries regarding the operation of the reciprocal system, you should contact the nearest office of the *Dirección Provincial de la Seguridad Social* – Provincial Directorate of the (National) Social Security Organisation.

2.2.4.2 Private health insurance

While you may think that it is not necessary to take out health insurance to cover you while you are in Spain, you are strongly advised to do so. There are three main reasons why we give you this advice. First, there are some important things which are not covered by the E111 scheme, such as repatriation, the use of the air ambulance (which can cost up to £10,000), compensation for loss of a limb or eye and, if you happen to be an employed person, loss of earning capacity. Additionally, what are classed as 'dangerous sports', such as skiing, mountaineering, rock climbing and sub-aqua activities, would not be covered by the E111 and, even under a private insurance policy, you would need to pay an extra premium. Second, if you find that, in spite of your best efforts, your only means of getting treatment is from a private doctor or hospital in Spain, you will have no worries with regard to charging: if you hand over the insurance form to the relevant doctor or hospital staff, the chances are that you will not be charged and, even if you are charged (which may occur in the case of minor treatment by a doctor) you can rest assured that, provided that you keep all relevant receipts, you will be reimbursed in full when you return to the UK (a useful additional safeguard is to produce your Form E111 at the same time as your insurance policy document). Third, as you will have seen from 2.2.4.1, the operation of the reciprocal scheme in Spain can sometimes be subject to bureaucratic delays and complications, adding to the already stressful situation in which you find yourself while a long way from home.

2.2.4.3 Comprehensive travel insurance

Given that, in addition to medical insurance, you will need to take out additional insurance to cover things like your luggage and personal effects, delays, cancellation, personal liability and legal fees, you would be well advised to take out a comprehensive insurance that covers all these eventualities. There are many companies which can offer you the cover which you require, but one company that has many years of experience in providing it, at a very reasonable cost, particularly for students, is Endsleigh. You should study their brochure entitled 'Students studying abroad insurance', which offers both 'standard' and 'premium' cover, and make up your mind what is most appropriate for your own circumstances.

If, by any chance, you are planning to take a car to Spain, this will require additional insurance and you should look into this as a matter of urgency before you depart for Spain.

2.2.4.4 Medication

Needless to say, if you have a health problem for which you must take regular medication, you must ensure, well before you go, that you have ordered from your doctor a supply that will last you throughout your stay in Spain and beyond. It is also a useful precaution to find out, just in case of loss or theft, that you know what the name of the product, or its nearest equivalent, is in Spanish. Another vital precaution, in reality only common sense, is that you should always keep your medication close to you and, if you fly to Spain, you should certainly keep it in your hand luggage (apart from anything else, you may need it on the plane).

You will be pleased to know that no special injections are needed for Spain. However, if you are contemplating a trip to North Africa while there, check before you leave the UK what the requirements are for countries like Algeria, Morocco and Tunisia, and ensure that you have your 'jabs' while still in this country. In the case of such countries, it is almost certain that you will need some injections and you should allow four weeks for a whole course to be taken.

2.2.5 **Financial arrangements**

If you are a full-time undergraduate student, your placement tutor will no doubt have provided all relevant information about the position regarding tuition fees, etc. if appropriate, and will probably have given you general advice about other aspects to be taken into account (accommodation, travel, food, everyday expenditure, etc.). If you are an independent student, it is vital that you find out what fees you will have to pay and when the university concerned expects you to do so. (For many courses for foreigners in Spanish, for example, you will be expected to send a deposit – which can usually be done by credit card.) In general, you are likely to find that the cost of living is rather lower in Spain than the UK – although, up to January 2002, this will depend on the exchange rate and precisely where you are located. Madrid and Barcelona, for example, are more expensive than the provincial capitals and the latter are usually more expensive than the smaller towns. The safest approach is to assume that the cost of living is the same as in the UK and budget to that effect, allowing extra sums for weekend and vacation travelling, as well as for contingencies.

As a full-time first-time undergraduate, you will be eligible, if you require it, to apply for a student loan. Loans are now adminstered by your local education authority (LEA) and you should contact them at an early stage to find out, among other things, how to apply, how long you will have to wait to be paid and what maximum amount you can expect to receive for any one academic year.

These days, things in Spain are very much simpler than they used to be in the days before the cash dispenser or ATM (*cajero automático*) was invented. In reality, once you have sorted out your source(s) of funding, the only steps you need to take before you depart for Spain are: (i) to ensure that you have enough in your bank or building society account on which to draw during the whole of your stay in Spain; and (ii) to make sure that you take with you enough cash in pesetas or euros[2] to tide you over during the journey, especially if you are travelling overland, and during the first day or so of your stay. Once in Spain, you will find that most places of any size (even small towns of say 5,000 people) have banks with cash dispensers; they are less plentiful than in the UK but abundant enough to meet most people's needs. These days, there really is no great advantage to taking travellers cheques; although, if you do

2 Spain is part of the euro zone launched on 1 January 1999. Euro notes and coins will be in circulation from 1 January 2002 and the peseta will no longer be legal currency from 1 March 2002.

decide to take some (for example, in order to pay large bills, such as your rent advance, rather than carry cash around), it is best to take them in pesetas or euros.

2.2.6 **Travel arrangements: travelling to Spain**

Obviously, the quickest way for you to travel from the UK to Spain is by air. In addition to the three London airports, Heathrow, Gatwick and Stanstead, which offer flights to Spain several days per week, a number of regional airports, including Birmingham, Edinburgh, Glasgow, Luton, Manchester and Newcastle, operate charter flights to a number of Spanish destinations, including Alicante (for the south-east), Barcelona and Girona (for the north east), Málaga (for the south), Palma (for the Balearics) and Las Palmas and Tenerife (for the Canaries). The advantages of these flights are that they are direct and, being charter flights, quite cheap. The disadvantages are that they usually operate only on certain days of the week (except from London), they are often less comfortable than scheduled flights and are organised for a fixed duration, usually a maximum of four weeks. Thus, if you intend to be in Spain for a longer period, the return portion of your flight will be worthless – although it has to be said that many students, both English and Spanish, do avail themselves of such cheap flights and nowadays are able to obtain quite economical one-way return flights by booking at the last moment or taking a standby flight. Another major snag, obviously, is that the number of Spanish cities served by such charter flights is very restricted.

Otherwise, London Heathrow, via both British Airways and Iberia (the Spanish national airline), operates daily scheduled flights to most of these destinations plus, of course, Madrid. In addition, Iberia offers almost daily flights to Bilbao, Granada, Jerez, Santiago, Seville and Valencia; with the exception of Jerez and Santiago, these operate from Heathrow and Manchester. The advantages of these flights are that they generally offer greater comfort, there is a greater selection of days and times for travel, and return tickets can be obtained for much longer periods than for a charter flight. Moreover, unlike charter flights, return dates can usually be changed at relatively short notice – although depending on the airline or the particular flight, there may be a penalty to pay. The disadvantages are that they tend to be more expensive than the charter flights – although Iberia currently offers substantial discounts for travellers under the age of twenty-six – and, for many people at least, necessitate a prior cross-country journey. Another disadvantage is that, apart from

Barcelona and Madrid, these journeys necessitate a change of aeroplane. In recent years, some very competitively priced scheduled flights via Amsterdam, Brussels and Paris, for example, have become available from operators like KLM, Sabina and Air France respectively; these provide a useful alternative route, particularly for Britons living in Scotland or the north of England – although, again, a change of flight is involved.

The traditional way of travelling to Spain for UK students was to use a mixture of public transport methods, involving train or bus to a channel port, ferry across to France and (usually) train down to and through Spain. While this method is obviously still available, it can be quite time-consuming, especially if your destination is southern Spain, and may not necessarily be much cheaper than a charter flight. However, it does have the distinct advantage that you will see much more of Spain as you travel towards your destination; even before arriving (especially if this is your first visit), you will learn a lot about the Spaniards and their way of life.

An alternative, though not strongly recommended, way of travelling to the north of Spain is to drive down to either Plymouth or Portsmouth (a disincentive for many people!) and catch one of the ferries that ply the route to Santander in northern Spain, though never more than twice a week. Apart from the timetable limitations, the cost these days is also very off-putting, together with the risk of upset stomachs in the Bay of Biscay! None the less, for those averse to flying, it remains a possibility. This service is operated by Brittany Ferries.

2.2.7 **Things to take with you**

Clearly what you take with you to Spain is a very personal matter. At the top of your list, of course, will be clothes. To some extent, your choice here will be limited by your mode of travel: clearly, you will be most restricted if you travel by plane. Another factor will, naturally, be the climate of the region concerned and the time of year when you will be living there. If, for example, you are heading for one of the universities in Bilbao on the north coast in the first semester (end of September to end of January), you can assume that the weather will not be very different from that in the UK at that time of year. On the other hand, if you are going to the *Universidad de Málaga* on the south coast for the second semester (February to June), you should take the minimum of winter wear since by March temperatures of twenty to twenty-five degrees are quite common, rising to thirty to thirty-five in May and June. In general, you should not be tempted to empty your wardrobe at home and take every item of clothing you possess. Remember that, whether you are in a hall of residence or a flat, you are likely to have (indeed, you should insist on having) access to a washing machine. And if you do forget to take something or suddenly find that you need an item of clothing, you will not find that, in general, clothes and footwear are more expensive in Spain than in the UK – and it might be rather nice to purchase something authentically Spanish, with that little bit of extra style!

There are certain electrical goods, hopefully not too heavy, which you will perhaps want to take with you, such as a hairdryer, curling tongues and travel iron. You should have these checked before you go and, if necessary, re-plugged to avoid possibly embarrassing fusing situations. In any case, you should take an international adaptor with you, since UK square three-pin plugs are not compatible with the round, two-pin plugs used in Spain. For more than one reason, it is a good idea to take a small but good quality portable radio with you (possibly combined with tape recorder); apart from providing relaxation and entertainment, listening to Spanish channels is an excellent way of both improving your understanding of spoken Spanish and learning about current affairs, national and local, in the country. Depending on where you are in Spain, you may be able to receive UK channels (for example, Radio 4), but a surer way of being able to receive news from the UK is to make sure that your radio has a short wave band. Another useful piece of equipment is a small torch – for those maddening, unannounced power cuts!

While they are obviously rather bulky, you should try to make room for a good quality Spanish dictionary and perhaps a good reference grammar recommended by your tutors. Otherwise, on the whole (unless you take one or two light paperbacks) you should leave your other books at home and make a resolution that, while you are in Spain, you will try to read only in Spanish (novels, non-fiction, newspapers, magazines, etc.). Newspapers and magazines are available, not usually in shops, but in the numerous kiosks (*kioskos*) which you will see on Spanish streets.

It is very likely that you will want to take a camera with you and you should not be discouraged from doing this, since this may well be the stay of a lifetime in an exciting (and very photogenic) new country. If you do take one, these days you do not need to take more than a couple of films with you, since nearly all the brands common in the UK are now available in Spain and at roughly the same price. On the whole, however, you are advised to leave developing until you come home: this tends to cost rather more in Spain and at times the quality is not of the best.

One item which it is a good idea to take is a light, compact sleeping bag for when you want to go off travelling and exploring or simply staying overnight at a Spanish friend's house. If you intend to do a lot of travelling while in Spain (during *puentes* and vacations), you may well decide that it is better to go to Spain with a large rucksack rather than a suitcase. At the very least, you should pack a small knapsack which will come in very handy on all sorts of occasions – not least when you do your weekly shop!

From the point of view of security, one essential item you should take is a money belt. Particularly in the big cities, pickpocketing and handbag snatching (often from passing motorbikes) are rife. In general, handbags – however elegant for going out with in the evening – should be left at home. In any case, a word of general advice: never carry around with you more money than you need for any one particular outing.

2.2.8 **Language preparation**

The real key to acceptance and involvement when you are in Spain is, of course, the extent to which you can communicate effectively in the language. The chances are that you are already learning the language. Indeed, you may be one of those who, after completing your A-level, moved on to study it at a high level at university, in which case you obviously have a head start. If, on the other hand, you have little or no knowledge of Spanish, quite apart from making a resolution to study it while you are there (the best place to learn the language), you should take every opportunity to learn as much as you can before you go.

If you are planning things well ahead, it may be possible for you to attend a taught class (strongly recommended if feasible) in a local school, college or university. These normally start in September and may last for a term or a whole year. These days many opportunities exist, both for day-time and evening tuition, and Spanish – often taught by competent and qualified native speakers – is one of the most popular languages among part-time students. While conversation is clearly a key element of any course, on its own it will only take you to a certain level; while you may shudder initially at the idea of having to learn some grammar, it really is essential in the long run if you are to make real progress. If you live in London, Leeds or Manchester, you could make enquiries at the *Instituto Cervantes* which in all centres run courses at different levels in Spanish language and culture (see addresses in Appendix II).

If, however, you have only a limited time before you go, at the very least you should buy or borrow a short, intensive Spanish course which includes tapes and/or videos. The secret is to learn a little and often. Half an hour per day for three or four weeks, for example, will do you much more good than two or three long sessions squeezed in just before you go. If there is any chance of conversing with a native speaker who happens to live in your area, grab this golden opportunity with both hands!

Once you get to Spain, you will soon reap the rewards of your efforts. Although it may well take you a few weeks to adjust to the sounds of the language while there (not quite the same as hearing it in the classroom, even on tape!), soon you will find it easier to understand your Spanish lecturers, as well as your Spanish friends and people in the street. You will certainly get lots of encouragement from the Spaniards, who will appreciate the fact that you have made the effort to learn their language. Be prepared to talk to everyone, from the humblest beggar on the street to the *Rector* of the university; you will always get a response. Conversation unlocks so many doors that the sooner you can master some Spanish, the better, from every point of view.

2.3
Living in Spain (what to do when you get there)

2.3.1 Choosing your accommodation

Finding the right accommodation is the vital pre-condition for having a happy and successful placement and you should give it very careful thought. However, it is very important to realise from the outset, especially if you have already been on a placement in France or Germany where more organised help is available, that in all probability you will have to take personal responsibility for this once you arrive in the country and, unless you have been able to avail yourself of the kind of opportunities suggested in 2.2.3, you may not be able to do much in advance.

Compared to the UK (and indeed many other European countries) Spanish universities have only limited accommodation of their own; there are very few halls of residence, let alone university-owned flats and houses. This is because, as has already been pointed out 2.1.2, a high percentage of students, for largely economic reasons, attend their home-town university and continue to live with their parents. Many universities now have an accommodation office (*oficina de alojamiento*) – to some extent in response to the demands of the growing numbers of foreign students in recent years – but they have limited experience and very limited resources compared to their British counterparts, and can offer only modest help to students. In fact, they tend to restrict their function to providing addresses and telephone numbers, leaving students to make direct contact with landlords/ladies and flat-owners. On the other hand, it is true that these days some of the larger universities are making more effort and have prepared their own directories of recommended private accommodation available. In a number of institutions, however, students who need accommodation, both Spanish and foreign, are still left to their own devices and must make full use of student noticeboards, the student newspaper (if available) and the local newspaper. In a limited number of cases, notably where a Socrates or Leonardo agreement applies, students may be able to obtain access to a place in a *colegio mayor* (hall of residence), but these are generally quite small and the normal rule is for Spanish students to have priority.

Hence, unless accommodation has been organised for you in advance or unless you have managed to obtain it via a contact of your own, you are strongly advised to arrive in the centre concerned at least a week before the start of your course. You will, of course, need to find temporary accommodation, in a guest-house (*pensión*) or *hostal* while you look for something more permanent. These are often conveniently situated in city centres. The *pensiones* offer both a room and meals (on request) but vary greatly in standard. The *hostales* are small hotels offering (normally) room only and basic accommodation but in many cases offer better value for money than their counterparts in the UK. It may, of course, be possible to book such accommodation in advance if you have been able to acquire details from the tourist office of the town concerned (see appropriate town information) or via the Spanish Tourist Office in London (see Appendix II). However, since the quality of the accommodation varies enormously, you may be well advised to shop around on your first day in the centre and actually view the accommodation before committing yourself. Availability of rooms is not usually a problem, however. If you decide to use the services of the local tourist office (*oficina de turismo*), remember that they often close in the afternoons (i.e. after 2.00 pm or 3.00 pm), in common with most official bodies in Spain.

While modestly-priced *pensiones* and *hostales* abound in city centres, when it comes to looking for your more permament base, you may well find that flats in the same area are very expensive. So it may be necessary to accept accommodation in an outlying suburb – hopefully on a regular bus route! One thing that students opting for a flat are strongly advised to avoid is taking one on the ground floor since in certain cities these are the most vulnerable to burglars.

If you decide to rent a flat, you will be expected to sign a contract with the owner. We have provided you with a sample contract form in Appendix III. These are available from *estancos* – those typically Spanish shops which are a cross between a tobacconist's and a post office. While this can be irksome, it is in your own interests – as well as those of the landlord/lady – to do so. It is vital that it is clear to you from the outset what the terms of the contract are, in particular its duration and the arrangements for deposit and payment. Some flat-owners are not happy to let for less than a year, so if you are on placement for one semester only, signing up in such a case should be avoided – unless, of course, you know someone who is coming out to Spain the following semester and could occupy the flat/room (see 2.2.3). It is also essential to to make sure that all parties involved have written evidence of deposits paid etc. Flats can be found via local newspapers, student noticeboards or special agencies; the latter are usually very helpful but will charge a fee.

2.3.2 **Registration at university**

Apart from those enrolled on special Spanish language courses, all students are required to register on their chosen course on the first day of term in the *secretaría* of the relevant university centre. The form to be filled in is the registration form (*impreso de inscripción*). This is the time too when, if you are not a full-time student based in the UK, you must pay your registration fee (*matrícula*) and your tuition fees (*tasas académicas*).

As a Socrates or Leonardo student, it is possible that an introductory meeting will have been arranged for you at which you will be given your timetable and list of subjects, as well as other information about your course of studies and the facilities available. If you have not been told before you leave the UK about such a meeting, you should make it your business, as soon as you arrive in the centre, to find out if, when and where this is going to take place. One of the very first things you should do when you arrive on campus is to enquire which is the notice board most relevant to you.

Spanish students are left to fend for themselves much more than their British counterparts and are not 'spoon-fed' to the same extent. You will find that the equivalent of a 'freshers' week', with course inductions etc. is quite rare in Spain. Spanish students are expected to rely on notice boards and draw up their own timetables for the list of subjects which they must study in any one year of the course.

2.3.3 **Medical matters**

In general, the range of services available to students at Spanish universities does not compare favourably with those on offer in the UK for the reasons given in 2.1.2. While nearly all British universities can boast of having on campus or close by a medical centre with full-time doctors and nurses present, such facilities – though in some cases they are excellent – are quite rare in Spain. Where they do exist, they tend to be associated with the university hospital (*clínica universitaria*) attached to the medical faculty of that university. Otherwise, some universities have reached an agreement with a state or private hospital in the town concerned whereby students can receive emergency treatment or medical attention. These fall into two main categories: residential hospitals (*hospitales*) and (large) outpatients' hospitals (*ambulatorios*). In most cases, it is the latter to which you are likely to be taken or directed.

However, this general lack of dedicated facilities should not lead you to any false assumptions with regard to the quality of the treatment you will receive from a Spanish doctor or in a Spanish hospital. The Spanish National Health System (SNS), in which the vast majority of Spaniards are registered, has made giant strides in recent years and is generally held in high esteem by the Spanish people. Spain, incidentally, has one of the best ratios in the world for the number of doctors per thousand head of population.

Having an illness or suffering an accident is probably the last thing on your mind as you arrive in your new destination. However, soon after arriving (indeed it could be done at registration – see 2.3.2), you should make a point of finding out what to do in case of a health problem and where to turn for help, whether on the campus or in the town. You should also enquire where the nearest *farmacia* is located in case you need to buy medicines or even take advice on minor health matters.

If you suffer from a serious complaint (for example, if you are a diabetic or are subject to occasional fits) you should ensure that your closest friends are aware of the problem and what to do in an emergency situation. You should also inform the academic authorities at the host university, in particular your tutor.

2.3.4 **Adapting to Spanish patterns of study**

In the UK you will no doubt have worked out over time a pattern and approach to studying that suits you, and the discipline of doing this will have stood you in good stead. Adaptability, however, is also a commendable quality and one which now, faced with living and studying/working in a very different social and academic environment, you would do well to exercise, albeit not all the time. Life in Spain in general and student life in particular are very different from those of the UK. The fact that the Spanish day, with meals at very different times, and the academic day (see 2.1.1.3), which is strongly influenced by this, – to say nothing of the effects of the climate – is a world away from what you are used to at home means that, realistically, you have no choice but to adapt, in large measure, to the Spanish way.

Much will depend, of course, on your timetable of lectures. One thing that you will observe straight away is that on average Spanish courses involve more contact hours than those in the UK, so that, if you are following a normal course for Spanish students, you will have sessions of continuous lectures, with few 'free periods' which in the UK you might consider devoting to private study in the library. However, whether you have lectures in the morning or evening, you will find that the middle of the day (say from 2.00 pm to 5.00 pm) is time for you to spend as you please. The sensible thing is to do what the Spanish do and use this time for having your main meal of the day (*comida*) and then relax watching Spanish TV (the 3 o'clock news or *telediario*) or reading a Spanish newspaper or novel. In the summer, especially in the centre and south of the country, this is the hottest part of the day and thus it makes little sense to fight against fatigue by trying to work. If your lectures are not until the evening session, the (cooler) morning is the best time for private study. Logically, if your lectures are in the morning, the best time is in the early evening. However, this is precisely the time (say from 7.00 pm onwards) when young Spaniards like to frequent their favourite bars, often staying until the evening meal/supper (*cena*) calls them home anywhere from 9.00 pm to 10.00 pm. Sometimes they will tend to make *tapas* (see 2.4.1) a tasty substitute for *cena* and will stay in the bars until midnight or after. When, you ask yourself, do the Spaniards study? The fact is that many, who seem to manage on the minimum of sleep, work very late at night/early morning. Thus you are faced with a dilemma, particularly if you are one of those who needs plenty of sleep and have morning lectures starting at 9.00 am. This is where adaptability can have its limits and where will power comes into play. Probably the best solution – and one that is often adopted by Spanish students – is to agree with the group of friends that you will only go for a 'hard' night out at the weekend (Friday and Saturday). That, of course, is fine until a big fiesta occurs in the middle of the week, when you may once again have to be more flexible!

2.3.5 **Making contacts: *intercambios***

One of your top priorities soon after arriving should be to make as many acquaintances and friends as possible. While it is nice to have some of your UK friends or fellow students in the centre to whom you can turn at times, if you want to get the most out of your placement (which is, after all, a once-in-a-lifetime opportunity), you should wean yourself as quickly as possible from your dependence on them. The sooner you spend most of your time with Spaniards, the better from every point of view, academic, social and personal.

One very practical thing you can do to improve your spoken Spanish, as well as your knowledge of Spanish life, is to come to an agreement with a Spanish student or students whereby you exchange conversation sessions, alternating between speaking Spanish and English. If your attachment at the university is to an English department, you will have no difficulty in finding a person willing to enter into this kind of arrangement. Even if this is not the case, however, English is by far the most common foreign language studied in Spain and students from many other courses, whether as part of the course or not, will be keen to have some conversation practice with a native speaker. In fact, you will more than likely come across advertisements for *intercambios* on the student notice boards; if you don't, there is nothing to stop you taking the initiative and placing an advert of your own. Such *intercambios* have the great advantage that neither party pays a penny! However, it may well be possible to combine one or two of these with some 'one-way' lessons in conversational English for which you can charge a fee and improve your financial health!

2.3.6 **Keeping in contact with home**

If you are not constantly in touch with your family back home that is probably a good sign: you are no doubt having the time of your life, hopefully working hard as well as playing hard! However, try to put yourself occasionally in the position of your parents who may not always subscribe to the view that 'no news is good news' and may be wondering what has happened to you. You may be too busy to write a letter, but sending a postcard now and again costs little in time or money. These can be obtained at the nearest *estanco,* or from a stationer's (*papelería*). If you are living in a flat with no telephone, clearly there is no way in which your family can contact you and, therefore, the onus is on you to contact them from time to time. Telephone kiosks (*cabinas telefónicas*) are plentiful in Spanish streets these days, although you should look around to find one in a relatively quiet street, since main streets in Spain are very noisy indeed. The best time to ring is after 8.00 pm when the cheap rate becomes effective. However, do not be tempted to speak for too long because international calls from Spain are very expensive. To ring the UK, you should dial 00 44 followed by the local/STD code and the number (see Appendix IV for STD codes in Spain, as well as other useful codes and general information). One thing that you should avoid, unless it is a dire emergency, is to use a reverse charge call (*cobro revertido*) since the cost is astronomical; you may not be paying, but it might not be the best way of keeping on good terms with your family.

You may be tempted to take a mobile phone with you to Spain and, certainly, in most urban centres in the country, there is excellent coverage and reception. Before departing to Spain, you should check, however, that your server allows you to use it abroad. Some companies require two or three months' notice of intention to use one of their phones abroad and will charge a hefty deposit (returnable) if this is not given. But, if you feel that you can manage without a mobile, you should think very seriously about leaving it at home, since there is a great temptation to use it a lot when you do not have regular access to a phone as at home. The truth is that it can work out very expensive indeed, even for making local calls in Spain. Also remember that while abroad you are also likely to be charged for incoming calls. You have been warned.

2.3.7 **Keeping in touch with your home university/college**

If you are an undergraduate student on a full-time degree/diploma course in the UK, one of the first things you should do, once you have found settled accommodation, is to send your address (and, if applicable, telephone, fax number, etc.) to your home university or college. More than likely you will have been told before you depart to whom you should send this vital information. Quite possibly, your placement tutor will be visiting you in Spain and will need to know how to contact you in advance. Moreover, it is possible that, while you are away, changes may occur that may affect your final year academic programme (for example, the range of options open to you), so it is in your interest to be aware of such changes well before you return to the UK.

2.3.8 **Shopping in Spain**

If you are living in a flat and doing your own cooking, regular shopping is a necessity. However, it can also be a great pleasure and something which you can put to great advantage, especially from the language point of view. Shop assistants in Spain, especially in smaller shops (which still survive to a greater extent than in the UK), are nearly always willing to chat. In casual conversation, you may well find out many things about the language and the town in which you are staying which you will not be taught in the more formal atmosphere of the university. You may even make some useful contacts.

One of the things that you must be aware of when in Spain are the opening hours, very different from those of the UK. Normally, shops open about 9.00 am and close for lunch at 2.00 pm, opening again around 5.00 pm and staying open until 8.00 pm or even later, depending on the place and the time of year. Large supermarkets and department stores, like the *Corte Inglés*, have longer opening hours, remaining open at midday; sometimes they operate a '9 to 9' or '10 to 10' system as in this country. One of the great joys of living in Spain is being able to shop in the evenings, combining this perhaps with a visit to a bar or cafeteria, which is usually open all day long. At this time, even in winter, the pavements are thronged with people shopping, chatting or indulging in the traditional Spanish stroll, the *paseo*.

If you are lucky enough to be sharing a flat with Spanish students, you can probably save yourself a lot of time and expense by seeking their advice about where to shop and asking them which places are best for certain products. If you are living in a city, it will almost certainly have a large indoor market (*mercado*), which is open every day except Sunday. This is probably the best place to go for your main weekly shop to buy fresh meat, fish, fruit and vegetables. If you have been placed or are working in a smaller town, there is likely to be a weekly outdoor market (*mercadillo*) quite cheap and certainly colourful. However, don't despair if you are living in a *barrio* or district distant from the market, since the corner shops and small supermarkets, which you will find in nearly all districts, are not necessarily much more expensive than the market in the centre – a pleasant discovery for someone from the UK who is used to a quite dramatic difference! At all events, you should shop around literally to find the best buys. You should also pluck up courage to try those more exotic fruits and vegetables that are more common in Spain than in the UK. Another advantage of living with Spanish students is that the latter will be able to introduce you to a whole range of new dishes, helping to broaden your gastronomic repertoire!

These days there are very few things on sale in the UK which you cannot buy in Spain. Gone are the days in which travellers there had to take their 'Cornflakes' if they wanted their typically English breakfast. Gone too are the days when students were told that certain consumer goods, notably electrical, were prohibitively expensive. Today some things, like electrical and electronic gadgets, are probably about the same price as in the UK, while a wide range of things, including clothes and shoes, are on balance cheaper. Food and drink, either bought in shops or consumed in bars and restaurants, are considerably cheaper. Naturally, a major factor here at the time of writing (2001) is the strong pound, but the pound would have to drop considerably in value or the peseta rise substantially before this healthy situation for UK visitors to Spain would be radically changed. Even when the euro becomes the only legal currency in Spain (from 2002), it is unlikely that price differentials will change dramatically.

2.3.9 **Travelling in Spain**

Normally, it is presumed, as a student you will be largely dependent on public transport while you are in Spain – unless you are lucky enough to have a Spanish friend who owns a car! There is no doubt that over the last two or three decades the quality of transport services has greatly improved. The traveller has a choice between buses and trains – although students who are not short of money and wish to cover long journeys in a short time (for example, during a *puente*), could consider air travel since a number of the main provincial capitals are connected by a fairly reliable service (there are daily flights collecting most major cities, including Barcelona, Bilbao, Madrid, Seville and Valencia and Zaragoza).

Trains are generally a good deal cheaper than the UK but the price varies according to whether you take a luxury *Talgo* or a slower *Rápido* (or its night equivalent, the *Expreso*), and often you must pay a speed supplement (*suplemento de velocidad*). If Seville or Córdoba is your destination and Madrid your starting point (or vice versa), you may wish to try Spain's new high speed train, the AVE. Although this is more expensive than other trains, it offers a very smooth, comfortable ride and, what is more, it is very punctual – so punctual in fact that the operators offer you your fare back if it is only five minutes late! In general, travelling by train is a less harassing experience than in the UK; on long distance trains at least, standing passengers are not allowed and thus only seated places are sold. For this reason, you are advised to obtain your tickets at least a day in advance. Most major towns and cities have an office of Spanish Railways, *RENFE,* making it possible to do this in the city centre rather than trek to the station which may well be at some considerable distance.

Long-distance coaches (*autocares*), run by private companies and operating routes between the major towns and cities, are marginally cheaper than the trains and in general provide a good, reliable service. One example of these is Alsina-Graells, which operates mainly in Andalusia and, in addition to providing regular services between cities like Málaga and Granada, also covers areas where trains are non-existent, for example, the journey between Granada and Murcia or between Madrid and Soria. These coaches are usually quite comfortable; moreover stops are made at regular intervals to allow passengers to stretch their legs and visit a roadside bar or cafeteria. Most are now equipped with video – sometimes a mixed blessing! On most long services, tickets correspond to numbered seats, so it is a good idea to book the day before or arrive an hour early. No standing passengers are allowed – at least in theory! Another welcome prohibition for many UK travellers is that smoking is usually forbidden – though it is not uncommon for this to be flouted!

With regard to intra-city transport, all Spanish cities have their own municipal bus service plus a fleet of approved private taxis. In addition, Barcelona and Madrid have an underground system known in each case as the Metro. The Barcelona Metro is more efficient and much cheaper than its London counterpart. Both systems operate on the basis of a fixed rate per journey but offer good discounts to those who purchase either sets of ten journeys or season tickets.

The normal mode of transport within cities are the buses. These may be the conventionally-sized *autobuses* or the smaller, more economical *microbuses* with which we are now familiar in the UK. In most cases there is a single fixed price, however long or short the journey, and return tickets do not exist. Sets of (usually ten) *bonobús* tickets offer travel at a discount price and are a must if you are using the system frequently; they are normally available at newspaper or special kiosks in the city concerned. Passengers usually board at the back of the bus if there is is a conductor or, more frequently these days, at the front where the driver doubles up as conductor. Where a *bonobús* system is in operation, it is essential that passengers ensure that they punch their own tickets. Local buses in Spain provide very few seats and a large standing area; however, drivers are very lax when it comes to limiting those standing and passengers often find themselves crammed together like the proverbial sardines.

Taxis in Spain display different colours according to the city concerned and always sport a green light which is illuminated at night when in use. Taxi ranks are plentiful in Spanish cities and towns, and, of course, are always located at railway stations and airports. However, it is relatively easy to hail a taxi in the street; check, however, that it is not *ocupado* (engaged) but *libre* (free). Fares, which are generally much cheaper than in the UK, are charged via a metre as in this country, with a basic minimum charge and depend on the number of passengers and the amount of luggage. Tipping is expected but beware that the taxi driver has not already added an extra amount to the figure shown on the metre! For long distances, it is always advisable to agree a fare in advance.

If you are lucky enough to have taken a car to Spain, or if you are in a position to hire a car for use at weekends or during holidays, you will find that main roads and motorways are generally of a good standard these days. On the other hand, minor roads should generally be avoided, not least because travellers will find that in many areas the road surfaces are still poor and petrol stations are not as plentiful as in the UK. Drivers should also check in advance whether or not the motorway they would like to use is a toll one (*autopista de peaje*). These are, in fact, less common than, for example, in France and there are many good quality dual carriage-ways (*autovías*) which enable you to make rapid progress, free of charge, from one destination to another. Hiring a car need not be too expensive (generally cheaper than in the UK) but it is certainly advisable to shop around since prices do vary quite considerably. One thing that it is vital to check is that the deal offered includes fully comprehensive insurance and not just third person, fire and theft, which is all some companies are prepared to offer.

2.3.10 **Making the most of your time in Spain**

Although you may have been to Spain before (perhaps on holiday) and, although you may envisage going again in the future either for pleasure or for work, the kind of experience you will have while on placement, whether as a full-time undergraduate or an independent student, will be unique and one of which you should take full advantage. The benefits of a stay in a foreign country – and particular at a foreign university – are nearly always positive and varied, ranging from the academic to the social and personal.

2.3.10.1 Academic

If you are a full-time student your home university will have no doubt given you particular tasks to perform while attached to the university concerned. These may well include, in addition to attending certain lectures, the preparation of a project or dissertation relating to some aspect of Spanish life and culture. Your university no doubt also expects that in general you will return with a much enhanced ability to understand, speak and read the language. However, the latter will not happen automatically just by your being in Spain: you will need to work at it on a daily basis and, as far as possible in a country that does not really like regularity, you are advised to build certain good practices into your daily routine, in addition to the lecture programme and other requirements of your home university. Each day, ideally, you should resolve to do some extended listening, speaking and reading. With regard to listening, why not make a habit, perhaps after lunch, of always listening to the radio or watching the TV news? Speaking can be catered for in various ways. If you are sharing a flat with Spaniards, you will have little choice but to converse in Spanish. Otherwise, you may be involved in one or more *intercambios* as suggested in 2.3.5. With regard to reading there are various options, but ideally, at the very least, you should get into the habit of reading every day a good national newspaper like *El País* or *El Mundo,* or your local paper (local papers are often of very good quality). It is also a good idea always to be reading a good book, a contemporary Spanish novel or collection of short stories, for example. It might seem rather a chore at the time but, with at least some of your reading (perhaps certain newspaper articles), you should make a point of looking up and noting down new vocabulary under various headings. Another activity which may well be of value to you academically when you return to the UK (especially if you are a full-time student) is to collect newspaper cuttings on themes related to the subjects which you are likely to be studying in your final year. Never again will you have such an excellent opportunity to collect up-to-date material, which may well be of use from both a background and language point of view.

Even if you are an independent student, with no formal requirements imposed on you from above, you will probably benefit from organising your spare time to include at least some of the activities suggested above.

2.3.10.2 Social and personal

It would, however, be sad if, after your placement, you felt that the only gains were academic. In a country such as Spain, where in general the people are so open and communicative, you have a golden opportunity to make new friends and acquaintances and to enjoy their company in settings very different from those which you are used to in the UK. You should take every opportunity to talk to Spaniards of all ages and classes;

that way you will learn an enormous amount about their country and their attitude to life (from the personal point of view, you may find this very stimulating and instructive). The traditional meeting places for the Spanish are the bars and cafeterias, of course. However, if your host university, or indeed the local commmunity, does happen to have clubs and societies (musical, sporting, religious, photography, etc.), find one that interests you and join. This is an excellent way to meet people with your own interests and can open many doors for both your placement and the future. In the past, students who have had some of the most successful placements have been those who have become involved in such things as the local rugby team, the local branch of their Church (not all churches in Spain are Catholic), a gym or fitness club, an amateur theatre group, the local branch of a political party or an environmental group.

One thing that you must not fail to do while in Spain, in whichever part, is to use your weekends and your vacations to travel. Spain is a big country of enormous climatic, geographical and cultural contrasts, which has even been described as a mini-continent. You are almost certain to enjoy and benefit personally from this experience and, as shown in 2.3.9, travelling is Spain is cheaper than in the UK. One obvious thing to do is to visit your university friends in other towns. On the other hand, you may well have made a Spanish friend at the university who lives in a different part of the country and who invites you to his/her home (and being invited to the home of a Spanish person is a great honour, not to be refused). If you have no ready-made accommodation to rely on while travelling, don't worry: camping and youth hostels (*albergues juveniles*) are very cheap and reasonably-priced *pensiones* or *hostales* (see 2.3.1) are never far away.

After this great combination of living in a (very welcoming) foreign country, with its very different life and culture, studying in one of its universities and travelling round and meeting people from its various and varied regions, it would be very surprising if you did not return to the UK with your horizons broadened and with the personal satisfaction of having not only survived but prospered.

2.4
Living with the Spanish

It is an obvious truism to say that great differences exist between British and Spanish cultures, each to some extent representing an archetype of the Anglo-Saxon and Latin way of life. However, this has not always been a necessary barrier between the countries, and often the syndrome of 'the attraction of opposites' has come into play. On the other hand, in recent years Spain has to some extent been shedding some of the characteristics that once enabled propagandists of the tourism industry to claim that *'España es diferente'*. None the less, cultural changes, linked to social changes but with deeper roots, take time to come about and it will still be many years before Spain has ceased to be noticeably different. Indeed, many Spaniards are themselves still convinced – and are indeed proud to tell you – that 'Spain is different'.

2.4.1 **Eating and drinking out in Spain**

Per head of population Spain probably has more eating and drinking places (bars, cafeterias, restaurants) than all other countries in Europe. These basic human needs are almost elevated into an art form in Spain. The fact is, however, that in, general, eating and drinking out are not done for their own sake: they offer an opportunity for Spanish people to indulge in their favourite pastime, i.e. communicating. Visitors are much more likely to be invited out to a bar or restaurant than to be taken to the home of their Spanish contact or friend.

There used to be a clearer distinction between bars and cafeterias: the former tended to specialise in alcoholic drinks and *tapas* while the latter normally offered coffee, chocolate and (less frequently) tea, as well as a variety of sweetmeats and cakes, etc. Today that distinction has been blurred considerably – although there are still some bars which do not provide coffee. Another change is that many bars, which formerly concentrated on drinks only, now provide substantial meals both for locals and tourists, so that even the distinction between bar and restaurant is also tending to disappear.

One thing that all the bars and cafeterias have in common is that in most cases they stay open from 7.00 am till midnight or even later and that alcoholic drinks are available at any time of day. Breakfast Spanish-style (which most Spaniards take in a bar or cafeteria) is available any time from 7.00 am till midday. Usually this consists of white coffee (*café con leche*) plus a selection of cakes and biscuits, but may consist of the traditional chocolate with fritters (*chocolate con churros*). One thing that will surprise you in a Spanish bar is the number of people (usually men) taking an alcoholic drink, such as aniseed (*anís*) or brandy, for breakfast!

Soon after midday in many bars, the cake trays on the counter are replaced by trays of hot and cold *tapas* offering great temptations to all but the most determined slimmers. In many bars, what is on offer here is displayed in chalk on a makeshift blackboard above the bar. Prices are usually for *raciones,* portions which are substantial enough to provide a one-course meal. However, don't hesitate to ask for a *tapa* or *tapita,* a small amount of the dish concerned, to sample with your wine or beer. Traditionally these were always provided free of charge but, sadly, this custom is now dying out in most places except in certain cities in the south of Spain (e.g. Almería, Granada and Jaén) and bars in certain rural areas.

From about 5.00 pm the *tapas* trays are replaced by those provided for the 'breakfast' (cakes, etc.) as customers come in for a late afternoon drink and snack known as the *merienda.* About two hours later, the *tapas* appear again and the 'mid-day' routine is repeated. In fact, not all bars follow this 'chop and change' routine and many have *tapas* available for most of the day.

These days beer (*cerveza*) is becoming a serious rival to wine in Spanish bars, especially among the young and women. Most bars have installed systems for providing draught beer as an alternative to the well-known brands of bottled beer such as Águila, Cruzcampo, Estrella, Mahou and San Miguel. Draught beer is normally drunk out of ¼ litre measures known as *cañas* or from ⅓ litre measures (tall thin glasses) known as *tubos.* Occasionally stout or *cerveza negra* is also available. These days alcohol-free beer (*cerveza sin alcohol*) is becoming increasingly common and is usually marketed simply as *sin* (without).

It is worth pointing out that prices in some bars and cafeterias can vary according to whether you sit or stand at the bar (the cheapest way), sit inside the premises or sit outside on the terrace (the most expensive way). Where this policy is applied, there is usually a menu available that explains the different prices.

As visitors will soon discover, Spaniards are not the world's most patient people and have little notion of the word 'queue'. Thus, in order to be served in a bar, British people have to learn to be assertive (see 2.4.8) and voice their requests as loudly as possible – partly to be sure of being heard above the general hubbub!

In its ubiquitous restaurants, in both town and country, Spain offers a bewildering choice of eating houses and cuisine from traditional regional specialities to standard 'international' dishes. In fact, there is no such thing as traditional Spanish cooking but an infinite variety of regional cuisines. On the other hand, because of vastly improved communications and the impact of the tourist trade, certain regional dishes like *paella* (originally from Valencia) can now be tasted in virtually every part of Spain. Restaurants are classified according to a system of forks (one to three, the latter being the best), monitored by the relevant regional tourist board.

In choosing a restaurant the recommendations of locals are usually the best guide, but check the prices before you go in! It is consoling to know that nearly all restaurants display their menus at the door and that the vast majority, certainly at midday, offer a table d'hote menu known as the *menú del día* or sometimes, not very flatteringly, the *menú turístico*. These days the *menú del día*, a favourite with students, offers by far the best value for money at midday, often including three courses plus bread and wine. The à la carte menu is called simply *la carta;* this is usually divided into starters (*entremeses*), fish (*pescados*), meat (*carne*) and sweets (*postres*). Main courses of either fish or meat dishes are not accompanied by heaps of potatoes and vegetables as in the UK but are served with perhaps just a sauce (with fish) or French fries and a tiny amount of salad (with meats). Vegetables are sometimes taken as a course on their own from a separate list on the menu or as a starter.

Apart from city-centre restaurants, if you have transport, it is worth considering a meal out at a wayside inn known as a *venta*. These are often located in local beauty spots, sometimes high up in the hills. Also worth consideration, but only if you are feeling flush, is a meal at one of Spain's high-class state-run hotels called *paradores* which are often exquisitely converted palaces or monasteries, usually set in beautiful natural surroundings. The price may be high but the value is second to none.

Do not be afraid to order a good quality wine, preferably one from the region (if appropriate) with your meal; prices are very reasonable compared with the UK and the kind of unprincipled 'marking up' that sometimes happens in this country is not the norm in Spain. On the other hand, you need not be ashamed to order a beer, soft drink (*refresco*) or even water; not every Spaniard, believe it or not, drinks wine with a meal! In most places tap water (*agua del grifo*) is perfectly drinkable and free, but you will have to pay for the often recommended mineral water which may be sparkling (*agua mineral con gas*) or still (*agua mineral sin gas*).

One of the great delights of eating out in Spain is the chance to eat outdoors in the summer, either on the animated terrace of a city restaurant or outside a seafront restaurant or popular bar known as a *merendero* or, particularly in the south, a *chiringuito*. The latter often provide the opportunity to try fish and other seafood (*mariscos*) brought in direct from the sea.

Restaurants often indicate on the bill that a service charge is not included. However, even where it is, the normal custom is to leave a tip (say five per cent of the bill – less than in the UK) if you have been satisfied with the meal and the service. In fact, the chances are that you will certainly have been very happy with everything, since Spanish waiters take a great pride in providing an efficient and cordial service to their customers.

2.4.2 **Time**

In one major way, Spaniards still seem to have changed very little and this concerns their concept of time. The writer Anthony Trollope once said: 'Men have no idea of time in any country that is or has been connected with Spain'. This may be rather an overstatement but contains an element of truth, as does the popular perception of a country where procrastination has become embodied in the one word *mañana* – tomorrow. The point is that quite often it does not literally mean 'tomorrow'; it may indeed mean 'next week' or 'next month'. The message, then, for anyone living in Spain and particularly for the British academic attempting to set up links there or the student trying to obtain an interview about a project, is not to expect to get things done too quickly. Contacts may need reminding about what needs to be done, although if the reminding is overdone, it may be construed as 'pestering', in which case the cause is lost. In general, the British have had to learn to be very patient and tactful in their dealings with the Spanish people.

2.4.3 **The Spanish day**

Closely tied to the question of time is the nature of the Spanish day or *jornada*. The morning (also *mañana*) is very long; for most working people, it begins at 9.00 am (or even earlier) and stretches until 1.30 pm or 2.00 pm. It is quite common for working people at all levels to pop out to a nearby bar or cafe mid-morning to have coffee and a light snack. This is normally referred to as *el desayuno* (breakfast), although in time it hardly corresponds to its English counterpart! If you visit a Spanish contact during the morning, it is highly likely that, rather than being offered coffee at the workplace, you will be invited out to an adjacent bar where business and pleasure can be easily combined.

On the way home from work, it is quite common (though not the rule everywhere) to call in again at a bar to take a pre-prandial drink and one or two *tapas*. Most working Spaniards return home to have their lunch (*almuerzo* or *comida*) with their families. This is rarely taken before 2.00 pm and, being the main meal of the day, may well last a couple of hours. The traditional evening work shift normally starts at 4.30 pm or 5.00 pm and lasts till 7.30 pm or 8.00 pm. The evening meal (*cena*) is taken very late in Spain, rarely before 9.00 pm or 10.00 pm, and is generally much lighter than the *almuerzo*.

A pattern that has been in operation for a number of years now is the *jornada intensiva* which is from 8.00 am to 3.00 pm – theoretically without a break. This is favoured by many government departments, banks and other official institutions. Thus, it is vital that appointments, for example in connection with a project or dissertation, are made for the morning, but neither too early nor too late. Even when you arrive punctually for an appointment, do not be surprised if your contact has popped out for a quick (or maybe not so quick!) *desayuno*. Another point to remember is that banks are open only from 9.00 am to 1.30/2.00 pm most of the year; as compensation, they are open at these times on Saturday mornings too, but remember to check on arrival, for in summer in certain regions they are closed!

One great attraction for visitors from the UK is that shops are open for more hours than in this country. Even if they close for a couple of hours in the middle of the day, they stay open in the evenings from 4.30 pm or so until at least 8.00 pm. As we have already seen (2.3.8), large chain stores do not normally close at 'midday' and are often open from '9 to 9' or from '10 to 10'. In these cases Sunday shopping is also beginning to appear on the Spanish scene. Needless to say, as in the UK, small shopkeepers complain bitterly about such developments.

Increasingly in Spain, the traditional patterns are giving way to various alternative forms more familiar in northern Europe. For example, in the big cities, where large national and multinational companies are based, the working day, at least for office staff, is 9.00 am to 6.00 pm, with an uncharacteristically short one-hour break for lunch around 1.30 pm.

2.4.4 **Hospitality**

The majority of Spanish people are very friendly, generous and hospitable. You may well receive some hospitality during your visit. This usually takes the form of an invitation to have a drink or a meal out in a bar or restaurant; if you receive an invitation to your friend's home, you are being offered a special privilege and clearly regarded as a someone special. Reciprocating this hospitality while you are in Spain is well nigh impossible as Spaniards take it as a matter of honour to pay for guests and visitors to their country. However, what you can do – apart from offering the same kind of hospitality when your Spanish friend comes to the UK – is to take with you a small gift. If you do happen to be invited to a meal at your friend's home, however, a small present (e.g. a bunch of flowers or a box of sweetmeats or chocolates) will be much appreciated. (Incidentally, you will find that the shop assistants concerned are prepared to spend a lot of time wrapping your gift and maximising its outward attractions!)

Spaniards who know each other well are very effusive and demonstrative when they meet each other whether in private or in public, indulging in not only a handshake but the traditional Spanish embrace or *abrazo* followed (except where just men are concerned) by a social kiss on both cheeks. As a student or member of academic staff, you, of course, are likely to be met with just a handshake (usually very firm), certainly in the early stages of your acquaintance; if in time this is followed by a friendly tap on the arm or shoulder (from a male), you can be assured that you are making progress!

2.4.5 **Smoking**

The trend away from smoking that has occurred in the UK and other European countries over recent years has not yet taken root in Spain, in spite of some goverment attempts to discourage this national vice. A high percentage of Spanish people of both sexes smoke and it is seen by many as an essential ingredient of socialising. In many public places non-smokers may find the intensity of the atmosphere too great to bear. On the positive side, however, it has for many years been against the law to smoke in such places as cinemas and theatres and, in theory at least, smoking is not allowed on buses or trains.

2.4.6 **Noise**

In Spain one thing you must be prepared for (and this really is a culture shock) is the increase in the volume of noise to which you will be subjected wherever you go. Being a very extrovert and energetic people, they express themselves confidently and vociferously, constantly interrupting each other and giving the impression not only that they are shouting, not talking, but also that they are not listening to what others have to say to them. A visit to any Spanish bar at 'breakfast' time or in the evening will illustrate this: not only will the serried ranks of customers be all talking at once, but barmen will be shouting their orders to the kitchen behind the bar, the wall-mounted television will be blaring full-blast (often without viewers – unless there is a football match on!), the fruit machine will be gushing out either coins or its innane, monotonous chime and out in the street car engines will be revving and horns honking. Yet this vibrant atmosphere (*ambiente*) casts a spell on most foreign visitors whose eardrums in time adapt to these assaults and who find compensation in the warm and friendly nature of the locals and the lack of restrictions on drinking hours.

2.4.7 ***Machismo***

Male domination in this traditionally patriarchal society is only slowly beginning to recede. Over recent years, and particularly since the advent of democracy, more liberal attitudes from northern Europe have made some impact on the role and status of women. Many more women, for example, now go out to work than did so twenty-five years ago, and many more gain access to higher education; in fact, there are now more females than males studying in Spanish universities. In legal terms, their position is also much stronger: married women, for example, are no longer subject to their husbands as they were before 1975 (see 1.1), contraceptives are now more freely available, a divorce law was introduced in 1981 and a limited abortion law in 1985. A government department devoted to women's affairs, the *Instituto de la Mujer*, has been making attempts in recent years to improve the lot of women. A symbol of women's new status is that an increasing number now serve in Spain's police services and in the armed forces – something unheard of in Franco's day. At the social level, however, the attitudes of men are changing only slowly. It is true that now more men, especially of the younger generation, see marriage as a partnership in which domestic duties are shared, but too many still cling to traditional attitudes and see women as either inferior or potential sex objects. If you are a female student, you should be aware that there is always a risk of undue and over-assertive attention from certain Spanish males and, on certain occasions, you may need to adopt self-protection strategies.

2.4.8 **Assertiveness**

Visitors to Spain must also learn to be assertive, one of the key characteristics of the Spaniards. It is only counter-productive to behave in the reserved and mild way allegedly typical of the British; being 'backward in coming forward' may well mean that you have to wait ages to be served in a Spanish bar or shop, or that you may well miss the bus for which you have been queuing but for which the local Spaniards have only been waiting! Assertiveness also applies to conversation and, in order to be heard and to make get your point of view across, especially in a group, you may well have to interrupt in a thoroughly non-British way!

2.4.9 **Sense and sensibilities**

One very important consideration to bear in mind when in Spain is not to upset their national or local sensibilities. This is only common sense. Some Spaniards themselves are adept enough at denigrating their own country but are often less than pleased when foreigners do it for them. Even in the more enlightened times of the new millennium, Gibraltar is still a thorny issue with many people in Spain and is a subject to be avoided. If the topic does crop up, try to change the subject of conversation as soon as possible and certainly avoid rising to any kind of bait that may be offered. If you can think of something positive to say about Spain and the Spanish people, do so; underneath their many criticisms of their country they are, none the less, a very proud people. They are proud of their local region, town or even village and compliments about these are just as appropriate. What must be avoided at all costs, as well as criticism of their local homeland (*patria chica*), is telling people from Madrid how beautiful Barcelona is (or indeed vice versa) or telling the Catalans how impressed you are with the people of Andalusia. It is also prudent to avoid telling the Spanish how much better things are in the UK – if indeed they are!

2.4.10 **Involvement and participation**

If you are going to spend any length of time in Spain, you should be prepared to get involved in as many social and cultural activities as possible. The Spanish are a very spontaneous people and it may be that, at a moment's notice, you are invited to a family occasion or a public fiesta. Don't complain that you haven't been given much notice – if you are free, accept the invitation and go. Furthermore, don't simply go but make an effort actively to join in whatever activities are going on. Join in the Spaniards' zest for life. In this way, you are more likely to be accepted into authentically Spanish circles and learn more about the Spanish way of life.

2.5
Working in Spain

2.5.1 **Finding work**

Although most UK students spending time in Spain will enrol full-time on university courses in Spain, they and many non-enrolling students will search for some kind of employment. In many respects, the job-finding network for Spain is now well established and much the same as in the UK. Despite this and the wealth of information available from university placement officers, books, leaflets and the Internet, it is still true to say that many students still find it difficult to find a job in Spain. Where a work placement in Spain is an integral part of your studies, you will generally find it easier to obtain advice and practical assistance in finding work, as some kind of system will be in place with its own network of contacts and employers. Generally, arrangements should be made before you travel to Spain, but there are some cases where students – those on study placements, for example – decide to try and find work to help finance their stay or travels. In these and other cases, the type of work you are looking for and your particular qualifications and attributes will often dictate how you go about finding a job in Spain. There are a number of standard routes to follow when looking for work and some of the most important sources and procedures are described below.

2.5.1.1 University placement officers/tutors

Every UK university that sends students on a work/study placement will have staff (placement tutors) who are responsible for assisting their students in finding a suitable placement. They should also have a database of addresses of current and past employers of their students, as well as contact details for their counterparts in Spanish universities. Helpful advice and tips from students who have successfully completed a work placement in Spain will also be available. Placement tutors will offer practical help and advice in finding a job, from choosing a town or city to helping you construct a *curriculum vitae* (CV) and writing a letter of introduction (*carta de presentación*) in Spanish. Their experience will be invaluable in helping you decide upon the best course of action.

2.5.1.2 University careers service

Students often overlook the fact that their own university careers guidance officers can offer a great deal of assistance in finding work in Spain. In addition, the careers office library will generally have a wide range of books and pamphlets which will not only offer practical guidance but will also include details of organisations, agencies, companies and other employers whom you might wish to contact. The careers service might also be able to offer you useful information through its databases and the Internet.

2.5.1.3 The press

English-language newspapers do not generally carry advertisements for jobs in Spain except in relation to UK-based companies or to the European Union. International newspapers such as the *International Herald Tribune* contain advertisements for management, technical and professional staff. *Overseas Jobs Express* (*OJE*) is a particularly relevant publication. This fortnightly newspaper for international job hunters contains numerous categories of work, from seasonal opprtunities to permanent jobs. It also includes valuable advice and feature articles on work abroad, health and other matters. Its website is *www.overseasjobsexpress.co.uk* and you can find its postal address in Appendix II.

The principal newspapers in Spain are *El País*, *El Mundo*, *La Vanguardia*, *Diario 16* and *Ya*, with Sunday editions carrying the largest recruitment sections (*trabajo vacante* or *ofertas de empleo*) though there are vacancies advertised on other days. *El País* also has its own website (*www.elpais.es*), as does *El Mundo* at *www.el-mundo.es*. The libraries of universities where Spanish is taught should also hold current copies of at least one major Spanish newspaper so that you can keep up to date with the latest vacancies. You can, of course, advertise yourself in both the national Spanish newspapers and in Spanish regional newspapers (listed in *Benn's Media Directory Europe* and *Willings Press Guide*, again available in university libraries). Publicitas Limited, in London, is one of the largest publishers representatives and deals with a number of Spanish newspapers (see Appendix II for address) and they can help you place an advertisement in the classified sections of these papers. It is also worth noting that English-language newspapers such as *Sur in English*, *Costa del Sol News* and *Lookout* circulate on the Costa del Sol, and they too advertise job vacancies.

2.5.1.4 Books and annual publications

There are numerous guidebooks and reference works which, besides offering advice about finding work in Spain, often include addresses of potential employers and agencies. The *How to...* series of books and the annually updated publications on vacation work, such as *Summer Jobs Abroad*, are particularly informative and well regarded. Your university, careers service or local public library should have some of these books and the most important of them are listed in the bibliography. However, it is important to note that, even if you are using a relatively up-to-date book, some of the addresses and other information may have changed since publication. This can often be the case with web sites and you need to be aware that you may need to corroborate details through other sources. The *Yellow Pages* (*Páginas Amarillas*) of major towns and cities will supply you with details of companies or organisations which may be able to offer you work in a particular field. The Spanish Embassy, the Spanish Chamber of Commerce and the Cervantes Institute (addresses in Appendix II, as well as main post offices (*Correos*), should be able to help you locate copies. Spanish companies are listed by products, services and provinces in *Kompass Spain*, available in public and university libraries in the UK and in chambers of commerce offices in Spain. The *Europa Yearbook* is another informative directory which includes addresses and other information for Spanish banks, universities, radio and television stations and newspapers.

An important annual Spanish publication is the *Guía de las empresas que ofrecen empleo: España y Portugal* (*Guide to Companies offering Employment: Spain and Portugal*) (see bibliography for full details). Although primarily aimed at graduates, this two-volume work contains a wealth of useful information relating to finding work in Spain, and includes: preparing a CV in Spanish; types of work in Spain (full time, temporary, franchises and work placements); an A-Z of all the major employing companies in Spain (including many multinationals); and an exhaustive list (over 2,000) of addresses of public and private organisations and agencies which can offer advice on finding work in Spain.

2.5.1.5 Employment services

(i) INEM

Spain's employment offices are managed by the *INEM* (*Instituto Nacional de Empleo* – National Employment Institute), which is part of the Ministry of Labour and Social Affairs (*Ministerio de Trabajo y Asuntos Sociales*). It is the only employment and recruitment agency permitted to operate in Spain for permanent work. As an EU citizen you have the same rights as Spanish nationals and can use the services of their employment offices (*oficinas de empleo*). To register with them as a job seeker (*demandante de empleo*), you simply have to show your passport, residence card (*tarjeta de residencia*) (see 2.5.4.1) and have an address. They will inform you, free of charge, of job offers, employment promotion measures, vocational training and benefits and grants information. Again, a good level of Spanish will be necessary to make the most of their services. You can find employment office addresses in the telephone directory (under *INEM*) or on the Internet (*www.inem.es*).There is at least one office in all the provincial capitals and other Spanish cities. Use the office that corresponds to you according to your place of residence in Spain.

(ii) EURES (European employment services)

EURES (*http://europa.eu.int/jobs/eures*) is a co-operative network which was established by the European Commission and the national employment services of the EU member states. It facilitates access to jobs and has one database on job offers and another providing general information on living and working conditions in Spain. The network allows member states to exchange information on job vacancies and you can also have your personal details circulated to the employment service in Spain. This is not always a reliable or quick way of finding work and a lot will depend on your having a sufficient level of Spanish to undertake the work you may be offered. Euro-advisers (*euroconsejeros*) are specially trained staff who administer the EURES network in Spain and can also advise on any aspect of working in Europe. They are available at the *INEM* provincial offices (addresses under *INEM* on the town information). However, it is advisable to call into your local job centre before you leave for Spain. There, staff can contact the Overseas Placing Unit Employment Service on your behalf. This Unit administers the EURES system in the UK and it also provides information on living and working conditions in Spain. It is worth pointing out that job centre vacancies (including those for work in Spain) are also advertised on the Internet (*www.employmentservice.gov.uk*).

(iii) Private agencies and ETTs

Private employment agencies in Spain can only operate as temporary employment firms (*empresas de trabajo temporal/ETT*). These private enterprises offer temporary jobs by hiring workers to provide their services to other companies. They charge for their services and you can find their names and addresses in the *Páginas Amarillas* under *Empresas de trabajo temporal* or by enquiring at an *INEM* office where they keep a register. In addition to general temporary agencies there are also agencies, including non-profit employment agencies, which will only charge you for actual costs incurred (phone calls, etc.) These specialise in specific fields such as banking, secretarial work, hotel and catering, and nannying. Other temporary recruitment agencies like Manpower can be found in cities and large towns. Some UK employment agencies who deal with work abroad are registered with the Recruitment and Employment Confederation (REC). REC is a trade association of recruitment agencies and may be able to recommend an agency to help you in your search for work. You can write to them or visit their web site at *www.rec.uk.com* Appendix V includes some useful web sites relating to job vacancies.

2.5.1.6 Chambers of commerce (*Cámaras oficiales de comercio e industria*)

Offices of the Spanish chambers of commerce both in the UK and Spain may be useful sources of company and business information but, as they receive so many requests for information, you may find that at best you receive a standard reply with a selection of general web sites. You can check their Spanish web site at *www.camerdata.es/* or contact their addresses listed in Appendix V.

2.5.1.7 *COIE*

The *COIE* (*Centros de orientación e información de empleo* – centres for employment guidance and employment) were set up by *INEM* as employment guidance centres at fourteen state-run universities in Spain. They provide information on careers and the labour market, as well as drawing up lists of vacancies and courses. Although primarily aimed at young graduates looking for their first job, if you have the language capability and other relevant credentials or experience, you may find that they can help. All the addresses of the *COIE* are included in the appropriate town information and are listed under the addresses in volume two of the *Guía de las empresas que ofrecen empleo.* Other individual universities have their own *Bolsa de Trabajo* (Employment Agency) but these are chiefly concerned with their own students, although they do now work at the European level. You may find it useful to look at their combined job offers web site at *www.trabajos.com/ofertas*.

2.5.1.8 National and international exchange organisations

There are a number of organisations, based in the UK or with UK offices, which can provide both advice and practical help in finding work in Spain. The Central Bureau for International Education and Training (CBIET) in London (see 2.5.2.2 and 2.5.2.4) administers and co-ordinates a number of schemes (including the Language Assistant Scheme and Socrates programme) and publishes a wide range of material about official work schemes, exchanges, working holidays and voluntary work in Spain. It oversees the work of IAESTE UK (International Association for the Exchange of Students for Technical Experience) which provides international course-related vacation training and placements for thousands of university-level students in over sixty countries (including Spain) in the fields of engineering, science, agriculture, architecture, management and related fields. You should apply directly to IAESTE at the Central Bureau in London in the autumn term for placements beginning in the following summer.

You should also contact the Central Bureau for information relating to Leonardo, an EU action programme which provides support for young people to benefit from vocational training and work experience in another EU member state. The three-week to three-month placements are aimed at young workers, job seekers and those undertaking initial vocational training. Similarly, the CIEE (Council on International Educational Exchange) helps students to work and study abroad. Although based in New York, the Council has offices in London and Madrid and produces an annual *Work Abroad and Study Abroad* booklet which you should find in your university's careers library.

The Brussels-based specialist organisation *AIESEC*, the French acronym for the International Association for Students of Economics and Management, organises career-related placements in over eighty countries (including Spain) through its work abroad programme. *AIESEC* has an office in London. Placements relate to the fields of accountancy, business administration, computing, marketing, economics and finance for between six and seventy-two weeks. It should be stressed that usually very few placements are available due to the imbalance in the numbers of outgoing and incoming students.

The addresses of these organisations, together with many other useful addresses relating to voluntary (VSO, GAP, etc.) and vacation work in Spain, can be found in Appendix II.

2.5.1.9 Applying speculatively

As already mentioned, you can arrange to advertise in a *Situations wanted* section of a local or regional Spanish newspaper. You can do this yourself or use a UK media agency like Publicitas Limited. However, there is nothing to stop you approaching potential employers directly. In all cases send a covering letter or *carta de presentación* together with your CV. A number of the books noted in the bibliography, plus some of the larger language dictionaries, include sample letters and CVs in Spanish. If possible, you should endeavour to write both in Spanish, although it would be inadvisable to try to do this if you have little or no knowledge of the language. Similarly, you should not claim a level of spoken or written Spanish that, in reality, you do not possess. If you are writing from the UK, it helps to enclose a pre-addressed envelope and/or an international reply coupon so that the employer feels under some obligation at least to acknowledge your letter. Depending on your areas of interest and expertise, you might find it useful to start by writing to UK subsidiary or multinational companies. University, careers and public libraries will have sources of addresses such as the publications mentioned in 2.5.1.4, as will tourist guides (for example, *Fodors*, *Rough Guide*, *Lonely Planet* or *Michelin*) if you are interested in working in an hotel, restaurant, theatre, museum or art gallery. Many companies see advantages in employing a native English speaker, particularly if you can also speak Spanish to a reasonable level.

2.5.1.10 Networking

Networking, which originated in the USA, consists of making business and professional contacts. It is particularly useful in Spain where it is common to use such links, although as a student you may feel that you do not have any relevant contacts. However, other students on your course who have worked in Spain, visiting Spanish exchange students and teachers and tutors could form the basis of a potentially productive network. If you can actually carry out some of this networking in Spain, through friends, relations or other students, this can be an even faster way of making progress.

2.5.2 **Types of employment**

There are numerous kinds of work opportunities in Spain and it is often your own circumstances and abilities which will determine the type of employment that you undertake. Examples of the most common areas of work for UK students are described in the following sections.

2.5.2.1 Work placements

Work placements are usually arranged in one of two ways: (i) through your own university or college as the recognised format for the obligatory period of residence abroad for your study programme; or (ii) through the Spanish educational institution to which you have been attached. However, you may find that you are required to find your own placement and make your own arrangements. In some cases, students can request a particular work placement, usually when they have an interest in a specific type of work or where they have already made some initial arrangements. Obviously, as has already been noted above, it is often very difficult and frustrating to try to find work by yourself and Spanish bureaucracy often complicates matters. Where a placement has been arranged for you, your tutor will usually give you a named contact. In addition, you will find information relating to where to go for help in the town and university information in this book.

Once you begin your placement you need to be aware of the distinct ethos that prevails in the Spanish workplace. The nature of the Spanish working day has gradually moved more towards the pattern that exists in northern Europe, but there are still a large number of companies and organisations where you will experience the traditional Spanish work regime. The nature of the Spanish day has already been examined in some detail in 2.4.3.

Whatever system applies where you are working, you should always remember that your placement is designed to benefit you in terms of your career and personal development. You should try to ensure that you keep a written diary or record of your day-to-day experiences to help chart your progress and also to assist you when you come to produce the report normally required at the end of your placement.

2.5.2.2 Jobs with EU organisations

The Central Bureau for International Education and Training (CBIET) produces a list of EU-sponsored vocational and training programmes in their regularly updated *Info Sheet* on Europe. These programmes have a built-in obsolescence (around three years) but are worth following up because most of the funding comes from the European Union. EU action programmes for vocational training are also worth investigating.

Students with a background in information technology, tourism or marketing are eligible for placements in Spain. You must have some relevant experience and a GCSE in Spanish. Because of their reliance on EU funding, programmes change each year and details tend to become available in March.

The office of the European Commission in London (see Appendix II) issues several free fact sheets relating to working in the European Union. The Commission also has offices in Edinburgh, Cardiff and Belfast. If you are interested in working for the Commission as an administrator, translator, secretary, etc., you will need to compete in open competitions held at regular intervals. The London and regional offices will be able to advise on forthcoming dates and send you the relevant application forms.

2.5.2.3 Teaching English as a Foreign Language (TEFL)

There is a thriving market for English language teachers in Spain and this area of work is one of the most popular among students. The entries for language schools occupy around twenty pages of the Madrid *Páginas Amarillas*, but the days are gone when any native speaker of English can expect to be hired by a language academy without the necessary qualifications It is now generally accepted that you need to have some TEFL training and qualifications if you wish to teach English in Spain. The majority of employers demand qualifications and experience and there are only limited possibilities for candidates without either.

One of the most widely recognised initial qualifications is the Certificate in the Teaching of English as a Foreign Language to Adults offered by the Royal Society of Arts Examination Board/University of Cambridge Local Examinations Syndicate (RSA/UCLES). Details of the syllabus are available from UCLES (see Appendix II). Approved courses, normally four to five weeks' full-time tuition, are offered at a number of centres throughout the UK and these details together with costs are available from the English Language Information Unit of the British Council (see Appendix II). You should also contact this address if you are keen to pursue a career in TEFL as they have details covering all general and specialist courses. It is worth pointing out that it is significantly cheaper to undertake this course at a language school in Spain, something worth considering if your course contains a placement period in Spain. After obtaining the Certificate and two years' teaching experience, you can apply to take the Diploma course. Alternatively, Trinity College Dublin offers a Certificate in Teaching English to Speakers of Other Languages (TESOL). Details of the syllabus and courses can be obtained from the College (see Appendix II).

The AGCAS careers information booklet *Teaching English as a Foreign language and Teaching Abroad* (CSU, 2000) describes all aspects of this area of work and contains useful addresses and further readings. It is available from your careers service library. Three other very informative publications are: (i) the *English Language Teaching Guide* (EFL Ltd.), a regularly revised work which contains guidance on qualifications, how to find a job and numerous addresses and contacts; (ii) *Teaching English Abroad*, by Susan Griffith (Vacation Work Publications); and (iii) *Teach English in Spain*, by Penny Johnson (In Print Publishing). Many teaching jobs, particularly those in smaller schools, are only advertised locally in Spain. Those advertised in the UK tend to be for the larger schools, international agencies and government institutions.

The British Council regularly recruits English language teachers and supervisory staff, but these are usually for two-year placements in its language centres in Spain. There are currently seven of these, in Barcelona, Bilbao, Granada, Las Palmas, Madrid, Palma de Mallorca and Valencia. For most teaching posts it is necessary to have advanced qualifications and two years' experience. Further details are available from the British Council in London (see Appendix II). The Council also publishes *Teaching Overseas*, a free guide which explains how it recruits its teachers abroad. British Council and other vacancies are normally advertised in *The Guardian* (Tuesdays), *The Times Educational Supplement* (Fridays) and *EL Prospects*, a vacancies supplement to the *EL Gazette* (monthly, *www.elgazette.com*). It can also be subscribed to separately.

Some commercial language schools with bases in the UK also have branches in Spain. These are often referred to as 'chain schools'. Recruitment for all branches of these schools is generally dealt with at the central office, thus saving you the trouble of having to apply to every branch. Inlingua is one of the largest chain schools in Spain with over thirty branches in towns and cities, while Berlitz has schools in Barcelona, Bilbao, Madrid, Palma de Mallorca, Seville and Valencia. International House, an educational trust which specialises in TEFL and teacher training courses in TEFL, has twelve schools which are all affiliated to the central organisation which is responsible for recruitment and training. Linguarama has schools in Barcelona, Madrid, Seville, Valencia and Pamplona.

The demand for private tuition in English is high and Spain has the largest number of private language schools of any country in Europe, offering English classes for both children and adults. The quality of the schools and the rates of pay vary considerably, but experienced, qualified teachers will generally have an advantage over newcomers. Most recruitment in Spain is done on the spot. September is the best time to look, as this is after the summer holiday and before the beginning of the academic year. Schools usually only offer part-time work and, because statutory employee entitlements start operating only after twelve months' work, nine-month contracts tend to be the norm. The maximum number of teaching hours per week allowed by law is thirty-three, but contracted teachers can expect a punishing schedule with close to this number of hours, often at inconvenient times. If you are in Spain and keen to teach English privately you should consider advertising in local schools, universities and shops, as this can often bring results and, if successful, recommendations are often made by word of mouth. To advertise in advance you should contact Publicitas Limited and some of the local Spanish newspapers listed in *Willings Press Guide* or *Benn's Media Directory Europe*. Qualified applicants might want to make use of the English Educational Services (Madrid) recruitment agency (see Appendix II for details). This agency assesses and recommends qualified teachers to private schools all over Spain and applicants can either contact the agency in Spain in September or write well before travelling to Spain, since interviews are held regularly in London and occasionally in Dublin for client schools in Spain.

While still in the UK you should obtain a list of language schools in Spain from the Education Office of the Spanish Embassy (see Appendix II). They can send you a list of the 350 members of *FECEI* (*Federación Española de Colegios de Enseñanza del Inglés* – the National Federation of English Language Schools), together with the leaflet *Teaching English as Foreign Language*.

2.5.2.4 Teaching assistantships

If you are in the fortunate position of being able to spend a whole academic year in Spain, one of the most profitable ways of using your time – and of improving your Spanish – is to work as an English language assistant in a Spanish school or college. For many years now, the Central Bureau for International Education and Training (CBIET) has been operating a scheme that has allowed hundreds of students or graduates of Spanish to do precisely that. The greatest advantage of this scheme is that you have the opportunity to become totally integrated into a Spanish work and social environment. You may be the only native

English-speaking person working in the school (and indeed the only one living in the area), so that you are obliged to speak Spanish all the time – except when you are in the classroom, of course! Another benefit of an assistantship is that, if you are contemplating teaching as a career, this scheme will give you an excellent opportunity to experience something at least of what is involved – and, indeed, to decide whether you like it or not. There is no obligation, however, for applicants to commit themselves beforehand to becoming a career teacher.

You are eligible to participate in this scheme if you are a native speaker of English, aged between twenty and thirty, and have completed at least two years of higher education in the UK. Normally, applicants are either third-year students on a full-time degree course at a British university or recent graduates of the same. In practice, most applicants are students (and in a few cases) graduates of Spanish, but this is not an essential requirement and those from other disciplines may apply. However, clearly, you could not do the job without having an ability to communicate reasonably well in the language; hence, the CBIET fixes A-level or an equivalent in Spanish as the minimum requirement.

Application forms (AD/F2) are available from the CBIET whose offices are based in London (see Appendix II). These must be filled in neatly and in triplicate (photocopies of AD/F2 will not be accepted). Applicants should obtain a medical certificate from their doctor and attach this, plus one photocopy, to the application forms. Undergraduate and final year students whose degree courses include a foreign language must apply through their university department of languages. Normally, all the documentation is given to the nominated/responsible person in the department who, after writing a confidential reference, will send the form, together with those of other applicants from the university, to the Central Bureau. Those whose courses do not include a foreign language should hand all the forms to their nominated academic referee who will write their report and submit it with the dossier to the CBIET. Other applicants, such as serving teachers and graduates otherwise employed at the time, who fall into the category of independent candidates, should return the application and medical forms to the Central Bureau and ensure that the academic report is forwarded at the same time by the chosen referee. In addition, such candidates should arrange for a confidential reference to be sent to the Bureau by their current or most recent employer.

All forms should reach the CBIET before 1 December in the academic year before that for which the application is made. Applications from independent candidates are acknowledged by the end of January. The likely outcome of applications is made at the latest by early May. Almost always, candidates are asked to attend an interview in London at which a representative from the *Ministerio de Educación, Cultura y Deporte* (*MEC*) is present. These interviews normally take place in February and March.

The CBIET stresses that there is usually a high demand for assistantship posts in Spain. For this reason, priority is given to undergraduates for whom the year abroad is a compulsory part of their course. A waiting list system operates during the summer and early autumn; those on this list may have to wait until as late as September before being offered a post, and not all are successful. Sadly, the Bureau's official brochure for applicants also states: 'Graduates, although welcome to apply, should note that their chances of obtaining a post are low'.

For the academic year 2000–2001 there were some 140 posts available in Spain. Although the 'Language area notes: Spanish' of the Bureau's brochure entitled *Appointment of English language assistants abroad* states that 'posts are available throughout Spain', it also makes it clear that, in certain regions (for example, coastal ones, Andalusia and Valencia), only a limited number of posts are available. On the back of the application form you are asked either to state that you have no area preference or to choose one area from each of three area groups and put them in order of preference (see Figure 2.1). You will be pleased to know that the Central Bureau's literature states: 'Almost all applicants are placed in one of their preferred areas; the majority obtain an offer of a post in the area of first choice'.

If you are lucky enough to be offered a post, you will be working in one of the following types of school/college: (i) an *Instituto de Bachillerato* (*IB*), which prepares 14–18 year olds for their secondary leaving certificate; (ii) an *Instituto de Enseñanza Secundaria* (*IES*), a standard 11–16/18 secondary school; and an *Escuela Oficial de Idiomas* (*EOI*), which offers quite advanced courses in English to students aged approximately 15+ with linguistic promise; or (iv) an *Escuela de Hostelería y Turismo* (*EHT*), which caters for students aged 14+ who are training to work in the catering and tourism industry. If you are allocated a post in Navarre, you may be asked to work in a primary school.

It is possible that, before leaving for Spain, your university has run a short preparatory course. However, in any case, prior to taking up your appointment, you will be expected to attend a compulsory two-day induction course in Madrid at the end of September run by the *MEC*. According to the CBIET brochure, the aim of this course is 'to provide an overview of the way schools are organised, what is expected of a language assistant and how to deal with any problems that may arise'.

Additional help is provided by way of a report compiled by your predecessor at the school where you will be teaching.

The period of appointment is from 1 October to 31 May. You will, of course, be entitled to the same holidays at the school or college concerned, usually about two weeks at Christmas and ten days at Easter. You will be expected to work no more than twelve hours per week. With regard to accommodation, although schools and colleges are usually willing to help out (sometimes by providing furnished lodgings within the school), your best bet is probably to contact the current English assistant (if applicable), who will probably by then have been living in the area for several months and be able to give you sound advice. He or she might even be able to arrange things for you in advance! If you prefer to make your own arrangements, the CBIET undertakes to give you advice.

With regard to income, in the year 2000–2001, the monthly allowance was 95,000 pesetas (approximately £385), which, to quote the Central Bureau, should be enough 'to ensure a reasonable staandard of living for one person'. Although it will depend to some extent on where you have been posted, such is the current demand in Spain for English these days that the chances are that you will be able to supplement your income by giving private conversation classes in the language. Prior to leaving for Spain, you should take advice from the previous assistant at the school regarding banks in the centre concerned. You must open an account there immediately on arrival in order for your monthly allowance to be paid. You will also be able to transfer other monies from the UK to Spain – although you should take steps to prepare the way for this prior to your departure.

As an English assistant, you will usually work either in the classroom with the class teacher or (most often) on your own with a small group of students. Obviously, the exact duties vary from one school to another. However, in general, the role of an assistant is to build up the confidence and competence of the Spanish students in speaking English and also to teach them something about the British way of life. In this context, it is a good idea to take to Spain some relevant up-to-date material with you (photos, maps, tourist brochures, etc.) to use as background or supplementary material. If you have a particular hobby or interest, this can also spark off a postive reaction in your students and you may wish to bring related material into the classroom. You may also be interested to know that the British Council (address in Appendix II) may also be able to provide materials for classes. Specifically, when in the classroom, the activities in which you are involved are likely to include: role playing, pair work, language games, discussions and general conversation –

Figure 2.1 Designated areas for English assistants in Spain

Group A	*Group B*	*Group C*
Asturias	Aragón	Andalucía
Catalunya	(Islas) Canarias	(Islas) Baleares
Ceuta	Cantabria	Castilla y León
Extremadura	Castilla-La Mancha	Madrid
Galicia	Navarra	Murcia
Melilla	La Rioja	Valencia
País Vasco (Euskadi)		

Source: 'Appointment of English Language Assistants Abroad 2000/2001' (*CBIET*, 2000).

depending, of course, on the level and needs of the particular class of students. In addition, you may be asked to help out making recordings in English, either audio or video, and to help the full-time staff in the preparation of language teaching materials.

While you will be expected to take responsibility for your work, and indeed at times to use your own initiative, you will not be left to your own devices. Once at the school, you will be put in the charge of a mentor, usually the head of English or an experienced member of the department. They will be responsible for your programme at the school and will help you to plan your lessons, giving you a clear idea of the requirements of each of the groups with which you will be involved. When you are on your own with a group of students, naturally you are expected to keep good order. However, you can rest assured that, if you do encounter any problems of misbehaviour, you can always turn to your mentor, who is ultimately responsible for class discipline. The good news is that, in the main, Spanish students are very keen to learn and practise their English.

After nine months or so working and living in such an environment, it would be exceptional of you did not derive enormous benefit, both linguistic and personal, from this unique experience. The Central Bureau, in its very informative handout entitled *English language assistants abroad: 20 questions,* states very encouragingly: 'Every year, participants refer time and time again to greatly improved language skills, increased self-confidence and to a real sense of achievement. There are few better ways of getting involved with and feeling part of the community than working as an assistant'.

2.5.2.5 Au pair work

Au pair posts are open to males and females aged between eighteen and thirty, although employers tend to prefer females. They are popular with students as they offer one of the best ways of learning or improving language skills in a typical family environment and gaining experience of living and working in Spain. Duties include looking after children, housework, cooking and possibly teaching the children English. In exchange, lodging, food and pocket money (around 25,000 pesetas a month) are offered. Conditions do vary greatly and it is advisable to agree these before leaving the UK, although there is an argument for only finalising arrangements in Spain, so that you have the chance to visit the family, ask them questions, meet the children and inspect the home.

As an au pair, you can expect to be contracted to work for a minimum of six months and a maximum of a year, and most families require an au pair for at least the whole school year, from September to June. There are also summer au pair programmes of two to three months. If you do not speak Spanish, you will be required to attend Spanish classes, unless you are employed for the summer only. Working hours are officially limited to thirty a week, five hours a day (morning or afternoon), six days a week, plus a maximum of three evenings' baby-sitting. In addition, you should have one full day and three evenings free each week.

Your experience as an au pair will depend almost entirely on your family and, although most au pairs enjoy the experience and form lifelong friendships, others can be treated as servants or slaves, rather than members of the family. If you do have any problems, you should refer them immediately to the agency that found you your position. You should never remain with a family if you are unhappy about the way you are being treated.

For addresses of UK au pair agencies, you should consult: *The Au Pair and Nanny's Guide to Working Abroad* (Vacation Work, 1997); *Summer Jobs Abroad* (Vacation Work, annual); and *Working Holidays* (Central Bureau for Educational Visits and Exchanges, annual). All of them contain important information about au pair work as well as lists of all the principal agencies in the UK.

If you prefer, you can contact Spanish au pair agencies, though you will be required to pay a fee. Among the biggest and most reputable are:

Canary Islands Bureau (Urb. Santiago Edf. 4–5°, Santa Cruz de Tenerife, Las Canarias)

Centros Europeos Galve (Calle Príncipe 12–6°A, 28012 Madrid. Tel: 91 532 72 30)

GIC (Pintor Sorolla, Apt 1080, Monte Vedat, 46901 Valencia. Tel/Fax: 96 156 58 37). This agency was the founding member of the International Au Pair Association.

Relaciones Culturales Internacionales (see Appendix II)

S & C Agencia de Au Pairs (Avda Eduardo Dato 46, 20B, 41005 Sevilla. Tel/Fax: 95 464 24 47 Email: s&c@mundivia.es).

2.5.2.6 Seasonal/vacation work

As Spain is the most popular destination for British tourists, especially the coastal resorts and islands, it is not surprising that companies are keen to employ English-speaking students to help with their British guests. Seasonal jobs include most trades in the service industry: in hotels and restaurants; couriers and representatives; work in holiday camps and campsites; work in ski resorts; sports instructors; and jobs in bars, clubs and discos. Fluency in Spanish is normally required for the better jobs in the hotels and restaurants and with the courier companies. The hours for hotel, restaurant and courier work are often long and the pay is not particularly good. A day off a week is regarded as perfectly normal during the summer and in most cases staff work a minimum of ten hours a day. A list of the main hotels in the main towns and resorts is available from The Spanish National Tourist Office in London (see Appendix II).

You should also approach some of the main UK organisations which employ couriers, guides, and campsite representatives, including:

Airtours Holidays Ltd., Wavell House, Holcombe Road, Helmshore, Rossendale, Lancashire, BB4 4NB. Tel: 01706–909027 Fax: 01706 232328

Canvas Holidays, 12 Abbey Park Place, Dunfermline, Fife, KY12 7PD. Tel: 01992 553535/01383 644000

Club Cantabrica Holidays, Overseas Department, Holiday House, 146148 London Road, St Albans, Hertfordshire, AL1 1PQ. Tel: 01727 33141

Eurocamp PLC, Overseas Recruitment Department. Tel: 01565 625522/ 01606 787522 Fax: 01565 625517

Solaire International Holidays, 1158 Stratford Road, Hall Green, Birmingham, B28 8AF. Tel: 0121 778 5061

Thomson Tours, Greater London House, Hampstead Road, London, NW1. Tel. 0870 5502555.

Addresses and more information on seasonal/vacation work can be found in a large number of guidebooks, including:

Summer Jobs Abroad (Vacation Work, annual)
Working Holidays (Central Bureau for International Education and Training)
Work Your Way Around the World (Vacation Work, annual)
How to... A large number of the books in this series cover a variety of aspects of seasonal and vacation work in Spain.
Working in Tourism – the UK, Europe and Beyond (Vacation Work, annual)
Working in Ski Resorts – Europe and North America (Vacation Work).

Other seasonal work includes fruit picking and other agricultural jobs, though most of this is done by Spanish workers and North African migrants. Nevertheless, addresses and contacts for this type of work can also be found in these guidebooks.

2.5.2.7 Office and administrative work

A number of employment agencies specialise in placing people with language skills and sometimes have details of posts in Spain. However, it should be noted that these agencies do require evidence of fluency and professional or secretarial qualifications before placing candidates on their books. They include: Bilinguagroup, Euro-London Appointments, Merrow Employment Agency and Multilingual Services. Task Force Pro Libra places qualified librarians and information scientists and occasionally has details of posts in Spain. In addition, REC (Recruitment and Employment Federation) produces a free *Job Seeker's List*, covering professional and technical vacancies. They will send you a relevant list once you have told them your area of vocation. Addresses for all these organisations can be found in Appendix II.

2.5.2.8 Charity and voluntary work

The main areas of charity and voluntary work in Spain are education, health, agriculture, and social and community work, although there are rather fewer opportunities in Spain than in some other European countries due to the greater reliance on self-help and increasing government provision within public services. Voluntary Service Overseas (VSO) is the principal organisation sending volunteers abroad, offering work mainly in the field of education, but also other work requiring different skills. Current vacancies are posted on their web site, *www.vso.org.uk*.

International Workcamps provide opportunities for short-term voluntary work in a range of different fields, from conservation work to helping people with disabilities. Again, a good level of Spanish will generally be required. *Workcamp Organisers* is published by the Co-ordinating Committee for International Voluntary Service (which is part of UNESCO), based in France (see Appendix II for their address, or phone the London office on 020 7930 3504). Regularly revised, it contains details on over 300 voluntary service organisations worldwide and is free upon receipt of four international reply coupons. The Central Bureau for International Education and Training provides details on voluntary work and addresses to contact in the annually updated *Working Holidays* and in its *Volunteer Work*, while the Hispanic and Luso Brazilian Council (an organisation linking the UK, Spain, Portugal and Latin America) publishes the very informative *Spain: a Guide to Work Opportunities for Young People*. Another useful guide is the *International Directory of Voluntary Work* (Vacation Work, annual), which provides information on residential and non-residential voluntary work.

Many organisations and agencies arrange workcamp, charity and voluntary work placements in Spain and some of the most important are described below:

The British Trust for Conservation Volunteers (*www.btcv.org.uk*) is a registered charity promoting practical conservation work by volunteers. Recent projects have included working at a permanent research station near Sorbes, Almería, with the Sunseed Trust, planting trees and drystone walling. The Trust's details are as follows: Eastside, Huntingdon, Cambridgeshire, PE18 7BY. Tel: 01480 411784 Fax: 01865 721530.

Earthwatch (Belsyre Court, 57 Woodstock Road, Oxford, OX2 6HU. Tel: 01865 311600) is a charitable organisation which recruits volunteers for research and conservation projects. You will be expected to contribute towards the cost of the project.

The *Instituto de la Juventud* (*INJUVE*) (José Ortega y Gasset 71, 28006 Madrid. Tel: 91 401 66 52 Fax: 91 401 81 60 Email: svi@mtas.es) co-ordinates work on many archaeological and conservation projects in Spain, and their handbook *Campos de Trabajo* provides details of over one hundred projects throughout the country. The *Instituto* also organises volunteer work with archaeological digs in Spain.

Sci-Catalunya (Carrer del Carme 95, baixos 2ª, 08001 Barcelona) and *Sci-Madrid* (C/Valencia 2, 1°N, 28012 Madrid) organise international teams to work on projects ranging from: (i) working in centres for the disabled; (ii) working in drug addicts' rehabilitation centres; (iii) building greenhouses and nurseries; and (iv) the care of animals at injured animal centres. A good knowledge of Spanish or Catalan is essential on most camps.

Kursolan (C/Sándalo 5, 28042 Madrid. Tel: 91 320 75 00 Fax. 91 320 77 53) appoints monitors to take care of, and teach English and sports to, Spanish children. Applicants are expected to have relevant experience.

2.5.2.9 Self-employment

As in the UK, there are several ways to work in Spain on a self-employed or similar basis. These include franchises (*franquicias*), co-operatives (*cooperativas*) and limited liability companies (*Sociedades anónimas laborales/ SAL*). To work in Spain on a self-employed basis it is necessary to provide not only the documentation required for a residence permit (see 2.5.4.1) but also a large quantity of other material. The exact nature of the documentation required will depend on the proposed activity and, although complex, is basically the same as that demanded of a Spanish citizen. For details of the requirements, you should contact the Spanish Chamber of Commerce or Labour Office (Spanish Embassy) in London (addresses in Appendix II) or a British Council Office in Spain.

2.5.3 **Making an application**

If you are applying to an agency, UK organisation or directly to a Spanish firm, your focal point for selling yourself will be your introductory letter (*carta de presentación*) and your *curriculum vitae* (CV). The golden rules with this type of correspondence are:

- Be brief
- Be clear
- Write CV in Spanish (and covering letter, if possible).

You need to be able to show at a glance what your particular qualities are as the reader will probably have dozens of similar letters and CVs to deal with. Always type your letter and CV, avoid abbreviations and ensure that you give your contact information (telephone, postal address or email). Your introductory/covering letter is your opportunity to underline the relevance of your qualifications and experience to the requirements of the particular job or area of work. Your CV is a statement of information and is not the place for a 'hard sell' to an employer; your covering letter is more appropriate for this. It should occupy no more than a single A4 page, making it easy to read. Stick to the relevant headings (for example, education), emphasise your work experience and language skills, and list your interests and hobbies (briefly). Also make sure that you give the names of two referees and that you have already contacted them and obtained their permission. A good CV and an appropriate letter may enable you to exploit your 'added value' of being a native English speaker, particularly with large firms and international companies based in Spain. You will find a model CV in Spanish in Appendix III.

2.5.4 **Documentation**

Where work experience is organised through a higher education institution or through an established scheme, many of the routine formalities will be arranged for you, but there are various documents that you will need to ensure you obtain yourself. You will obviously need a valid passport and proof of student status will be a valuable asset. With an International Student Identity Card (ISIC), it is often possible to obtain reduced fares on planes, trains and buses, as well as a range of other shopping discounts. It currently costs £6 (with proof of full-time student status and a passport-sized photograph) from university Student Union offices. As well as providing additional proof of identity, it also functions as a phonecard and contains a helpline number. The student travel organisation TIVE, based in INJUVE (Tel: 91 347 77 00) (see 2.5.2.8), is well worth contacting since, among other benefits, they can provide cut-price travel and cards for Spanish youth hostels (*albergues de la juventud*).

2.5.4.1 Residence permit (*tarjeta de residencia*)

In recent years, paperwork has become a little easier for EU citizens working in Spain. Work permits as such no longer exist, but you will need to obtain a residence permit from the local authorities if you intend to stay more than three months. This must be done within thirty days of arrival. Application should be made to the local police headquarters (*comisaría de policia*) which deals with foreigners' affairs (*asuntos de extranjeros*). The documents necessary for the residence permit are as follows: (i) proof that you are a student enrolled on a recognised course or a contract of employment; (ii) three passport-sized photos; (iii) your passport; (iv) proof of income for the duration of your course/work; and

(v) proof of health insurance status, private or public (for example, form E111 or personal insurance policy – see 2.2.4). You may also find it useful to have your birth certificate available. This information can be confirmed either with the Labour and Social Affairs Office of the Spanish Embassy (20 Peel Street, London, W8 7PD. Tel: 020 7221 0098 Email: spanlabo@globalnet.co.uk) and at the British Consulate-General's Office in Madrid (C/Marqués de la Ensenada 16–2°, 28004 Madrid. Tel: 91 308 52 01). In addition, the British Embassy produces a document entitled *Settling in Spain*, which contains comprehensive information on entry and residence requirements (you should also register your arrival and current address in Spain with your nearest British Consulate office as soon as you arrive). When your application has been considered, you will receive a letter asking you to go to the *comisaría* to collect your resident's card, taking with you a copy of the application, passport and proof that you have paid 1000 pesetas into the Ministry of the Interior's account in a branch of the Argentaria bank. You must also ensure that you keep a copy of all the documents you submit. You will normally be given a type A residency permit, valid for twelve months and not automatically renewable.

2.5.4.2 Employment contract (*contrato de trabajo*)

Remember that you have the same rights as Spanish workers as regards salaries, working conditions and promotion. In Spain it is obligatory for all employees to have an employment contract, stating such particulars as job title, position, salary, working hours, benefits, duties and responsibilities and the duration of the employment. There are two main types of contract: (i) an indefinite term contract and (ii) a short-term contract (which is usually for a minimum of one year, but can be less for students in seasonal or temporary work). However, to facilitate the entry of young people into the labour market, two other types of contract have been established. One is a training contract (*contrato en prácticas*) aimed at assisting university and college graduates without work experience to find employment. The other is a contract for part-time work (*contrato a tiempo parcial*). In order to get any employment contract, you need to obtain a *NIE* (*número de identificación de extranjero*), a kind of national insurance number for foreigners from the *comisaría* where you applied for your residence card (this could be done at the same time). Some students have highlighted occasions of a Spanish Catch–22 situation, in that they have been unable to obtain a *NIE* until they have an employment contract, whilst some are told that they cannot be given the contract without the *NIE*! Your best option is to try to obtain your employment contract from the agency or company first and then take it along with your other documentation when you apply for your residence card. In this way, you should receive your *NIE* and *tarjeta* around the same time. It is important to note that without a *NIE* you will not be able to open a bank account or take out an insurance policy in Spain. If you have any doubts or queries relating to your own circumstances, it is advisable to contact the offices mentioned above in 2.5.4.1 or check the British Embassy in Spain's *Settling in Spain* document. Alternatively, advice on employment law, contracts and related matters can be sought through the English-speakers' department of the trade union *Comisiones Obreras* (*CCOO*), either at its Madrid headquarters (C/Lope de Vega 38. Tel: 91 536 51 00) or at its local and regional offices.

Before signing a contract, carefully check the terms and conditions of engagement and make sure that you fully understand what is in it. As it will be in Spanish, you may wish to obtain an English translation, or ask an independent native Spanish speaker to go through it with you.

2.5.5 **Tax, social security and health insurance**

2.5.5.1 Tax

In Spain income tax is called *impuesto sobre la renta de las personas físicas* (*IRPF*), or simply *la renta*, and is deducted at source. As individual circumstances are different, it is advisable to investigate your tax position carefully before you start work. Discuss your tax situation with your employer to establish how much tax and national insurance will be deducted. You can also obtain free tax advice at your local tax office in the UK (ask for their leaflet *Going to Work Abroad*), at the local provincial tax offices in Spain or by visiting the Inland Revenue web site at *www.inlandrevenue.gov.uk*. EU member states have entered into tax agreements in order to avoid double income taxes on people travelling or residing in different EU countries.

VAT in Spain is known as *IVA* (*impuesto sobre el valor añadido*) and ranges from 4 per cent on goods considered to be basic necessities to the general 16 per cent rate.

2.5.5.2 Social security

The Spanish social security system is managed by the *Instituto Nacional de la Seguridad Social* (*INSS*) and you can obtain information about benefits relating to health, illness and unemployment from their local offices or at their web site, *www.seg-social.es*. The Department of Social Security (DSS) (*www.dss.gov.uk*) also publishes a series of leaflets (for example, *Social Security Abroad*) and it is advisable to call into your local office for up-to-date information and guidance.

Basically, your social security rights in Spain under EU legislation are the same as those that apply throughout the EU. Contributions (*cotizaciones*) and benefits (*prestaciones*) are both high in Spain. When you start work there, you will contribute to the Spanish social security system and, in doing so, gain the right to benefits. Contributions are calculated as a percentage of your gross income and are deducted at source by your employer. Make sure that you are aware of what your contributions are likely to be before you start work.

If you are entitled to the contributory part of job seeker's allowance and have been claiming this for at least four weeks in the UK, you may continue to receive it for up to three months in Spain, while you actively seek work there. You must first tell your Employment Service job centre in the UK (where you are registered) of your intention to look for work in Spain well in advance of your departure date. Your job centre will advise the DSS Overseas Branch which will determine whether conditions are met and send you form E303 before you leave. This form, which secures payment of your unemployment benefit in Spain should be taken to a local employment office (*oficina de empleo*) as soon as possible after your arrival in Spain. It is also advisable to request form E301 before leaving, if you have worked in the UK, in order to account for the periods worked in order to calculate eventual benefits in Spain.

If you become unemployed in Spain, you should contact the local Spanish employment office or an INSS office which will give you advice about claiming benefits. If you wish to become a self-employed worker in Spain, you should contact the Spanish Embassy (Commercial Office) in London, a regional Consular Office or any *oficina de empleo* if you are in Spain. They will advise about regulations concerning setting up as a self-employed worker and social security contributions and benefits information.

2.5.5.3 Health insurance

It is essential that during your stay in Spain you are insured against accident and illness, either through the social security system, private health insurance or both. Health care in Spain is provided by the *Instituto Nacional de la Salud* (*INSALUD*). Before you travel to Spain you should request information from your local DSS office. As a minimum cover, they will recommend that you acquire Form E111 available from post offices. As already indicated in 2.2.4.1, this entitles you to free health benefits in the event of accident or illness; however, even with Form E111, it is still likely that you may be expected to pay for some of your costs (dental, for example) and so you are advised to investigate taking out private health insurance, either through a company (BUPA, etc.) in the UK or one of the large number of Spanish private health companies which are listed in the Yellow Pages (*Páginas Amarillas*) under *clínicas médicas*.

If you are working in Spain and therefore contributing to the Spanish Social Security system, you will receive a social security card (*cartilla de la seguridad social*) containing your personal details and affiliation number. This card entitles you to free medical and hospital treatment in the Spanish health system. This also covers 40 per cent of the amount of medical prescriptions. The only dental treatment covered by the social security system is extractions. The local offices of the *INSS* can give you a list of all the national health centres and hospitals in Spain. About 40 per cent of hospitals in Spain are private hospitals.

If you receive medical treatment in Spain make sure you retain all your medical bills, receipts and other documentation and return these together with your E111 to the Overseas Branch of the DSS in Newcastle upon Tyne (DSS, Overseas Group, Newcastle upon Tyne, NE98 1YX).

2.5.6 **Legal assistance**

During your stay in Spain, it is important to remember that you are subject to Spanish law. In the event of any legal problem, either consult with a lawyer or, if particularly serious, with British Embassy or consular officials. The services of a lawyer are guaranteed to anyone in custody in all police and legal proceedings.

2.5.7 **Validation of UK qualifications**

If you are a graduate seeking long-term employment in Spain – and, in particular if your aim is to find a job as a teacher in the public sector (normally better paid than in its private counterpart) – you will find that it is essential at some stage to have your degree or diploma validated by the Spanish authorities. Experience has shown that this process of *convalidación* can be time-consuming and frustrating, sometimes taking years to complete. You can seek initial advice through the Education Office of the British Council or your nearest *Instituto Cervantes* (see Appendix II). If your aim is to teach in the public sector in Spain, you will need to request the required forms from the *Subdirección General de Títulos, Convalidaciones y Homologaciones* of the *MEC* in Madrid (address in Appendix II).

2.5.8 **Checklist**

Before you take up or look for employment in Spain, ensure that you have the following documents:

- Valid UK/EU passport
- Copy of your birth certificate
- Form E111 and any other forms recommended by your Social Security Office
- Translated CVs, letters of introduction, references, and degree and course information
- Other documents that you deem appropriate, for example, your driving licence
- Some passport-sized photographs.

In addition, you should check that:

- You have a job contract and fully understand its terms and conditions.
- You know the method and frequency of payment of salary
- You know what travel arrangements need to be made and whether you or your employer will pay
- You have accommodation in Spain
- You have adequate medical coverage
- You have sufficient funds to cover your costs until you are paid or to cover the cost of your return home if this becomes necessary
- You have been to your local DSS office and found out what rules apply if you are visiting Spain to look for work
- You have taken out a travel insurance policy that covers luggage, accidents and personal liability
- Your language competence is appropriate for the work you are intending to do.

2.6
Returning to the UK

Just as you should take time and care to prepare in advance for your trip to Spain (see 2.2), so you should not neglect to prepare in a sensible and systematic way for your return to the UK. This is especially true if you are a full-time student, for you will have been part of a large and long-standing operation that may have taken years to build up. However, even independent students need to make some preparations for coming home.

2.6.1 **Academic matters**

As a full-time undergraduate, it is more than probable that the academic authorities in your home university will be expecting you to bring back at the very least a certificate of attendance (*certificado de asistencia*) relating to your formal studies at the host university and it is quite possible that you will have been asked to take examinations and to take back the results of these, with (where appropriate) the corresponding number of credits attained. As an independent student, who has just completed, for example, an intensive course in Spanish leading perhaps to one of the *Diploma Española de Español como Lengua Extranjera* (*DELE*) examinations, you will also be interested in obtaining, where possible, the results and certification. If you are unable to obtain the documents you require before leaving Spain, you should ensure that you leave your home address in the UK with the *secretaría* of the appropriate teaching centre.

2.6.2 **Leaving your accommodation**

If you have been lucky enough to be lodged in a *colegio mayor*, do make sure that you have paid all your bills (always ask for receipts) and handed the keys back to the warden before your departure. If you have been living in a flat, likewise ensure that you have no outstanding bills; while you may well have paid your rent a month in advance, you may still be liable for other bills like electricity (*luz*) and water (*agua*). So, well before you leave, make sure that you have had the metres read and that you know what you owe. One important consideration, of course, is the deposit (*fianza*) that you will almost certainly have paid at the start of your tenancy and which you must have paid back to you. Do check that you have not left anything behind before you finally move out of your accommodation; even if you leave a forwarding address with your landlord/lady, you cannot be sure that things left behind will be passed on.

2.6.3 **Financial matters**

Needless to say, any outstanding financial transactions should be completed before you leave the country, as they are always likely to be much more complicated from a distance. If you have, by any chance, opened a bank account while in Spain (in general something not to be recommended), unless you have a very good reason for leaving it open (e.g. you are returning in the near future to live in Spain), you should close it before you leave. Banks in Spain charge quite high sums to keep accounts open and their statements can come think and fast, eating into what monies you have left in the account! One final point: try not to end up with a lot of Spanish cash, because you are likely to lose out badly in the UK when changing it back into sterling; far better to spend it on an extra present for your Mum or Dad or an extra bottle of good Spanish wine – if you can fit it into your luggage!

2.6.4 **Travel arrangements**

If you flew to Spain on a charter flight, the likelihood is that the return part of your ticket will long ago have expired. Well before you plan to return to the UK (say a month), you should make enquiries and hopefully secure a booking for your return journey – although, depending on the airport and the airline involved, this may not be easy if you plan to return by the same method because of the nature of charter flights. If you want to be absolutely certain of obtaining a flight back in advance (and assuming you have been living near a major airport), you should consider catching a scheduled flight, even though the cost will be quite high. If you plan to return overland, say by train and Britanny Ferries, while a train journey need only be booked a day or two in advance, you would be well advised to enquire into ferry reservations several weeks beforehand. Travel agents (*agencias de viajes*) are plentiful in Spain and you should have no problems in sorting out all your arrangements with one of them. Whichever method of transport you plan to use, the secret is to plan ahead and not leave things until the last minute.

2.6.5 The farewell (*despedida*)

Particularly if you are a full-time undergraduate and have had regular contact with one or more of your tutors or lecturers at your host university, or if you have had a lot do with staff in one or more of the student services, it is only courtesy to take your leave of them and thank them for their help. The same applies to wardens of halls of residence and landlords or landladies. Even if you feel that they may not deserve very effusive thanks, at least go through the motions. The reason for this is that these contacts, especially those at the university, are vital to the formal links established over time between your home university and your host institution in Spain. For the sake of other students who will follow in your footsteps, you should do your best to leave a good impression. This does not mean, however, that you should keep silent if there have been genuine problems, but in most cases it is probably best if these are aired to your placement tutor when you return to the UK.

While the above *despedida* may, in some cases at least, appear to be no more than an obligation, it is highly likely that you will want to say farewell in style to the (perhaps many) friends you will have made while in Spain. Spaniards set great store by *despedidas* and would be somewhat miffed if you sneaked off back to the UK without saying goodbye. The probability is, in any case, that they will have organised a party of some sort and, although you might be busily engaged organising your return journey, you can be sure that this will be an occasion not to be missed. But, if you are leaving for home next morning, don't forget to set your alarm clock.

Part 3
Towns and their universities

Introduction

In this section, the data will be presented as follows: basic information about the city or town concerned, followed by essential facts and figures about the university, universities or university campus/campuses located within its boundaries. In each case, a two digit general heading for the location (e.g. *Granada*) is followed by a three digit sub-heading for the town concerned (e.g. *Ciudad de Granada*), and then by a parallel three digit sub-heading for the following information giving the university or universities located there (e.g. *Universidad de Granada*). The latter includes in brackets the official acronym of the university concerned; such acronyms are commonly used both formally and informally. In a number of two digit headings, the alternative vernacular name for the location is given in brackets; these apply in the three autonomous communities of Spain, where regional languages (and hence regional spellings of place names) are co-official with their Castilian counterparts, i.e. the Basque Country, Catalonia and Galicia. Thereafter, in the following three digit sub-headings, only the Castilian forms are normally given – the exceptions being the cases of a few universities, notably in the Basque Country and Catalonia, where the regional spelling or title of the university governs the acronym (for example, *Universidad/ Universitat de Lleida = ULLE* and *Universidad de Mondragón/ Mondragón Unibertsitatea = MU*) or where the vernacular name is somewhat different from the Castilian form (e.g. *Universitat de les Illes Balears*). It is recognised that these days a number of place and university names are probably quite widely known in their vernacular forms (for example, *Universitat de Girona*). However, apart from the fact that, within any one autonomous community, there is not always common agreement whether to use the Castilian or regional forms (Galicia is very much a case in point), the authors have opted to give preference to the Castilian forms in the interests of presentational consistency.

(a) **Town information**

Information is provided under two major headings: (i) basic information and (ii) sources of information. The first section includes: location; status (for example, regional/provincial capital); population; geography and climate; history and main historical sites; nature of town (industrial, tourist, port, etc.); main areas of interest for visitors; places worth visiting in the surrounding area; travel and transport information; major economic activities; and major employers. The second section provides the names, addresses, telephone, fax numbers, etc. of official bodies where students are likely to find information on the town and province where they are living. Examples of these are the tourist office, the town hall (*ayuntamiento*) and the chamber of commerce (*cámara de comercio*). In addition, details are given of the local employment office, the *INEM* (*Instituto Nacional de Empleo*), and of the university employment guidance and information centre, *COIE* (*Centro de Orientación e Información del Empleo*). (The latter may seem more appropriate in the university information, but in fact the COIEs are seen very much as a local resource for the whole community.) Finally, if a city or town is twinned with a counterpart in the UK, this is indicated at the end.

Readers should note that the addresses for most of the companies listed under 'Major employers' can be found in the *Guía de las empresas que ofrecen empleo: España y Portugal* (see 2.5.1.4), details of which are given in the bibliography.

(b) **University information**

These comprise four sections: (i) basic information; (ii) teaching centres; (iii) student services; and (iv) courses in languages. The first section includes: the name of the autonomous community, province (if appropriate) and town in which the university is located; its status (public or private) and, in brackets, its date of foundation; the main address of the university, as well as telephone, fax, email and Internet numbers; the main campuses (usually, but not always, within the city concerned) plus, if appropriate, any satellite campuses (usually, but not always, in other towns within the province); and, finally, information on the approximate number of full-time students and academic staff.

The second section outlines, in English, the faculties, higher technical schools (ETS) and university schools (EU) which operate within the university; this gives the reader an overall view of the kinds of subject areas taught in the institution concerned. (A complete list of degree and diploma courses for Spain as a whole is given in Appendix I). A plus sign (+) followed by town name will indicate that the subject area is also available at a satellite campus in another town. Depending on the size and nature of the university, this section may also include the names of other university centres; the most common of these are the university institutes, such as the *ICE*s (*Institutos de Ciencias de la Educación*) which provide teacher training for graduates (see 1.4.7.2).

The third section includes, where available, details of information offices, accommodation offices, health centres and university centres offering courses in Spanish especially designed for foreign students. In addition to the names, in Spanish, of such centres, telephone, fax and email numbers are provided where it has been possible to obtain them. The fourth section makes a distinction between full-time language degree courses for Spanish students, which may be relevant and of interest to British students of modern languages involved in official exchanges with a partner institution in Spain (an Erasmus/Socrates programme, for example), and full-time and/or part-time courses in Spanish language (and culture) offered specifically for foreign students. Such courses are normally, though not always, provided by the *Cursos para Extranjeros* department, whose name, address, etc., where available, is given in the third section. It should be noted that some minor university campuses (including, in some cases, those located in small provincial capitals like Cuenca, Lugo, Teruel and Soria, as well as those situated in even smaller towns) have not been included due to lack of space. Should readers require information on these towns, they should consult the guide books included in the bibliography, which will give details of tourist offices and other useful organisations.

It should be stressed that the authors have made every effort to ensure that the information which they have provided is accurate and up to date. However, it is well known that in Spain such things as telephone and fax numbers (and sometimes the names of departments within universities) change with remarkable frequency. Nevertheless, in attempting to contact a given university, readers and would-be students in Spain must not be discouraged: if the switchboard (*centralita*) numbers do not respond, other numbers are given (for example, the information office or department of international relations) where contact may well be easier and, indeed, more appropriate. Conversely, if one of the latter fails to respond, the *centralita* is more than likely to be able to give you the number(s) you require. While university web sites vary greatly in the amount of data they carry and in the regularity with which they are updated, in the main they are very valuable sources of data.

3.1 Alcalá de Henares

3.1.1 **Ciudad de Alcalá de Henares**

Basic information

Location and status: Central Spain, 30 km north-east of Madrid. Located within Comunidad de Madrid.

Population: 166,525

Geography: Landscape of palm and fruit trees, vineyards, pinewoods and vegetables.

Climate: Hot summers and cold winters; very cold at night in winter. Similar climate to Madrid.

History: Under Roman rule before being destroyed in 1000 and rebuilt in 1038 by Alfonso VI who granted with it the surrounding lands to the archbishop of Toledo.

Main historical sites: Gothic church of San Justo (built in 1136 and called La Magistral). University (original being moved to Madrid). Former archbishop's palace (now a seminary that contains documents of Inquisitions of Toledo and Valencia).

The town: One of Europe's most ancient university towns. Now a modern industrial town. Many Renaissance style buildings.

Main areas of interest: Birthplace of novelist Miguel de Cervantes, Emperor Ferdinand I and Catherine of Aragón. The house that Cervantes was born in, Calle Mayor 48, now contains a museum which reflects living conditions in the sixteenth century. University buildings.

Surrounding area: Nuevo Baztán (20 km); Loeches (13 km); Sierra de Guadarrama.

Travel and transport: Regular trains (every 15–30 minutes) and buses (every 15 minutes) from Madrid. To the west is the airport of Barajas, round which bypasses have been built bearing north-west and south-west.

Major economic activities: Manufactures chemicals, cotton goods, perfumes, pottery, electrical and domestic appliances. Famous for iced almonds.

Major employers: Autoestático, S.L. Alcalá Industrial, S.A. (Grupo Cointra), Ibérica AGA, S.A., L'Oréal S.B., Realizaciones Publicitarias, S.L.

Sources of information

Tourist Office: Callejón de Santa María 1, Alcalá de Henares. Tel: 91 889 26 94

INEM: Paseo de la Estación 9, 28807 Alcalá de Henares. Tel: 91 888 08 66 Fax: 91 883 48 16

COIE: COIE de la Universidad de Alcalá, Plaza de San Diego s/n, Antiguo Palacio de San Pedro y San Pablo. Tel: 91 885 40 58/98 Fax: 91 885 40 95 Email: coieuah@coie.alcala.es

Town hall: Plaza de Cervantes 1, 28801 Alcalá de Henares Tel: 91 888 33 00

Chamber of commerce: As for Madrid

Twin town: Peterborough

3.1.2 **Universidad de Alcalá de Henares (UAH)**

Basic information

Autonomous community: Comunidad de Madrid

Province: Madrid

Town: Alcalá de Henares

Status: Public (1499; 1977)*

Address: Plaza de San Diego s/n, 28001 Alcalá de Henares (Madrid)

Tel: 91 885 40 00 Fax: 91 885 40 95 Web site: www.alcala.es

Main campus: Plaza de San Diego

Satellite campus: Guadalajara

Students: 18,664

Staff: 1,314

Teaching centres

Faculties: Arts; economics and business; environment; law; medicine; pharmacy; science

Higher technical schools: N/A

University schools: Business (Guadalajara); nursing and physiotherapy; nursing (Guadalajara); teacher training (+Guadalajara)

Student services

Information office: Centro de Información Universitaria (CIU), Plaza de San Diego s/n, Alcalá de Henares. Tel: 91 885 40 03/06 Fax: 91 885 40 95 28001 Email: ciu@ciua. alacala.es

Accommodation office: Oficina de Alojamiento, Campus Universitario Vivienda A-8.4, Ctra Madrid–Barcelona, 28805 Alcalá de Henares. Tel: 91 880 98 95

Health centre: Servico Médico, Campus Universitario, 08808 Alcalá de Henares. Tel: 91 887 81 00

Spanish courses for foreign students: Cursos para Extranjeros, Antiguo Colegio de los Irlandeses, Escritores 4, 28801 Alcalá de Henares. Tel: 91 881 23 78

Courses in languages

For languages undergraduates: The Faculty of Arts offers degree courses in English and Spanish philology. Details can be obtained from: Colegio Mayor de San Ildefonso, Plaza de San Diego s/n, 28801 Alcalá de Henares. Tel: 91 885 40 88

Spanish for foreign students: Three types of course are on offer: (1) a one-year Spanish language and literature course, especially for foreign graduates with knowledge of Spanish; (2) three-month courses in Spanish language and culture at all levels are offered in the autumn, spring and summer terms; (3) intensive language and culture courses are offered at all levels during July and August (4–5 hours of tuition each day).

* Refounded in 1977 after old Universidad Complutense was closed in 1836.

3.2 Alicante (Alacant)

3.2.1 **Ciudad de Alicante**

Basic information

Location and status: South-east Spain, 422 km from Madrid. Located within Comunidad Valenciana. Capital of Province of Alacant (Alicante).

Population: 276,000

Geography: Located on Mediterranean. Beaches known as Costa Blanca. Lush vegetation grows on coast, as well as forests of pine, oak and holm oak. Rugged peaks inland.

Climate: Mild, winter resort. Pleasant winter climate. In summer it is very hot.

History: The city was founded by Phocaean Greeks in 325 BC. It was captured by the Romans in 201 BC, who called it Lucentum (City of Light). Was under Moorish domination during the years 718–1249. It was besieged by French in 1709 and by federalists of Cartagena in 1873.

Main historical sites: Baroque town hall (1701–60). Church of Santa María (fourteenth century). Renaissance Collegiate Church. Cathedral of San Nicolás de Bari (eighteenth century).

Town: Port city. Dominated by Benacantil hill (721 feet). Winter resort with beaches that attract tourists. Second largest city of the Comunidad Valenciana.

Main Areas of interest: Church of Santa María. Palacio de la Diputación. Museo de Arte. Castle of Santa Bárbara, sixteenth-century fortress overlooking city. During the last week of June it has the famous Fiesta de Sant Joan, with its own Fallas (see Valencia).

Surrounding area: Balcón del Mediterráneo affords a superb view overlooking the bay. Elche – Palm Forest (20 km)

Travel and transport: Excellent road, rail and air transportation facilities. Newly extended airport of El Altet is only 8 km from city centre (many direct flights from UK). Most roads converge on the palm-lined Esplanada de España, skirting the harbour. Alicante is the gateway to Costa Blanca.

Major economic activities: Commercial port, wine, raisins, vegetables, esparto grass, tomatoes, bricks, cigarettes, aluminium utensils, furniture and embroideries, textiles, chemicals and tourism (vitally important to local economy).

Major employers: Bull. Econet Medio Ambiente, S.A., El Pozo Alimentación, S.A., Fundación para el Desarrollo de la Formación Empresarial (FUMDESEN), Grupo Fimestic, Hatmix, S.A.

Sources of information

Tourist office: Oficina de Turismo, Esplanada de España 2, 03002 Alicante. Tel: 96 521 22 85 Tourist Line: 96 520 00 00

INEM: Pintor Aparicio 15, 03003 Alicante. Tel: 96 522 85 42

Town hall: Plaza del Ayuntamiento s/n, 03002 Alicante. Tel: 96 520 51 00

Chamber of commerce: Cámara de Comercio, Industria y Navegación, San Fernando 4, 03002 Alicante. Tel: 96 520 11 33 Fax: 96 520 14 57

3.2.2 **Universidad de Alicante (UAL)**

Basic information

Autonomous community: Comunidad Valenciana
Province: Alicante
Town: Alicante
Status: Public (1979*)
Address: Sant Vicent del Raspeig, 03690 Alicante. Tel: 96 590 34 00 Fax: 96 590 34 64 Web site: www.ua.es
Main campus: Sant Vicent del Raspeig
Satellite campuses: Elche+; Elda; San Juan
Students: 30,000
Staff: 1,200

Teaching centres

Faculties: Arts; economics and business; law; medicine (San Juan); science

Higher technical schools: Higher polytechnic school

University schools: Business sciences; labour relations (Elda); nursing; optics and optometry; social work; teacher training

Institutes: Criminology; geography; international economics; Valencian language studies; water and environmental sciences

Student services

Information office: Oficina de Información al Alumno, Apartado de Correos, 03080 Alicante. Tel: 96 590 34 00 Fax: 96 590 34 64 99

Accommodation office: See *Oficina de Información al Alumno* or contact Asociación para la Promoción del Voluntariado, Aulario 1, Planta 2ª, Apartado 99, 03080 Alicante. Tel: 96 590 37 53

Health centre: See *Oficina de Información al Alumno*

Spanish courses for foreign students: Cursos Internacionales, Cátedra Rafael Altamira, San Vicent del Raspeig, 03690 Alicante. Tel: 96 66 11 50; 66 12 00 Fax: 96 66 88 67

Courses in languages

For languages undergraduates: The Faculty of Arts offers degree courses in Catalan, English, French and Hispanic philologies. The same Faculty also runs a degree course in translating and interpreting, the languages offered being English and French.

Spanish for foreign students: Spanish language and culture courses are offered at all levels during July and August. Accommodation can be provided at a modest cost on the main campus at Sant Vicent del Raspeig.

* The Universidad de Alicante claims to be the heir to the former Universidad de Orihuela, which existed between 1610 and 1808 and which is now a campus of the new Universidad de Miguel Hernández (see 3.16.2).

3.3 Almería

3.3.1 **Ciudad de Almería**

Basic information

Location and status: South-east Spain, in Andalucía. Capital of Province of Almería. Located on Mediterranean, 563 km from Madrid.

Population: 167,350

Geography: Altitude of 614 feet above sea level on hillside where Rivers

Rivillias and Guadiana meet. An ancient port city. Situated on beautiful bay.

Climate: Mild, sunny climate. Year-round swimming possible. Winter is warm and dry. Summer is hot inland; hot winds can raise shade temperatures to thirty-six degrees centigrade.

History: Known to Romans as Urci or Portus Magnus. Known to Moors as al-Mariyah (Mirror of the Sea). A thriving town and port under Moors. Captured by Catholic Monarchs, Ferdinand and Isabella of Castile, in 1489. Devastated by earthquake in 1522. After 1960 it became popular with film-makers.

Main historical sites: Gothic cathedral (1524–43) built in form of fortress. Bishop's palace and seminary built in 773 by Amir of Córdoba. Ruined castle of San Cristóbal overlooks city and harbour.

Town: Has Morrocan rather than European appearance due to dazzling whiteness of many of its buildings.

Main areas of interest: La Alcazaba (fortress). Cathedral. Church of Santiago. Gypsy district of La Chanca.

Surrounding area: Dunes along Cabo de Gata, a rugged and unspoiled natural park. Hinterland (e.g. Sierra de Gador) is very hilly and arid, north African in appearance. Remains of old mines, including gold. 'Little Hollywood' is located abour 25 km north of Almería; set open to public when not filming. Prehistoric site of Los Millares at Benahadux.

Travel and transport: Growth in airport facilities since 1960, due to film industry. Charter flights from European countries and regular national services. Regular national bus services as well as train. Boat services to Spanish destinations.

Major economic activities: Intensive cultivation under plastic of citrus fruits and vegetables, especially tomatoes. Metalworking, canning and salting of fish, refining of oil and sulphur, manufacture of chemicals. Tourism, especially at nearby resort of Roquetas de Mar.

Major employers: Port. Major cement complex (including quarry, plant and port) was built in late 1970s at Carboneras Beach. El Pozo Alimentación, S.A., Blockbuster Vídeo España, S.L., Contratas y Obras Empresa Constructora, S.A.

Sources of information

Tourist Office: Oficina de Turismo, Hermanos Machado s/n, Edificio Servicios Múltiples, 04004 Almería. Tel: 950 21 00 00

INEM: Avenida Cabo de Gata 120, 04007 Almería. Tel: 950 24 23 23 Fax: 950 24 23 78

Town hall: Plaza de la Constitucion s/n, 04003 Almería. Tel: 950 21 00 00
Chamber of commerce: Cámara de Comercio, Industria y Navegación de Almería, Conde Ofalia 22, entresuelo, 04001 Almería. Tel: 950 23 46 39/23 44 33 Fax: 950 23 48 50

3.3.2 **Universidad de Almería (UALM)**

Basic information

Autonomous community: Andalucía
Province: Almería
Town: Almería
Status: Public (1993)
Address: Ctra de Sacromonte s/n, 14120 La Cañada de San Urbano, Almería. Tel: 950 21 50 80/05 Fax: 950 21 55 75 Email: CIDU@ualm.es Web site: www.ualm.es
Main campus: La Cañada de San Urbano
Satellite campuses: N/A
Students: 16,000
Staff: 700

Teaching centres

Faculties: Economics and business; experimental sciences; humanities and education; law
Higher technical schools: Higher polytechnic school
University schools: Labour relations; nursing

Student services

Information office: Centro de Información y Documentación Universitario (CIDU), Ctra de Sacromonte s/n, 04120 Cañada de San Urbano, Almería. Tel: 950 21 50 80/05 Fax: 950 21 52 80 Email: CIDU@ualm.es
Accommodation office: See *CIDU*
Health centre: See *CIDU*
Spanish courses for foreign students: Currently being set up. Contact *CIDU*

Courses in languages

For languages undergraduates: The Humanities Faculty offers a long-cycle degree course in Spanish philology.
Spanish for foreign students: Currently being set up

3.4 Ávila

3.4.1 **Ciudad de Ávila**

Basic information

Location and status: Situated in north-west central Spain. Capital of Province of Ávila. Located on River Adaja, 115 km north-west of Madrid

Population: 49,800

Geography: 3,715 feet above sea level on high Castilian plateau (*Meseta*). Devoid of water and trees.

Climate: In winter, access roads can be blocked with snow and at night temperature plummets, even in summer. Influenced by African winds that bring heat and dryness to land. Continental climate. Rains heavily for about twenty days per year. Over 3,000 hours of sunlight per year. Boiling in summer but freezing in winter.

History: Pre-Roman site called Abula or Avela fell to Moors *c*. 714. Recaptured for Christians by Alfonso VI in 1088.

Main historical sites: Renowned old quarter (Romanesque/Gothic) surrounded by excellently preserved city walls (eleventh century); declared World Heritage Site by UNESCO.

Town: Ávila de Los Caballeros. Modern part of city outside walls. Noted tourist centre. Eighty-eight towers. Highest city in Spain.

Main areas of interest: Cathedral (first Gothic church in Castile). Twelfth-century churches of San Vicente, San Pedro and San Andrés. Fifteenth-century convent of San Tomás which contains tombs of Tomás de Torquemada (head of Inquisition). Sixteenth-century palace of Viceroy Blasco Nuñez Vela. Convent of Santa Teresa, built over her birthplace in 1636.

Surrounding area: Lofty Sierra de Grados and Sierra de Guadarrama. Alba de Tormes, where Santa Teresa died; her remains are in the Carmelite Convent. Fine views over city from Los Cuatro Postes.

Travel and transport: From Madrid, there are up to 12 trains a day to Ávila. Parking can be a problem. National destinations more easily reached by train but there are bus services.

Major economic activities: Tanning, flour milling, liquor distilling and manufacture of soft drinks and meat by-products.

Major employer: El Pozo Alimentación, S.A.

Sources of information

Tourist Office: Oficina de Turismo, Plaza de la Catedral 4, 05001 Ávila. Tel: 920 22 27 63

INEM: Plaza de Santa Ana 7, 05001 Ávila. Tel: 920 22 10 00 Fax: 920 22 95 30

Town hall: Plaza de la Victoria 1, 05001 Ávila. Tel: 920 21 13 00

Chamber of commerce: Cámara de Comercio e Industria de Ávila, Eduardo Marquina 6, 05001 Ávila. Tel: 920 21 11 73 Fax: 920 25 51 59 Email: ca500@camerdata.es

3.4.2 **Universidad Católica 'Santa Teresa de Jesús' de Ávila (UCAV)**

Basic information

Autonomous community: Castilla y León

Province: Ávila

Town: Ávila

Status: Private (1997)

Address: Los Canteros s/n, 05005 Ávila. Tel: 920 25 10 20 Fax: 920 25 10 30 Email: info@ucavila.es Web site: www.ucavila.es

Main campus: Los Canteros

Satellite campuses: N/A

Students: 350

Staff: 60

Teaching centres

Faculties: Humanities; science; social and legal sciences

Higher technical schools: Agriculture and forestry

University schools: Agriculture; business; computing; forestry

Student services

Information office: Servicio de Atención al Estudiante, Universidad Católica de Ávila, Los Canteros s/n, 05005 Ávila. Tel: 920 25 10 20 Fax: 920 25 10 30 Email: sae@ucavila.es

Accommodation office: See *Servicio de Atención al Estudiante*

Health centre: See *Servicio de Atención al Estudiante*

Spanish courses for foreign students: Summer Hispanic Study Program Universidad Católica de Ávila, Los Canteros s/n, 05005 Ávila. Tel: 920 25 10 20 Fax: 920 25 10 30 Email: belen.ares@ucacvila.es

Courses in languages

For languages undergraduates: N/A

Spanish for foreign students: The University runs an annual four-week course in Spanish language and culture in July at beginners, intermediate and advanced levels. Culture classes include Spanish art, history and geography, literature and music. Weekend excursions to local places of interest are also organised. Attendance certificates are granted to those who attend 90 per cent of the classes and 'regular credit certificates' are awarded to those who attend 90 per cent of the classes and pass the examinations.

3.5 Badajoz

3.5.1 **Ciudad de Badajoz**

Basic information

Location and status: South-west Spain, on River Guadiana, 401 km from Madrid. Capital of Province of Badajoz.

Population: 132,200

Geography: Desolate terrain. South bank of River Guadiana. Six km from Portuguese frontier. Lies on low range of hills crowned by Moorish castle. Lies at altitude of 614 feet above sea level.

Climate: Extremely hot and dry in July and August; dry and dusty. Cool and dry in winter.

History: Originated as Pax Augusta, small Roman town, then later flourished as Batalyaws under Moors. Freed from the Moors by Alfonso IX of León in 1229. Was known as the key to Portugal. Played strategic roles in both Peninsular and Civil Wars. Stormed by British forces under Duke of Wellington in 1812 and taken by Franco's Nationalist troops in 1936.

Main historical sites: Cathedral of San Juan (Gothic). Alcazaba – Moorish fortress. Museo Provincial de Bellas Artes (Museum of Fine Art).

Town: River flows between castle and hill, and fort of San Cristóbal, and is crossed by granite bridge built in 1596 and rebuilt in 1833 (Puente de Palmas).

Main areas of interest: Birthplace of Manuel de Godoy (favourite of King Charles IV). Archeological Museum. Museum of Contemporary Art. Puente de Palmas – bridge over River Guadiana.

Surrounding area: Bastioned wall with moat and outworks and forts on surrounding heights gives city appearance of great strength. Thirteenth-century castle. At Olivenza, 25 km away, is Church of Santa María Magdalena.

Travel and transport: Various frequent local and long distance bus services. Various long distance train services, including three daily trains that cross to Portugal.

Major economic activities: Transit trade with Portugal. Food processing and production of alcoholic and other drinks. Basketwork, blankets and wax.

Major employers: Blanca Pueyo, S.A., El Pozo Alimentación, S.A., Granjas Cantos Blancos, S.A., Grupo Fimestic, Hoteles Tryp, S.A., Nutreco España, S.A., Unide S. Coop.

Sources of information

Tourist Office: Oficina de Turismo, Pasaje de San Juan 1, 06002 Badajoz. Tel: 924 22 49 81

INEM: Avda Colón 6, 0671 Badajoz. Tel: 924 23 74 08 Fax: 924 24 30 32

Town hall: Plaza de España 1, 06002 Badajoz. Tel: 924 22 51 35

Chamber of commerce: Cámara de Comercio e Industria de Badajoz, Avda de Europa 4, 06004 Badajoz. Tel: 924 23 46 00 Fax: 924 24 38 53 Email: cci.badajo@cscamara.es

3.5.2 **Universidad de Extremadura (UEX)**

Basic information

Autonomous community: Extremadura

Provinces: Badajoz; Cáceres

Towns: Badajoz; Cáceres

Status: Public (1973)

Addresses: Avda de Elvas s/n, 06071 Badajoz. Tel: 924 28 93 00 Fax: 924 27 29 83 Email/Web site: www.unex.es

Plaza de los Calderos, 10071 Cáceres. Tel: 927 21 20 00 Fax: 927 21 12 68

Main campuses: Badajoz; Cáceres

Satellite campuses: Almendralejo; Mérida; Plasencia

Students: 19,179

Staff: 1,057

Teaching centres

Faculties: Arts (Cáceres); economics and business (Badajoz); education (Badajoz); law (Cáceres); librarianship and documentation (Badajoz); medicine (Badajoz); physical activity and sport (Cáceres); science (Badajoz); veterinary science (Cáceres).

Higher technical schools: N/A

University schools: Agricultural engineering (Badajoz); agriculture (Almendralejo); business (Cáceres; Plasencia); engineering (Almendralejo); industrial engineering (Badajoz); nursing (Mérida; Plasencia); polytecnic (Cáceres; Plasencia); teacher training (Almendralejo; Cáceres).

Student services

Information office: Servicio de Información y Orientación (SIO), Avda de Elvas s/n, 06071 Badajoz. Tel: 924 28 93 69 Fax: 924 27 63 67 Email: sio@unex.es
C/ Pizarro 8, 10071 Cáceres. Tel: 927 24 32 27 Fax: 927 21 30 23 Email: siocc@unex.es
Accommodation office: Oficina de Relaciones Internacionales, Avda de Elvas s/n, 16071 Badajoz
Casa Grande, c/ Pizarro 8, 10071 Cáceres
Tel/Fax/Email: see *SIO*
Health centre: Servicio Médico, Avda de Elvas s/n, Edificio Antiguo Rectorado, 16071 Badajoz
Casa Grande, c/ Pizarro 8, 10071 Cáceres Tel/Fax/Email: see *SIO*
Spanish courses for foreign students: N/A

Courses in languages

For languages undergraduates: The Faculty of Arts offers degree courses in English, French and Hispanic philologies.
Spanish for foreign students: N/A

3.6 Baeza

3.6.1 **Ciudad de Baeza**

Basic information

Location and status: Located in northern Andalucía, in Province of Jaén, 321 km south of Madrid.
Population: 15,150
Geography: Perched among olive groves and rolling landscape hills of northern Andalucía.
Climate: Mild. Summers not too hot and in winter temperatures rarely drop below freezing.
History: Originally settled by Romans; was won back from Arabs in 1227, making it the first Christian enclave in Andalucía.

Main historical sites: Old university and cathedral (sixteenth-century Gothic), in area of beautiful old stone buildings which has been declared a World Heritage Site.

Town: An elegant town with magnificent Renaissance buildings, erected by sixteenth-century architect Andrés de Vandelvira. Small, ancient and has a perpetual Sunday air. White, winding and cobbled.

Main areas of interest: Town Hall (declared National Monument), Corn Exchange, Plaza de los Leones. Palacio de Marquesa de Jabalquinto, now a seminary. Casa del Pópulo. Attractive main square.

Surrounding area: Canena – castle (12 km). Ibros – town walls (5 km).

Travel and transport: Although Baeza is on direct line from Madrid, nearest train station is 13 km from Baeza itself, at Linares. There is a connecting bus for most trains, except on Sundays.

Major economic activities: Olive oil and tourism.

Major employers: University, shops, restaurants and bars.

Sources of information

Tourist Office: Oficina de Turismo, Plaza del Pópulo s/n, 23440 Baeza. Tel: 953 74 04 44

INEM: Plaza de la Constitución 1, 23440 Baeza. Tel: 953 74 28 28

Town hall: Cardenal Benavides 1, 23440 Baeza (Jaén). Tel: 953 74 01 50

Chamber of commerce: As for Jaén

3.6.2 **Universidad Internacional de Andalucía (UIA)**

Basic information

Autonomous community: Andalucía

Provinces: Huelva; Jaén; Sevilla

Towns: Baeza (Jaén); La Rábida (Huelva); Sevilla

Status: Public (1994)

Addresses: (1) Rectorado, Monasterio Sta María de las Cuevas, Isla de la Cartuja, 41092 Sevilla. Tel: 954 46 22 99 Fax: (954) 46 22 88 Email: unia@uia.es Web site: www.uia.es.

(2) Sede Antonio Machado, Plaza de Santa María s/n, 23440 Baeza (Jaén). Tel: 953 74 27 75 Fax: 953 74 29 75 Email: machado @uniaam.uia.es Web site: www.uniaam.uia.es

(3) Sede Iberoamericana, Paraje La Rábida, 21819 Palos de la Frontera (Huelva). Tel: 959 35 04 52 Fax: (959) 35 01 58 Email: uniara@uniara.uia.es Web site: www.uniara.uia.es

Main campuses: Baeza; La Rábida; Sevilla

Satellite campuses: N/A

Specialist centres

Baeza: Andalusian centre for local development studies
La Rábida: Andalusian centre for Latin American studies

Student services

Information office: See *Rectorado, Sevilla*
Accommodation office: See main addresses above
Health centre: N/A
Spanish courses for foreign students: N/A

3.7 Barcelona

3.7.1 **Ciudad de Barcelona**

Basic information

Location and status: Capital of Catalonia (Catalunya) and of Province of Barcelona. Spain's second city and principal port. Located 621 km north-east of Madrid.

Population: 1,681,132

Geography: Seaport 150 km south of French frontier. Gentle slope in fertile plain between Rivers Besós and Llobregrat facing south-east to Mediterranean. Fringed by mountains.

Climate: Mild and agreeable. Winter is mild. Sultry summer heat tempered by sea breezes. High temperatures and humidity experienced in hottest months of July and August can be unpleasant.

History: Probably founded by Carthaginians in 230 BC. Roman Barcelona (ruled for six centuries) was probably overshadowed by Tarragona. Under Visigoths was temporarily the capital, then Muslims took it over in AD 713. At one point Barcelona held territory as far north as Provence. Arabs forcefully entered Barcelona in 716 and it was not until 801 that soldiers reconquered the city for the Franks. Barcelona was granted independence by French king as reward for Wilfred the Hairy's glorious fighting deeds for the Arabs. The Middle Ages were Barcelona's Golden Age. In the thirteenth century Barcelona was the leading city in Spain and leading port in the Mediterranean, remaining so until the discovery of America. In following years, importance moved southwards from Barcelona towards Madrid, and Barcelona rebelled more than once against the Bourbon dynasty. Because of this, it lost its autonomy and the Catalan language was outlawed. Barcelona did not make a comeback until the eighteenth century with Charles III. During the Spanish Civil War, it was capital of the Spanish Republic for little over a year in the final stages of the war.

Main historical sites: City hall. Cathedral. Palace of Generalitat. Casa Arcediano. Palace of Lloctinent and Royal Palace. Gaudi's buildings: Guell Park, Casa Batlló and Casa Mila have all been declared part of World Heritage Site, which includes his two more creative buildings, the Church of La Sagrada Familia and College of Santa Teresa de Jesús.

Town: Hosted 1992 Olympics. Spain's major Mediterranean port and commercial centre. This city is continually reinventing itself. Most European of all Spanish cities – progressive, stylish and cosmopolitan.

Main areas of interest: Numerous museums and art galleries, including those of Picasso and Miró. Barri Gotic (Gothic Quarter). Montjuic. World Exhibition Site of 1929. Ramblas Avenue. Olympic Village and Pac de Mer development. Harbour and Port Vel (Old Port). Nou Camp football stadium (one of largest in world).

Surrounding area: Fringed by mountains and close to Mediterranean coast (Costa Dorada). Attractive resort of Sitges is short train journey away and historic Benedictine monastery of Montsrerrat is only 52 kms away, and can also be reached by train.

Travel and transport: Excellent communications system, including Metro. Trains to the airport – 12 km south of city. Trains to beaches, nearby cities and long-distance domestic routes. Buses run from 05.00 or 06.30 until 22.30. Metros operates 05.00–23.00 (Mon–Fri); 05.00–01.00 (Sat) and 06.00–01.00 on Sunday. Cable-car between port and Montjuic. Taxis are plentiful and cheap. Dense traffic problem. Railways connect the city with suburbs as well as with the rest of Spain and France.

Major economic activities: Manufacturing, shipping and tourism. Automobiles (including SEAT), heavy machinery, chemicals and textiles. Active stock exchange. International banking and finance centre.

Major employers: Universities, Hewlett Packard Española, S.A., IBM España, S.A., SEAT, Revlon, S.A., Deloitte and Touche, S.A.

Sources of information

Tourist Office: Oficina de Turismo, Gran Vía de les Corts Catalans 658, 08010 Barcelona. Tel: 93 301 74 43; 317 22 46

INEM: Vía Layetana 18, 08003 Barcelona. Tel: 93 315 30 62

Town hall: Plaza San Jaime s/n, 0800 Barcelona. Tel: 93 402 70 00

Chamber of commerce: Cámara de Comercio, Industria y Navegación de Barcelona, Oficinas y Servicios, Avda Diagonal 452–54, 08006 Barcelona. Tel: 93 415 16 00. Fax: 93 416 09 84

3.7.2 **Universidad Autónoma de Barcelona (UAB)**

Basic information

Autonomous community: Cataluña (Catalunya)
Province: Barcelona
Town: Barcelona
Status: Public (1968)
Address: Campus Universitario Bellaterra 08193 Barcelona. Tel: 93 581 10 00 Fax: 93 581 20 00 Email: informacio@ub.es Web site: www.uab.es
Main campuses: Bellaterra (Cerdanyola del Vallés)
Satellite campuses: Badalona; Barcelona; Manresa; Mollet del Vallés; Sabadell; Sant Cugat del Vallés; Terrassa
Students: 36,856
Staff: 2,643

Teaching centres

Faculties: Arts; comunication science; economics and business; education; law; medicine; politics and sociology; psychology; science; translating and interpreting; veterinary science
Higher technical schools: N/A
University schools: Business (Manresa; Sabadell); computing (Sabadell; Sant Cugat del Vallés); environment (Mollet del Vallés Polytechnic); nursing (Barcelona x 2; Manresa; Terrassa); nursing and physiotherapy (Sant Cugat del Vallés).

Student services

Information office:
1) Oficina d'Informació, Gabinet del Rectorat, 08193 Bellaterra. Tel: 93 581 11 11 Fax: 93 581 20 00 Email: informació@uab.es
2) Oficina d'Informació, Campus Treball, 08193 Bellaterra. Tel: 93 581 14 72 Fax: 93 581 27 66

Accommodation office: Oficina de Relacions Internacionals, Edifici A, 08193 Bellaterra. Tel: 93 581 22 10; 581 27 53 Fax: 93 581 20 00; 581 32 64 Email: of.rel.internacional@uab.es
Health centre: Servei Assistencial de Salut, Edifici F, 08193 Bellaterra. Tel: 93 581 18 00; 581 19 00 Fax: 93 581 13 34
Spanish courses for foreign students: Servei d'Idiomes Moderns (SIM), Edifici M, 08193 Bellaterra. Tel: 93 581 13 25 Fax: 93 581 27 36 Email: iutm2@cc.uab.es

Courses in languages

For languages undergraduates: The Faculty of Arts in Bellaterra offers degree courses in Catalan, English, French and Hispanic philologies. The Faculty of Translating and Interpreting at Bellaterra offers a degree course in translating and interpreting in English, French and German.

Spanish for foreign students: See *SIM* or *Oficina de Relacions Internacionals.*

3.7.3 **Universidad de Barcelona (UB)**

Basic information

Autonomous community: Cataluña (Catalunya)

Province: Barcelona

Town: Barcelona

Status: Public (1450)

Address: Gran Via Corts Catalans 585, 08007 Barcelona. Tel: 93 403 54 17 Fax: 93 403 54 28 Email: udi@sacu.ub.es Web site: www.ub.es

Main campuses: Plaza Universitat; Bellvitge; Pedralbes; Vall d'Hebron

Satellite campuses: N/A

Students: 67,435

Staff: 3,000

Teaching centres

Faculties: Biology; chemistry; dentistry; economics and business; education; fine art; geography and history; law; geology; mathematics; medicine; pedagogy; pharmacy; philology; philosophy; physics; psychology

Higher technical schools: N/A

University schools: Business; librarianship *and* documentation; nursing x 4; social work; teacher training

Institutes: Criminology; education (ICE); Hispanic studies; hotel management; physical education; public health in Catalonia

Student services

Information office: Oficina d'Informació, Servei d'Atenció a la Comunitat Universitaria, Gran Via Corts Catalans, 585, 08007 Barcelona. Tel: 93 403 54 15 Fax: 93 403 54 29 Email: udi@sacu.ub.es; sest@org.ub.es

Accommodation office: Secció d'Allotjament, Servei d'Atenció a la Comunitat Universitaria, Gran Via Corts Catalans 585, 08007 Barcelona. Tel: 93 403 54 19; 403 54 21 Fax: 93 403 54 28 Email: allotjament@sacu.ub.es

Health centre: See *Servei d'Atenció a la Comunitat Universitaria*
Spanish courses for foreign students: Instituto de Estudios Hispánicos, Gran Via Corts Catalans 585, 08071 Barcelona. Tel: 93 403 55 19 Fax: 93 403 54 33 Email: est-hispa@dl.ub.es

Courses in languages

For languages undergraduates: The Faculty of Philology offers courses in Arabic, Catalan, English, French, Galician, German, Portugese, Slav and Spanish philologies. The School of Modern Languages offers courses of up to a year's duration in a variety of modern languages.
Spanish for foreign students: The *Instituto de Estudios Hispánicos* offers the following courses: (1) DELE preparation courses – basic and advanced levels (six-week course in October and November); (2) a *Diploma de Estudios Hispánicos* (Spanish language and culture) and a *Certificado de Suficiencia en Lengua Española* (language only) (both from mid-October until the end of May); (3) four-month courses in Spanish language (October to February; February to May); (4) intensive four-week courses in Spanish language (October to early April); (5) four week courses in business Spanish, conversational Spanish and writing in Spanish between early November and mid-April.

3.7.4 **Universidad Internacional de Cataluña (Catalunya) (UIC)**

Basic information

Autonomous community: Cataluña (Catalunya)
Province: Barcelona
Town: Barcelona
Status: Private (1997)
Address: Campus Iradier Inmaculada 22, 08017 Barcelona. Tel: 93 254 18 00 Fax: 93 254 18 50 Email: info@unica.edu Web site: www.unica.edu
Main campus: Iradier
Satellite campuses: Campus de L'Ebre; Sant Cugat

Teaching centres

Faculties: Health Sciences (San Cugat); humanities; journalism; legal and political sciences; social and economic sciences
Higher technical schools: Architecture
University schools: N/A

Student services

Information office: Vicerrectorat de la Comunitat Universitaria, Inmaculada 22, 08017 Barcelona. Tel: 93 254 18 10 Fax: 93 254 18 43 Email: mnassare@unica.edu

Accommodation office: See *Vicerrectorat de la Comunitat Universitaria*

Health centre: Mutua Cyclops, Ausías March 41, 08010 Barcelona. Contact via *Vicerrectorat la Comunitat Universitaria.*

Spanish courses for foreign students: Servicio de Idiomas, Campus Iradier, Inmaculada 22, 08017 Barcelona. Tel: 93 254 18 00 Fax: 93 254 18 50 Email: maria@unica.edu

Courses in languages

For languages undergraduates: The Faculty of Arts offers degree courses in the philologies of English, French, German and Japanese.

Spanish for foreign students: The *Servicio de Idiomas* runs a special course in Spanish for foreign students throughout each academic year.

3.7.5 **Campus of Universidad de Navarra (see** 3.35.2**)**

3.7.6 **Universidad Oberta de Cataluña (UOC)***

Basic information

Autonomous community: Cataluña (Catalunya)

Province: Barcelona

Town: Barcelona

Status: Public (1995)

Address: Avda del Tibidabo 39–43, 08035 Barcelona. Tel: 93 253 23 00 Fax: 93 471 64 95 Email: internet@uoc.es Web site: www.uoc.es

Main campus: Tibidabo (Barcelona)

Support centres: Bages (Manresa); Baix Camp (Reus); Gironés (Salt); Segria (Lleida)

Students: 4,000

Staff: 50

Courses offered

Degrees: Business administration and management; Catalan language and literature; computer engineering; documentation; educational psychology; English philology; humanities; law; management studies

Diplomas: Information systems engineering; management systems engineering; statistics

Student services

Information office: Progames Internacionals i Recerca, Avda del Tibidabo 45, 08035 Barcelona. Tel: 93 253 57 50 Fax: 93 211 01 26 Email: ariu@campus.uoc.es
Accommodation office: N/A
Health centre: N/A
Spanish courses for foreign students: N/A

Courses in languages

For languages undergraduates: The university offers degree courses in Catalan and English language and literature.
Spanish for foreign students: N/A

* The UOC is a huge, innovative virtual campus which takes the form of a large data network covering and interconnecting the whole of Catalonia. It has a broad and rapidly expanding programme of courses of continuing education in a wide range of disciplines. The university has a large virtual library and study is based on distance learning, periodic tutorials in support centres and the use of multimedia and interactive educational materials.

3.7.7 **Universidad Politécnica de Cataluña (UPC)**

Basic information

Autonomous community: Cataluña (Catalunya)
Province: Barcelona
Town: Barcelona
Status: Public (1971)
Address: Rectorat, Jordi Girona Salgado 31, 08034 Barcelona. Tel: 93 401 68 44 Fax: 93 401 62 10 Email: upcinof@info.upc.es Web site: www.upc.es
Main campuses: Nord (Jordi Girona); Sud (Avda Doctor Marañón)
Satellite campuses: Canet de Mar; Igualada; Manresa; Mataró; Sant Cugat del Vallés; Sant Just Desvern; Terrassa; Vilanova i la Geltru
Students: 47,062
Staff: 2,040

Teaching centres

Faculties: Computing; mathematics and statistics; nautical studies
Higher technical schools: Architecture (+Sant Cugat del Vallés); civil engineering; industrial engineering (+Terrassa); telecommunications
University schools: Agriculture; Business College of Savings Bank (Terrassa); industrial engineering (+Igualada +Terrassa); knitted fabric

engineering (Canet de Mar); multimedia; optics (Terrassa); photography; polytechnic (+Manresa +Mataró +Sant Just)

Institutes: Cybernetic engineering; energy techniques; textile research and industrial co-operation; technology and environmental modelling

Student services

Information office: Servei d'Informació, Imatge i Publicacions, Jordi Girona Salgado 1–3, Edifici BIB, 08034 Barcelona. Tel: 93 401 73 96 Fax: 93 401 68 95 Email: upcinfo@hi.sia.upc.es

Accommodation office: Oficina de Mobilitat Internacional (OMI), Jordi Girona Salgado 1–3, Edifici A-4, 08034 Barcelona. Tel: 93 401 69 37 Fax: 93 401 74 02 Email: omi@cri.upc.es

Health centre: Unitat de Suport, Campus Sud, Edificio SG, Avda Gregorio Marañón, 08028 Barcelona. Tel: 93 401 61 39 Email: uspisabel @sg.upc

Spanish for foreign students: See *Oficina de Mobilitat Internacional* (*OMI*)

Courses in languages

For languages undergraduates: N/A

Spanish for foreign students: See *OMI*

3.7.8 **Universidad Pompeu Fabra (UPF)**

Basic information

Autonomous community: Cataluña (Catalunya)

Province: Barcelona

Town: Barcelona

Status: Public (1990)

Address: Placa de la Mercé 10–12, 08002 Barcelona. Tel: 93 542 20 00; 542 17 00 Fax: 93 542 20 02 Email: webmaster@upf.es Web site: www.upf.es

Main campus: Placa de la Mercé (Barcelona)

Satellite campuses: Manresa; Mataró

Students: 6,560

Staff: 781

Teaching centres

Faculties: Economics and business; humanities; law; politics and public administration; social and communication sciences; translating and interpreting

Higher technical schools: N/A

University schools: Business (+Mataró); labour relations; management and public administration (Manresa)

Institutes: Advanced social studies; applied linguistics; audio-visual studies; history; international economics; territorial studies

Student services

Information office: Servei d'Atenció a la Comunitat Universitaria (SACU), Placa de la Mercé 12, 08002 Barcelona. Tel: 93 542 21 11 Fax: 93 542 21 31 Email: sacu@grup.upf.es

Accommodation office: See *SACU*

Health centre: See *SACU*

Spanish courses for foreign students: Español para Extranjeros, Facultat de Traducció i Interpretació, La Rambla 32, 08002 Barcelona.

Tel: 93 542 24 00/11 Fax: 93 542 22 95 Email: secretaria@fti.grup.upf.es

Courses in languages

For languages undergraduates: The Faculty of Translating and Interpreting (located in the Edifici Rambla) offers a degree course in translating and interpreting, involving English, French, German and Spanish.

Spanish for foreign students: the *Español para Extranjeros* programme of the Faculty of Translating and Interpreting offers the following options: (1) general Spanish language courses involving sixty hours' study, either over 4 weeks (intensive) or ten weeks (semi-intensive) throughout the year; (2) Spanish language for special purposes involving twenty hours' study; one course runs from mid-January to late March and another from mid-April to mid-June.

3.7.9 **Universidad Ramón Llull (URL)**

Basic information

Autonomous community: Cataluña (Catalunya)

Province: Barcelona

Town: Barcelona

Status: Private (1991)

Address: Sant Joan de La Salle 8, 08022 Barcelona. Tel: 93 602 22 00 Fax: 93 602 22 49 Email: urlsc@sec.url.es Web site: www.url.es

Main campuses: La Salle; Sant Gervasi; Sarria

Satellite campus: Roquetes (Tarragona)
Students: 13,410
Staff: NK

Teaching centres

Faculties: Communication sciences; economics; law (ESADE*); philosophy; politics and sociology; psychology and education

Higher technical schools: Administration and business management (ESADE*); architecture; design (ESDI+); electronic engineering and computing

University schools: Design; labour relations; nursing and physiotherapy; social education; social work; technical communications engineering; tourism (ESADE*)

Institutes: Chemistry (Sarriá); Ebro university observatory (Roquetes)

Student services

Information office: Servicios Centrales, Sant Joan de la Salle 8, 08022 Barcelona. Tel: 93 253 04 50 Fax: 93 418 80 65 Email: urlsc@sec.url.es
Accommodation office: See *Servicios Centrales*
Health centre: See *Servicios Centrales*
Spanish courses for foreign students: N/A

Courses in languages

For languages undergraduates: N/A
Spanish for foreign students: N/A

* ESADE = Escola Superior de Administració y Direcció d' Empreses
\+ ESDI = Escola Superior de Disseny

3.8 Bilbao (Bilbo)

3.8.1 Ciudad de Bilbao

Basic information

Location and status: Located in northern Spain, in Spanish Basque Country (Euskadi), 390 km from Madrid. Capital of Province of Vizcaya (Biscay).

Population: 372,054

Geography: Lies along mouth of River Nervión, 1 km inland from Bay of Biscay. Green and wooded countryside all along coast; green mountains project into sea. Large sandy beaches alternate with cliffs and islands.

Climate: Warm, humid climate with mild winters and hot summers. Temperate climate, depressingly damp in winter. Atmosphere rather polluted.

History: Lord of Biscay (Don Diego López de Haro) in 1300 gave the city a charter and privilege of self-government in an independent municipality. In 1511, it claimed the right to its own commercial tribunal that could issue laws in form of ordinances. In the eighteenth century, it derived great prosperity from intensive trade with American Colonies of Spain. The city was sacked by French troops in Peninsular War (1808–14) and besieged four times during Carlist Wars. It fell to Franco's Nationalist troops in 1937.

Main historical sites: Gothic-style cathedral of Santiago (fourteenth century). Plaza Nueva (nineteeth century). Renaissance style churches of San Antonio, San Juan and San Nicolás.

Town: Largest city in Basque country. A well-established industrial city and important port as well as commercial and banking centre. In Basque known as Bilbo.

Main areas of interest: Casco Viejo (Old Quarter). Arriaga theatre. Plaza Nueva. Museo de Bellas Artes (Museum of Fine Art). Gugenheim Museum.

Surrounding area: Durango (gateway to Duranguensado Massif). Limestone caves. Many historical villages are found dotted on hillsides further inland. Close to Bilbao are numerous little fishing ports and good beaches for bathing. Limestone caves of Las Cuevas de Pozalagua are well worth a visit.

Travel and transport: Regular buses and trains. An airport and a ferry port are nearby. Ferry service from Portsmouth.

Major economic activities: Metallurgical industry, chemical industries, textiles and building materials. Financial centre. Fishing, shipbuilding and ship repairing.

Major employers: AMS management systems, El Pozo Alimentación, S.A., Gestiones Sociolaborales, S.A. (Gestolasa), Grupo Fimestic, Hewlett Packard Española, S.A., IBM España, S.A.

Sources of information

Tourist Office: Plaza de Arriaga 1, Bilbao, Tel: 94 416 02 88

INEM: Gran Vía 50–60, 48011 Bilbao. Tel: 94 442 21 34; 442 80 78 Fax: 94 442 45 95

Town hall: Plaza Ernesto Erkoreka s/n, 48007 Bilbao. Tel: 94 445 52 00

Chamber of commerce: Cámara de Comercio, Industria y Navegación de

Bilbao, Alameda Recalde 50, 48008 Bilbao. Tel: 94 410 46 64 Fax: 94 443 61 71 Email: info@camaracombilbao.es

3.8.2 **Universidad de Deusto (UD)**

Basic information

Autonomous community: País Vasco (Euskadi)
Province: Vizcaya (Bizcaia)
Town: Bilbao
Status: Private (1886)
Address: Avda de las Universidades 24, 48080 Bilbao. Tel: 94 413 90 00 Fax: 94 413 90 10 Web site: www.deusto.es
Main campus: Bilbao
Satellite campus: San Sebastián
Students: 18,338
Staff: 655

Teaching centres

Faculties: Arts (+San Sebastián); computing; economics and business (+San Sebastián); engineering; law; philosophy and education; politics and sociology; theology
Higher technical schools: N/A
University schools: Legal practice; social work; theology (+San Sebastián); tourism (+San Sebastián)
Institutes: Basque studies; business management (international institute); co-operative studies; drug addiction; education; European studies; fiscal studies; human rights; labour relations studies; leisure studies; modern languages (+San Sebastián)

Student services

Information office: Oficina de Relaciones Internacionales, Avenida de la Universidades 24, 48007 Bilbao. Tel: 94 413 92 88 Fax: 94 413 90 69 Email: relaciones.internacionales@deusto.es
Accommodation office: See *Oficina de Relaciones Internacionales*
Health centre: See *Oficina de Relaciones Internacionales*
Spanish courses for foreign students: Departamento de Español para Extranjeros, Facultad de Filosofía y Letras, Avda de las Universidades 24, 48007 Bilbao. Tel: 94 413 93 14 Fax: 94 413 90 87 Email: jdiaz@fil.deusto.es

Courses in languages

For languages undergraduates: Both in Bilbao and San Sebastián, the Faculty of Arts offers degree courses in Basque, English and Hispanic philologies.

Spanish for foreign students: The *Departamento de Español para Extranjeros* offers a Spanish language course at various levels for foreign students during the academic year. Students may study for one semester (October–February or February–June) or for the whole year. The course provides four and a half hours of study per week. The department also offers an intensive three-week course in Spanish during September involving fifteen hours' tuition per week.

3.8.3 **Universidad del País Vasco (UPV) (Euskal Herriko Unibertsitatea/EHU)**

Basic information

Autonomous community: País Vasco (Euskadi)
Provinces: Álava (Alaba); Guipúzcoa (Gipuzkoa); Vizcaya (Bizkaia)
Towns: Bilbao; Leioa; San Sebastián; Vitoria
Status: Public (1968*)
Address: Ciudad Universitaria, Leioa, 48940 Bizkaia. Tel: 94 601 20 00 Fax: 94 464 95 40 Web site: www.lg.ehu.es
Main campuses: Álava (Vitoria/V); Bizkaia** (Bilbao/B and Leioa/L); Gipuzkoa (San Sebastián/SS)
Satellite campuses: Barakaldo; Eibar; Portugalete
Students: 65,000
Staff: 3,500

Teaching centres

Faculties: Chemistry (SS); computing (SS); economics and business (B+SS***); fine art (L); law (SS); medicine *and* dentistry (L); pharmacy (V); philology, geography and history (V); philosophy and education (SS); psychology (SS); science (L); social and communication sciences (L)

Higher technical schools: Architecture (SS); industrial engineering and telecommunications (B); naval engineering (Portugalete)

University schools: Business (B+SS+V); labour relations (L); nursing (L, SS; V); social work (SS; V); teacher training (B, SS; V); technical industrial engineering (B, SS, V; Eibar); technical mining engineering (Barakaldo)

Institutes: Applied business economics (B); applied industrial economics (B); Basque Institute of Criminology (SS); education (ICE-B); epidemiology and prevention of Ccardiovascular diseases; financial and actuarial studies (B); medicine (B); research and development of processes (B)

Student services

Information office: Servicio de Gestión Académica, Ciudad Universitaria, Campus de Leioa, 48940 Bizcaia. Tel: 94 464 21 55 Fax: 94 480 14 73

Accommodation office: See *Servicio de Gestión Académica* or Servicio de Relaciones Internacionales, Vicerrectorado General, Ciudad Universitaria, Leioa, 48940 Bizcaia. Tel: (94) 601 50 59 Fax: (94) 480 15 90

Health centre: See *Oficina de Información*

Spanish courses for foreign students: (1) University Studies Abroad, Facultad de Ciencias Sociales, Apartado 644, 48080 Bilbao. Tel: 94 464 77 00 Fax: 94 480 80 66 Email: fepmeegf@lg.ehu.es
(2) Cursos de Verano, Palacio de Miramar, Apartado 1042, 2080 San Sebastián. Tel: 94 21 33 77 Fax: 94 21 90 33

Courses in languages

For languages undergraduates: The Faculty of Philology, Geography and History in Vitoria (Álava) runs degree courses in Basque, English and French philologies.

Spanish for foreign students: The University 'Studies Abroad Consortium' offers intensive courses in Bilbao throughout the year in the Spanish and Basque languages. *Cursos de Verano* in San Sebastián offer intensive courses in Spanish Language in July and August.

* The UPV was first founded in 1968 as the *Universidad de Bilbao* and was reorganised in 1980 under its present title.

** This campus (the central administrative one) is sometimes known as the *Campus de Leioa.*

*** This is part of the Faculty of Economics and Business in Bilbao.

3.9 Burgos

3.9.1 **Ciudad de Burgos**

Basic information

Location and status: Located in northen Spain, 237 km from Madrid. Capital of Province of Burgos.

Population: 166,979

Geography: On lower slopes of castle-crowned hill overlooking River Arlanzón. Located 2,600 feet above sea level. Lies on northern meseta and its waters are carried into Atlantic or Mediterranean by Rivers Duero, Ebro and Cadagua. Scenery is mixed: barren land, mountains and valleys. A typical city of inland Castilian Spain.

Climate: Climate of Burgos is more notorious for its extremes than that of Madrid: very hot in summer and very cold in winter. Generally dry and sunny.

History: Founded in 884 as a strategic fortress town, and became a capital city under Philip II in nineteeth century. Until well into seventeenth century, its wealth came from wool exports. In the Peninsular War the French defeated the Spanish at Burgos. Then the French were besieged in the city (1812) by the British who eventually captured it in 1813. In July 1936 it became the official seat of General Francisco Franco's Nationalist government during the Civil War. Industrial development in the 1950s and 1960s brought a degree of prosperity to the city.

Main historical sites: Church of San Gadea where, according to tradition, El Cid made King Alfonso swear his innocence. One of finest Gothic cathedrals in Europe (eighty-four metres high). Gothic churches of San Nicolás and San Esteban. Monastery of Las Huelgas (most famous Cistercian monastery in Spain). Cathedral houses the remains of legendary hero El Cid.

Town: A small city with some outstanding medieval architecture.

Main areas of interest: Cathedral Monastery of Cartuja de Miraflores. Medieval textiles museum.

Surrounding area: Monastery of San Pedro de Cardeña. Santa Gadea del Cid. Benedictine monastery of Santo Domingo de Silos. Gorges of Yecla. Covarrubias.

Travel and transport: Good bus and train services to Bilbao, Madrid and other major cities. International buses to London and Agadir (Morocco).

Major economic activities: Agricultural centre, liquor, flour, woollen and leather goods, chemical fertilisers, chocolate, paper, large tourist trade, an extensive sports centre, military garrison.

Major employers: Desarrollo Ganadero Español, S.A. (DEGESA), El Pozo Alimentación, S.A., Kataforesis Burgos, S.A., L'Oréal, Unión Española de Explosivos, S.A.

Sources of information

Tourist Office: Oficina de Turismo, Plaza Alonso Martínez 7, 09003 Burgos. Tel: 947 20 31 25

INEM: San Pablo 8, 1°, 09002 Burgos. Tel: 947 32 23 56 Fax: 947 27 21 12

Town hall: Plaza de José Antonio 1, 09003 Burgos. Tel: 947 28 88 00

Chamber of commerce: Cámara de Comercio e Industria de Burgos San Carlos 1, 09003 Burgos. Tel: 947 20 18 44 Fax: 947 26 33 26 Email: formación.cociba@camerdat.es

3.9.2 **Universidad de Burgos (UBU)**

Basic information

Autonomous community: Castilla y León
Province: Burgos
Town: Burgos
Status: Public (1994)
Address: Hospital del Rey, c/ Puerta Romeros s/n, 09001 Burgos. Tel: 947 25 87 00 Fax: 947 25 87 44 Web site: www.ubu.es
Main campuses: General Vigón; Hospital del Rey
Satellite campuses: N/A

Teaching centres

Faculties: Economics and business; humanities and education; law; science; Theology Faculty of North of Spain*
Higher technical schools: Higher polytechnic school
University schools: Labour relations; nursing
Institutes: 'San Juan Bosco' Higher Institute of philosophy*

Student services

Information office: Centro de Orientación e Información al Estudiante (COIE), Edificio B, Plaza Misael Bañuelos s/n, 09001 Burgos. Tel: 947 25 87 42 Fax: 947 25 87 54
Accommodation office: See *COIE*
Health centre: See *COIE*
Spanish courses for foreign students: Relaciones Internacionales, Edificio

Rectorado, Hospital del Rey s/n, 09001 Burgos. Tel: 947 25 88 40 Fax: 947 25 87 36 Email: relin@ubu.es/intl@ubu.es

Courses in languages

For Languages Undergraduates: The Faculty of Humanities and Education offers language modules in English, French and Spanish as part of the diploma course in humanities.

Spanish for Foreign Students: Contact *Relaciones Internacionales.*

* These are run as private centres within the university. The Institute of Philosophy awards degrees of the *Universidad Pontificia de Comillas* (see 3.28.11).

3.10 Cáceres

3.10.1 **Ciudad de Cáceres**

Basic information

Location and status: Located in western Spain, 307 km from Madrid. Capital of Province of Cáceres. One of major cities of region of Extremadura.

Population: 84,319

Geography: Built on low east–west ridge, south of River Tagus. Extremadura – land beyond River Duero – is akin to the American Far West.

Climate: Hot dry summers and cool winters. Warm desert wind in summer.

History: Originating from the Roman town of *Norba Caesarina,* it was under Moorish control from the ninth century. It was reconquered for Christians by Alfonso IX of León in 1229. Noble Leonese families settled here in the fifteenth and sixteenth centuries and turned its walled nucleus into one of most impressive works of stonemasonry in Europe.

Main historical sites: Casa de las Veletas (now a museum). Gothic cathedral. Episcopal palace. Casa del Mono. Arab Walls (*Murallas Árabes*). Plaza de Santa María and Church of Santa María. Church of Santiago de los Caballeros. Ovando palace.

Town: Medieval town. Walls date from time of the Almohads and even preserve some Roman sections. Twelve of the thirty towers which once protected the enclosure are still standing. Remains little changed since the sixteenth century. Declared a World Heritage Site by UNESCO.

Main areas of interest: Old, historic town (*ciudad monumental*) up the hill is surrounded by turreted walls that are half Roman and half

Moorish. This part has several medieval palaces and is dominated by Gothic-style church of San Mateo (sixteenth century). Lower town contains law courts, town hall and palace of the bishops of Coria.

Surrounding area: Arroyo de la Luz (13 km). Church of La Asunción. Historic town and bridge of Alcántara (62 km to north-west)

Travel and transport: Bus station is 200m east of train station, just off Avenida de la Hispanidad. Daily bus and train local and long distance services. Five trains a day to Madrid; one to Barcelona, Lisbon and Seville.

Major economic activities: Cork, leather goods, pottery, cloth, exports grain, fruit, olive oil, livestock, wool, sausages, and phosphates from nearby mines. Textiles. Well known for hams.

Major employers: Banca Pueyo, S.A., Unide S. Coop.

Sources of information

Tourist Office: Oficina de Turismo Mayor 10, 10013 Cáceres. Tel: 927 24 63 47

INEM: Avda de la Hispanidad 3, 1005 Cáceres. Tel: 927 22 41 62 Fax: 927 21 13 71

Town hall: Plaza Mayor s/n, 10013 Cáceres. Tel: 927 24 80 00

Chamber of commerce: Cámara de Comercio e Industria de Cáceres, Plaza Doctor Durán 2, 10003 Cáceres. Tel: 927 62 71 08 Fax: 927 62 71 09 Email: caceres@camerdata.es

3.10.2 **Campus of Universidad de Extremadura (see** 3.5.2**)**

3.11 Cádiz

3.11.1 **Ciudad de Cádiz**

Basic information

Location and status: Located in south-west Spain, in western Andalucía, 663 km from Madrid. Capital of Province of Cádiz. Important seaport.

Population: 155,599

Geography: Nearby is southernmost point of Iberian Peninsula, on shores of the Straits of Gibraltar. Coast of Cádiz Province is bathed by waters of both Atlantic and Mediterranean. Located on large natural harbour.

Climate: Mild climate. Winters are generally temperate and summers agreeably warm, due to mild breezes from Atlantic.

History: One of oldest settlements in Spain. Originally an ancient Phoenician town (Gadir), founded *c.* 1100 BC. Later it was subjected to Roman rule. It was destroyed by Visigoths in the fifth century. The Moorish domination lasted from 711 until 1262, when Cádiz was captured and rebuilt by Alfonso X of Castile. Its golden age was in the eighteenth century when it enjoyed 75 per cent of Spanish trade with the Americas. First Spanish Parliament (*Cortes*) met here in 1812 during the Peninsular War.

Main historical sites: Two cathedrals: old cathedral (1252, rebuilt after 1596) and Baroque cathedral. San Sebastián and Santa Catalina castles. Torre de Vigía (100 feet high). Museo de Bellas Artes y Arqueológico. Oratories of San Felipe Neri and La Santa Cueva.

Town: Commercial port. Characterised by tall white houses with roof terraces and narrow inter-crossing roads opening out into charming small squares. Old part is African in appearance.

Main areas of interest: Old historic quarter (*casco antiguo*). Sea fortifications and waterside boulevards. Murillo collection in Fine Art Museum. Cádiz Historical Museum.

Surrounding area: Puerto Real – church of San Sebastián y San José (9 km). Puerto de Santa María (accessible by ferry from Cádiz). Chipiona.

Travel and transport: Train and bus connections to other parts of Spain. Ships to Canaries. Local ferries.

Major economic activities: Naval and mercantile shipbuilding yards. Exports wine, salt, olives, figs, corks, salted fish. Famous for tuna fish. San Lúcar de Barrameda produces celebrated 'Manzanilla' wine (like dry sherry).

Major employers: El Pozo Alimentación, S.A., Gestiones Sociolaborales, S.A. (GESTOLASA), Hoteles Tryp, S.A., Grupo Lettera, S.L.

Sources of information

Tourist Office: Oficina de Turismo, Plaza San Juan de Dios 11, 11003 Cádiz. Tel: 956 24 10 01

INEM: Avda de Andalucía 44, 11006 Cádiz. Tel: 956 28 01 91

Town hall: Plaza de San Juan de Dios s/n, 11005, Cádiz. Tel: 956 28 33 11

Chamber of commerce: Cámara de Comercio, Industria y Navegación, Antonio López 4, bajo, 11004 Cádiz. Tel: 956 22 3050 Fax: 956 25 07 10 Email: ccincadiz@camerdat.es

Twin Town: Rochester

3.11.2 **Universidad de Cádiz (UCA)**

Basic information

Autonomous community: Andalucía
Province: Cádiz
Town: Cádiz
Status: Public (1979)
Address: C/ Ancha 16, 11011 Cádiz. Tel: 956 01 50 00 Fax: 956 01 50 49 Email: www-team@uca.es Web site: www.uca.es
Main campus: Cádiz
Satellite campuses: Algeciras; Jerez; La Línea; Puerto Real
Students: 21,300
Staff: 1,600

Teaching centres

Faculties: Arts; economics and business; science (Puerto Real); education (Puerto Real); law (Jerez); medicine; marine sciences (Puerto Real); nautical sciences (Puerto Real)
Higher technical schools: Higher engineering school
University schools: Business studies (Jerez); health sciences (+Algeciras+ Jerez); labour relations (+Jerez); legal and economic studies of the *Campo de Gibraltar* (Algeciras); naval engineering (Puerto Real); nursing x 2; polytechnic (Algeciras); social studies; teacher training (La Línea)

Student services

Information office: Informació al Alumno, c/ Felipe Abarzuza 4, bajo, 11001 Cádiz. Tel: 956 22 38 08 Fax: 956 22 34 62 Email: serv.alumnos @uca.es
Accommodation office: See *Información al Alumno*
Health centre: See *Información al Alumno*
Spanish courses for foreign students: Cursos de Verano, Vicerrectorado de Extensión Universitaria, c/ Ancha 16, 11011 Cádiz. Tel: 956 01 50 80 Fax: 965 01 50 76 Email: vicerrec.extuniver @uca.es

Courses in languages

For languages undergraduates: The Arts Faculty offers degree courses in Arabic, English French, Hispanic and Slavonic philologies.
Spanish for foreign students: Cursos de Verano offer a four-week course in July (four hours' tuition per day) at various levels.

3.12 Cartagena

3.12.1 **Ciudad de Cartagena**

Basic information

Location and status: Located in Province of Murcia in south-eastern Spain, 439 km from Madrid, 49 km from Murcia, and 109 km from Alicante.

Population: 181,000

Geography: Central eastern part of Mediterranean coastline (Levante). Important port and naval base, surrounded by scrub and semi-desert.

Climate: Mediterranean, temperate. Hot summers, mild winters.

History: Originally the Iberian settlement of Mastia. Founded in 221 BC, Cartagena (*Quart Hadas*) was Hannibal's capital city and renamed Carthago Nova in 209 BC by the Romans. In 425 BC it was pillaged by Goths. Under the Moors it became an independent principality. In 1242 it was conquered by Ferdinand III of Castile. Its easily defended natural harbour lent itself to rebuilding and in the sixteenth century Philip II made it a great naval port. It was a loyalist naval base during the Spanish Civil War (1936–39). As a great commercial port, it was adversely affected by the increasing importance of Barcelona, Málaga and Alicante.

Main historical sites: Castle of La Concepción (twelfth century). Torre Ciega (Roman funeral monument). Castle of Monte Sacro. Churches of Santa María de Gracia and Santa María la Vieja. Arsenal dominating old part of town. Peral's submarine (see below).

Town: Uninspiring newer suburbs on the outskirts give way to the old part of town by the port, with narrow medieval streets, packed with bars and restaurants. Good views of town from the castle of La Concepción. Parts of the old town walls remain. The town hosts the International Nautical Week in June and the International Festival of Nautical Cinema in November.

Main areas of interest: Old part around port and promenade. Seafront houses prototype of submarine designed by Isaac Peral in 1888. Walk along the sea wall to the old military hospital. Lighthouse and Torres Park both offer great views of city. Naval Museum. Archaeological Museum (with excellent collection of pre-Roman and Roman artefacts). National Museum for Underwater Archaeology (Greek and Roman remains, including Roman galley).

Surrounding area: Costa Cálida (Warm Coast) stretches either side of Cartagena. San Ginés de la Jara Monastery (19 km). Numerous castles in hills surrounding city, for example, castle of Los Moros (half a day's trek to east of city). Mar Menor (Lesser Sea), north of Cartagena, broad lagoon with shallow waters, is popular resort area. La Unión (10 km) hosts Festival del Cante de las Minas (Miners' Songs) (10–27 August).

Travel and transport: Has new bus station (Plaza México) and two railway stations. Twelve buses a day to Los Alcázares on the Mar Menor. Four trains a day to Madrid. N-332 road takes you north-east to Los Alcázares and on to Alicante.

Major economic activities: Tourism, commercial port/dockyards, mineral exports, smelting industry, glass and esparto manufacturing.

Major employers: Dockyard/Naval Base, Banco de Santander Central Hispano, Argentaria, Repsol.

Sources of information

Tourist Office: Oficina de Turismo, Palacio Consistorial, Plaza del Ayuntamiento. Tel: 968 52 21 31

INEM: Plaza de España s/n, 30290 Cartagena. Tel: 968 50 31 54 Fax: 968 12 42 42

Town hall: Sor Francisca Armenda s/n, 30202 Cartagena. Tel: 968 12 88 02/10 Fax: 968 50 09 53

Chamber of commerce: Cámara de Comercio, Industria y Navegación de Cartagena, Plaza del Castellini 5–7, 30201 Cartagena. Tel: 968 50 70 50/54/58 Fax: 968 10 26 92 Email: ccincartagena@camerdata.es; admin@cofin-cartagena.es

3.12.2 **Universidad Politécnica de Cartagena (UPCT)**

Basic information

Auonomous Community: Región de Murcia

Province: Murcia

Town: Cartagena

Status: Public (1998)

Address: Paseo Alfonso XIII 22, Edificio el Regidor, 30201 Cartagena, Murcia. Tel: 968 32 56 76 Fax: 968 32 57 00 Email: relent.upct.es Web site: www.upct.es

Main campus: Paseo Alfonso XIII

Satellite campuses: N/A

Students: 6,000

Staff: 320

Teaching centres

Faculties: Business sciences

Higher technical schools: Agricultural engineering; industrial engineering; telecommunications engineering

University schools: Labour relations; technical civil engineering; labour relations; technical naval engineering; tourism

Student services

Information office: Servicio de Relaciones Internacionales, Universidad Politécnica de Cartagena, c/ San Juan 4, 30201 Cartagena. Tel: 968 50 76 87; 50 79 08 Fax: 969 32 14 32 Email: relint@upct.es

Accommodation office: Residencia Universitaria, Alberto Coloa, c/ Doctor Pérez Espejo s/n, 30203 Cartegena. Tel: 968 12 03 11/15 Fax: 968 12 04 11 Email: colao@plc.um.es

Health centre: See *Servicio de Relaciones Internacionales*

Spanish courses for foreign students: Servicio de Idiomas, Paseo Alfonso XIII 52, (Edificio de Minas, 2ª planta), 30203 Cartagena. Tel: 968 32 56 13 Fax: 968 32 54 35 Email: servicio.idiomas@upct.es

Courses in languages

For languages undergraduates: N/A

Spanish for foreign students: Spanish courses for foreign students are provided by the *Servicio de Idiomas.* Contact by phone, fax or email for details (see above).

3.13 Castellón de la Plana (Castelló de la Plana)

3.13.1 **Ciudad de Castellón de la Plana**

Basic information

Location and status: Situated in eastern Spain, 462 km from Madrid. Capital of Province of Castellón. One of three provinces of Comunidad Valenciana.

Population: 140,820

Geography: On a fertile plain near Mediterranean coast. Province of Castellón is more mountainous than flat, the inland landscape being of a rugged nature. There are numerous orange plantations.

Climate: Mediterranean climate: warm dry summers and mild winters

History: Originally founded on top of the nearby Magdalena Hill, it was captured from the Moors by Jaume I of Aragón in 1233. On petition of its inhabitants in 1251, it was moved to its present site on the fertile plain near the Mediterranean. It was made the provincial capital in 1833.

Main historical sites: Museum of La Diputación. Cathedral of Santa María (Gothic-style, fourteenth century). Seventeeth-century Town Hall. Bell tower of El Fadrí (sixteenth century). Capuchinos convent.

Town: A pleasant town, set amid attractive scenery. One of least expensive places to stay along this stretch of coast. Prosperous commercial centre.

Main areas of interest: Old town, fine art museum and beaches.

Surrounding area: Segorbe – cathedral of Vall de Uxó (28 km). Grutas de San José.

Travel and transport: Train station is located north-west of the town. Several bus stations.

Major economic activities: Through port of El Grau (4 km to east), exports oranges (from magnificent orange plantations along coastline), as well as almonds, hemp, and coloured tiles. A well developed tourist industry is based on the local beaches.

Major employers: Cerámica Saloni, S.A., Grespania, S.A., Mutua Intercomarcal, Contratas y Obras Empresa Constructora, S.A.

Sources of information

Tourist Office: Oficina de Turismo, Plaza María Agustina 5, 12003 Castellón de la Plana. Tel: 964 22 77 03 (Tourist Line: 22 10 00)

INEM: Castelldefels 1, 12004 Castellón de la Plana. Tel: 964 26 03 84

Town hall: Plaza Mayor 1, 12001 Castellón de la Plana. Tel: 964 22 40 00

Chamber of commerce: Cámara de Comercio, Industria y Navegación de Castellón de la Plana, Avda Hermanos Bou 79, 12003 Castellón de la Plana. Tel: 964 35 65 00 Fax: 964 35 65 10

3.13.2 **Universidad Jaume I de Castellón (UJCS)**

Basic information

Autonomous community: Comunidad Valenciana

Province: Castellón

Town: Castellón de la Plana

Status: Public (1991)

Address: Campus del Riu Sec, 12071 Castellón de la Plana. Tel: 964 72 90 41/42 Fax: 964 72 90 16 Email: rectorat@uji.es Web site: www.uji.es

Main campuses: Ctra de Borriol; Riu Sec
Satellite campuses: N/A
Students: 10,322
Staff: 979

Teaching centres

Faculties: Humanities and social sciences; law and economics
Higher technical schools: Technology and experimental sciences
University schools: N/A

Student services

Information office: Punt d'Informació de Centre, Campus del Riu Sec, 12071 Castellón de la Plana. Tel: 964 72 84 38 Fax: 964 72 90 16 Email: info@uji.es

Accommodation office: Borsa d'Habitatge, Campus del Riu Sec, 12071 Castellón de la Plana. Tel: 964 72 84 38 Fax: 964 72 90 16 Email: habitatge@uji.es

Health centre: See *Punt d'Informació*

Spanish courses for foreign students: Centro de Autoaprendizaje de Lenguas (CAL), Campus de Borriol, 12071 Castellón de la Plana. Tel: 964 72 92 29 Email: cal@nuvol.uji.es

Courses in languages

For languages undergraduates: The Faculty of Humanities offers degree courses in English philology, and translating and interpreting.

Spanish for foreign students: CAL offers self-tuition courses in Spanish (and Catalan) at various levels throughout the academic year on the Borriol Campus.

3.14 Ciudad Real

3.14.1 **Ciudad Real**

Basic information

Location and status: Located in south-central Spain, 198 km from Madrid. Capital of Province of Ciudad Real, in region of Castilla-La Mancha.

Population: 63,300

Geography: On fertile plain watered by Rivers Guadiana and Jabalón.

Climate: Continental: hot dry summers and cold winters

History: Founded in 1255 by Alfonso X El Sabio. In the late fifteenth century it became the seat of the Inquisition Tribunal.

Main historical sites: Gothic cathedral of Santa María la Mayor. Remains of fourteenth-century walls. Mudejar Gate of Toledo (1328, National Monument).

Town: Medieval walls are only highlight of the town.

Main areas of interest: El Corral de Comedias (seventeenth-century theatre). Provincial Museum.

Surrounding area: Carrión de Calatrava – ruins of castle of Calatrava la Vieja. Miguelturra – hermitage of El Cristo de la Misericordia. Natural Parks of Las Lagunas de Ruidera and Las Tablas.

Travel and transport: Ciudad Real is focus of road network. Bus station south of city centre and trains include high speed AVE to Sevilla (south) and Madrid (north).

Major economic activities: Agricultural processing and market centre, lumbering, flour-milling, liquor distilling, production of brandy.

Major employers: El Pozo Alimentación, S.A., Hoteles Tryp, S.A., Laboratorios Proyex, S.A., Unión Eléctrica Fenosa S.A., Adasa Sistemas, S.A.

Sources of information

Tourist Office: Oficina de Turismo, Avda Alarcos 31, 13001 Ciudad Real. Tel: 926 21 29 25; 21 20 03

INEM: Echegaray 3, 13002 Ciudad Real. Tel: 926 23 25 60

Town hall: Plaza Mayor 1, 13001 Ciudad Real. Tel: 926 21 38 95

Chamber of commerce: Cámara de Comercio e Industria de Ciudad Real, Lanza 2, 13004 Ciudad Real. Tel: 926 22 12 20 Fax: 926 25 38 13

3.14.2 **Universidad de Castilla-La Mancha (UCLM)**

Basic information

Autonomous community: Castilla-La Mancha

Provinces: Albacete; Ciudad Real; Cuenca; Toledo

Towns: Albacete; Ciudad Real; Cuenca; Toledo

Status: Public (1982)

Address: Casa Palacio Medrano, Paloma 9, 13071 Ciudad Real. Tel: 926 29 53 00 Fax: 926 22 38 94 Web site: www.uclm.es

Main campuses: Albacete; Ciudad Real; Cuenca; Toledo

Satellite campuses: Almadén; Talavera de la Reina

Students: 28,500

Staff: 1,170

Teaching centres

Faculties: Arts; chemistry (+Toledo); economics and business (Albacete); fine art (Cuenca); legal and social sciences (Toledo)

Higher technical schools: Agricultural engineering (Albacete); humanities (Toledo); industrial engineering

University schools: Agriculture; computing; labour relations (+Albacete +Cuenca); nursing (+Albacete +Cuenca); nursing and physiotherapy (Toledo); polytechnic (Albacete +Almadén); social work (Cuenca); teacher training (+Albacete +Cuenca +Toledo); technical architecture (Cuenca).

Student services

Information office: Servicio de Información al Estudiante (SIE), Edificio Servicios Generales, Campus Univeritario, 13071 Ciudad Real.
Tel: 926 29 53 10/00/07 Fax: 926 29 53 01 Email: jtomas@sie-cr.uclm.es
NB If required, ask this office for details of SIEs in Albacete, Cuenca or Toledo.

Accommodation office: Contact SIE and ask for details on either *Bolsa Vivienda Joven* (flats) or *Alojamiento Solidario* (lodgings with older people) for the campus at which you wish to study.

Health centre: See *SIE*

Spanish courses for foreign students: Vicerrectorado de Extensión Universitaria, Ronda de Julián Romero 18, 16071 Cuenca. Tel: 969 22 82 11 Fax: 969 22 89 84

Courses in languages

For languages undergraduates: The Faculty of Arts in Ciudad Real provides degree courses in English, French and Spanish philology.

Spanish for foreign students: The *Vicerrectorado de Extensión Universitaria* runs summer courses in Spanish language and culture at various levels in Cuenca.

3.15 Córdoba

3.15.1 **Ciudad de Córdoba**

Basic information

Location and status: Located in southern Spain, in Andalucía, 400 km from Madrid. Capital of Province of Córdoba.

Population: 318,000

Geography: Lies on southern edge of Sierra Morena and on right bank of River Guadalquivir.

Climate: Summers are searingly hot; winters are generally mild.

History: One of leading cities of the medieval world. It was occupied by Romans in 152 BC. In AD 711 Córdoba was captured and largely destroyed by Muslims. Abd ar-Rahman I, leader of Spanish Muslims, made Córdoba his capital in 756. It grew rapidly under his rule and became the largest and probably most cultured city in Europe. It was sacked by French in 1808 for its part in fomenting rebellion against Napoleonic rule. It was one of the first cities occupied by Francoist forces in the Spanish Civil War.

Main historical sites: Great Mosque (La Mezquita). Alcázar de los Reyes Católicos. San Lorenzo Church (Romanesque/Gothic). Roman Bridge, walls and gates. Church of San Pablo. Historical and Archeological Museum.

Town: Whitewashed houses and narrow, winding streets, squares that shelter convents, homes and taverns.

Main areas of interest: Recently the Mosque and the old Jewish quarter (La Judería) were declared World Heritage Sites.

Surrounding area: Medina Azahara, ancient palace of the Moorish kings (6 km).

Travel and transport: Railway station – modernised in early 1990s to take the high speed AVE en route to Madrid or Seville; provides services to most parts of Spain. New bus station to west of the train station provides national bus service. The centre is easy to walk round as it is so compact.

Major economic activities: Textile manufactures, brewing and distilling industries, manufacturing of gold and silver ornaments and products in copper, bronze, and aluminium.

Major employers: El Pozo Alimentación, S.A., Grupo Alcántara, Grupo Fimestic, Hoteles Tryp, S.A., Mutua Intercomarcal.

Sources of information

Tourist Office: Oficina de Turismo, Torrijos 10, 14003 Córdoba. Tel: 957

47 12 35; 48 31 12; 47 20 00

INEM: Madre de Dios 9, 14010 Córdoba. Tel: 957 25 84 46

COIE: Edificio Escuela Universitaria de Enfermería 4°, 14001 Córdoba. Tel: 957 47 31 25 Fax: 957 21 81 22

Town hall: Capitulares 1, 14001 Córdoba. Tel: 957 47 20 00

Chamber of commerce: Cámara de Comercio e Industria de Córdoba, Pérez de Castro 1, 14003 Córdoba. Tel: 957 29 61 99 Fax: 957 20 21 06

Twin Town: Manchester

3.15.2 **Universidad de Córdoba (UCO)**

Basic information

Autonomous community: Andalucía

Province: Córdoba

Town: Córdoba

Status: Public (1972)

Address: Alfonso XIII 13, 14001 Córdoba. Tel: 957 21 80 00 Fax: 957 21 80 30 Email: prensa@uco.es Web site: www.uco.es

Main campus: Menéndez Pidal (Córdoba)

Satellite campus: Bélmez

Students: 21,000

Staff: 1,066

Teaching centres

Faculties: Arts; economics and business (ETEA)*; education; law; medicine; science; veterinary science

Higher technical schools: Agriculture and forestry; higher polytechnic school

University schools: Education; labour relations; mining engineering (Bélmez); nursing; polytechnic; teacher training

Student services

Information office: Servicio de Información al Estudiante, Avda Menéndez Pidal s/n, 14071 Córdoba. Tel: 957 21 80 34 Fax: 957 21 80 30 Email: informacion@uco.es

Accommodation office: Oficina de Relaciones Internacionales, c/ Ángel de Saavedra 5, 14071 Córdoba. Tel: 957 49 11 91 Email: ori@lucano. uco.es

Health centre: See *Servicio de Información al Estudiante*

Spanish courses for foreign students: Servicio de Lenguas Modernas, Edificio EU Enfermería, Avda Menéndez Pidal s/n, 14071 Córdoba. Tel: 957 21 85 56; 21 81 32 Fax: 957 21 89 96 Email: idiomas@uco.es (si1diarc@uco.es)

Courses in languages

For languages undergraduates: The Faculty of Arts offers degrees in English and Hispanic philologies.

Spanish for foreign students: The *Servicio de Lenguas Modernas* offers five kinds of course: (1) three-week intensive courses at six levels between October and June; twenty hours of tuition per week; (2) a four-week intensive summer course at three levels; (3) two semester-long courses (October–February; March–June) for Erasmus or Socrates students from foreign universities; the total tuition for each is forty-five hours and each is worth four and a half credits; (4) month-long courses in Spanish for special purposes (e.g. catering, medicine, tourism) according to student demand; (5) this course comprises additional grammar classes for students on the above courses who wish to prepare for the DELE; exams are held in May and November.

ETEA = Escuela Técnica Empresarial Agrícola

3.16 Elche (Elx)

3.16.1 **Ciudad de Elche**

Basic information

Location and status: Located in south-eastern Spain in Province of Alicante, 409 km from Madrid and 22 km inland from the city of Alicante.

Population: 193,000

Geography: Lies on River Vinalopó with west bank housing newer section and east bank older town. Surrounded by forest of over 300,000 palm trees (*El Palmeral*) – debate as to whether this was planted by Phoenicians or Moors.

Climate: Summers are hot, winters generally mild.

History: Of Iberian origin, the site was originally settled around 5000 BC (at L'Alcúdia) where a fifth-century stone bust, *La Dama de Elche*, was discovered in 1897 (now held in Madrid). It was inhabited by Greeks, Carthaginians, Romans and Moors. Under Arab domination, the Roman name of *Ilici* was changed to *Elx*. The Muslims' irrigation systems were responsible for converting region into rich agricultural district.

Main historical sites: Church of Santa María (seventeenth century). La Calahorra (Moorish tower). Palace of Altamira (fifteenth century).

L'Alcúdia (southern outskirts) – Archaeological Museum.

Town: Combines historic with industrial. Ancient walls and major parks and monuments can be found in older town on east side of river.

Main areas of interest: Palm forest. Narrow streets of old walled city (*Vila Murada*). Municipal Park. Huerto del Cura (private palm forest garden). Museums (Archaeological and Contemporary Art). Fiesta and mystery play (*Misteri d'Elx*) during first two weeks of August.

Surrounding area: Alicante, beaches and Santa Pola (coastal resort).

Travel and transport: Train and bus stations north of centre (Avenida de la Libertat). Hourly buses and 16–18 trains daily to Alicante.

Major economic activities: Agriculture (citrus fruits, figs, almonds, dates and cotton). Palm Grove (*El Palmeral*) produces dates and palm fronds. Olive oil, esparto and hempen sandals (*alpargatas*).

Major employers: Econet, Medio Ambiente, Logic Control, Blockbuster Video.

Sources of information

Tourist Office: Oficina de Turismo, Parque Municipal, 03202 Elche. Tel: 96 545 27 47; 545 38 31

INEM: Mariano Benlliure 6, 03201 Elche. Tel: 96 538 30 27

Town hall: Plaza de la Fruta s/n, 03202 Elche. Tel: 96 545 35 41 Fax: 96 542 30 70

Chamber of commerce: (Uses Alicante) Cámara de Comercio, Industria y Navegación, San Fernando 4, 03002 Alicante. Tel: 96 520 11 33 Fax: 96 520 14 57

3.16.2 **Universidad Miguel Hernández de Elche (UMH)**

Basic information

Autonomous community: Comunidad Valenciana

Province: Alicante

Town: Elche

Status: Public (1996)

Address: Avda del Ferrocarril s/n, 03202 Elche, Alicante. Tel: 96 665 86 00 Fax: 96 665 86 32 Email: registrogeneral@umh.es Web site: www.umh.es

Main campus: Avda del Ferrocarril (Elche)

Satellite campuses: Altea; Orihuela; San Juan

Students: 6,900

Staff: 800

Teaching centres

Faculties: Experimental and technical sciences; fine art (Altea); medicine (San Juan); social sciences and law (Elche; Orihuela)

Higher technical schools: Engineering (industrial, materials, systems and telecommnications); engineering (agricultural, food industries, gardening and horticulture and oenology) (Orihuela)

University schools: N/A

Student services

Information office: Servicios Esudiantiles, Avda del Ferrocarril s/n, 03202 Elche (Alicante). Tel: 96 665 86 41 Fax: 96 665 86 80 Email: servalu@umh.es

Accommodation office: Relaciones Internacionales, Avda del Ferrocarril s/n, 03202 Elche (Alicante). Tel: 96 665 87 10 Fax: 96 665 86 32 Email: rel.internacionales@umh.es

Health centre: Hospital de Elche Huertos y Molinos s/n, 03202 Elche (Alicante). Tel: 96 667 90 00

Spanish courses for foreign students: See *Servicios Estudiantiles* or *Relaciones Internacionales*

Courses in languages

For languages undergraduates: N/A

Spanish for foreign students: The University offers courses at various levels in Spanish language during the summer.

3.17 Gerona (Girona)

3.17.1 Ciudad de Gerona

Basic information

Location and status: Located in north-east Spain, in Catalonia, 721 km from Madrid. Capital of Province of Girona.

Population: 72,800

Geography: Lies on River Oñar in foothills of Los Ángeles mountains, a short distance inland from Mediterranean coastal area known as Costa Brava (Rugged Coast). Bordering on frontier with France and provinces of Barcelona and Lleida. Coastline is magnificent. There is also a fine mountain region.

Climate: Mild climate which attracts tourists all year round.

History: A fortified site of Iberians and Romans, when known as Gerunda. It passed to the Visigoths and was later conquered in AD 714 by Muslims. Retaken by the Franks, the city was lost again in 793 and recaptured by Louis of Aquitaine in 797. Girona took active part in seventeenth- and eighteenth-century wars between Spain and France and was besieged several times.

Main historical sites: Collegiate Church of San Félix. Monastery of San Pedro de Galligans. Cathedral (fourteenth to sixteenth century). Arab baths. Provincial Archaeological Museum.

Town: Ancient walled city standing on hill. Inner city, packed with narrow streets, one of most beautiful and best preserved in Spain. Industrially important.

Main areas of interest: Old historic quarter (*casco antiguo*). City walls. Art Museum.

Surrounding area: Banyoles – Main Square and boating lake (18 km). Caldes de Malavella – Roman baths (18 km). Besalú – medieval village (33 km). Olot (48 km): Zona Volcánica (National Park of the Garrotxa region). Costa Brava.

Travel and transport: Train station in Plaza de España, across river in new part of city. Bus station on Carrer Rafael Masó i Valentí. Girona airport is 12 km south of city centre. Regular buses and trains to Costa Brava and inland towns. No airport bus service. Parking difficult in old part of town.

Major economic activities: Milk pasteurisation, filtering, freezing, and preserving, flour mills, distilleries, biscuit and confectionery and soft drink factories. Textile production considerable. Paper mill, publishing house, several chemical factories, soapworks. Heavy machinery. All-year-round tourism.

Major employers: Logic Control, S.A., Mutua Intercomarcal, SAT Mutua Accidentes de Trabajo.

Sources of information

Tourist Office: Oficina de Turismo Rambla de la Llibertat 1, 17004 Girona. Tel: 972 22 65 75; 21 62 96

INEM: Creu 2 y 4, 17002 Girona. Tel: 972 20 50 60

Town hall: Plaza del Vi 1, 17004 Girona. Tel: 972 41 90 00

Chamber of commerce: Cámara de Comercio, Industria y Navegación, Gran Via Jaume I 46, 17001 Girona. Tel: 972 41 85 00 Fax: 972 41 85 01

Twin Town: Wakefield

3.17.2 **Universidad de Gerona (UDG)**

Basic information

Autonomous community: Cataluña (Catalunya)
Province: Gerona (Girona)
Town: Gerona (Girona)
Status: Public (1991)
Address: Rectorat, Plaça de Sant Domenec 9, 17001 Gerona. Tel: 972 41 80 11 Fax: 972 41 80 31 Web site: www.udg.edu
Main campuses: Barri Vell; Emili Grahit; Montilivi
Satellite campus: Sant Feliu de Guíxols
Students: 14,000
Staff: 735+

Teaching centres

Faculties: Arts; education; economics and business; law; science
Higher technical schools: Higher polytechnic school; public relations
University schools: Nursing; tourism x 5 (+Sant Feliú de Guíxols)
Institutes: Agrofood technology; aquatic ecology; Catalan language and culture; computational chemistry; computing applications; education (ICE); environment; research on quality of life

Student services

Information office: Informació General, Edifici 'Les Aligues', Plaça de Sant Domenec 3, 17071 Gerona. Tel: 972 41 80 68 Fax: 972 41 80 31 Email: academica5@aligues.udg.es
Accommodation office: Servei d'Allotjament Universitari (SAU), Edifici 'Butinyanes', Alemanys 9, 17071 Gerona. Tel: 972 41 81 16 Fax: 972 41 80 31 Email: cde@cde.udg.es
Health centre: See *Informació General*
Spanish courses for foreign students: N/A

Courses in languages

For languages undergraduates: The Faculty of Arts offers degree courses in Catalan and Hispanic philologies.
Spanish for foreign students: N/A

3.18 Granada

3.18.1 **Ciudad de Granada**

Basic information

Location and status: Located in southern Spain, in Andalucía, 430 km from Madrid. Capital of Province of Granada.

Population: 287,850

Geography: Lies along River Genil in rugged landscape on north-western slope of snow-capped Sierra Nevada, 2,260 feet above sea level. Scenic diversity characterises land. Extensive fertile Genil plain. At confluence of Rivers Darro and Genil.

Climate: Very hot and dry in summer with mild-to-cool winters.

History: Site of an Iberian settlement in fifth century BC and also of a Roman one. It was established as an independent kingdom by Ibn Ahmar in 1238. It was the final stronghold of the Moors (Nasrid Dynasty) in Spain, and fell to the Catholic Monarchs, Ferdinand and Isabella, in January 1492. One of the first cities to be occupied by Franco at start of the Civil War.

Main historical sites: World-famous Moorish Palace/Fortress of the Alhambra and adjoining Generalife, summer palace of Moorish kings. Renaissance Palace of Carlos V. Gothic cathedral of Santa María de la Encarnación, with tombs of Ferndinand and Isabella. Sixteenth-century Royal Chapel (*Capilla Real*). Palace of La Madraza.

Town: Evocative and enchanting with underlying Moorish atmosphere. One of Spain's most frequently visited tourist centres, Granada contains many notable architectural and artistic monuments. As last Moorish capital on Iberian Peninsula, holds great symbolic value.

Main areas of interest: In north-east of the city, opposite Alhambra, is the Albaicín quarter, oldest part of Granada. Nearby are gypsy caves of Sacromonte, famous for (watered-down) flamenco shows for tourists.

Surrounding area: Sierra Nevada Ski Resort (33 km). Fuente Vaqueros, birth-place of García Lorca (17 km). Guadix – cave houses. Unique mountainous district of La Alpujarra, south of Granada.

Travel and transport: Airport bus service. New bus station. Airport is 17 km west of centre. Regular bus and train services.

Major economic activities: An active trade in agricultural produce, manufactures liquors, soap, paper, coarse linen and woollen fabrics. Venue for international festivals of music.

Major employers: University, El Pozo Alimentación, S.A., Estudio de Informática, S.L., Grupo Fimestic, Mutua Intercomarcal.

Sources of information

Tourist Office: Oficina de Turismo, Plaza Mariana Pineda 10, 18009 Granada. Tel: 958 22 66 88

INEM: Cartuja, Curro Cuchares, esquina Polo, 18014 Granada. Tel: 958 15 31 04

Town hall: Plaza del Carmen s/n, 18009 Granada. Tel: 958 24 81 00

Chamber of commerce: Cámara de Comercio, Industria y Navegación, Paz 18, 18002 Granada. Tel: 958 26 30 20 Fax: 958 26 22 14 Email: ccigranada@camerdata.es

3.18.2 **Universidad de Granada (UGR)**

Basic information

Autonomous community: Andalucía

Province: Granada

Town: Granada

Status: Public (1526)

Address: Hospital Real, Cuesta del Hospicio s/n, 18071 Granada. Tel: 958 24 30 25 Fax: 958 24 30 66 Web site: www.ugr.es

Main campuses: Cartuja; Fuentenueva; Realejo

Satellite campuses: Almuñecar; Ceuta; Guadix; Lanjarón; Melilla; Motril

Students: 58,960

Staff: 2,590

Teaching centres

Faculties: Arts; dentistry; economics and business; education; fine art; law; librarianship and documentation; medicine; pharmacy; politics and sociology; psychology; science; physical activity and sport; translating and interpreting

Higher techncial schools: Architecture; civil engineering; computing

University schools: Business Studies (+Melilla); health sciences; labour relations (+Melilla); nursing (+Ceuta +Melilla); social work; teacher training (+Ceuta *and* Melilla); technical architecture

Other centres: Andalusian institutes of: land science; geophysics and prevention of seismic disasters; criminology AND institutes of: biotechnology; theoretical and computational physics; water; regional development; neuroscience; nutrition and food technology; women's studies; peace and conflict studies AND Centre for continuing education AND School of Arab studies.

Student services

Information office: Centro de Información y Documentación del Universitario (CIDU), Edificio Comedores Universitarios, Avda Severo Ochoa s/n, 18071 Granada. Tel: 958 24 31 02/37 Fax 958 24 31 34 Email: CIDU@ugr.es
or Oficina de Relaciones Internacionales, Facultad de Ciencias Económicas, Campus Cartuja, 18071 Granada. Tel: 958 24 37 32 Fax: 958 24 37 28 Email: emprerin@ucartuja.ugr.es

Accommodation office: Servicio de Alojamiento, Vicerrectorado de Estudiantes, Avda Severo Ochoa s/n, 18071 Granada. Tel: 958 24 40 72 Fax: (958) 24 31 34

Health centre: Centro Juvenil de Orientación para la Salud, Pabellón Severo Ochoa, Avda Severo Ochoa s/n, 18071 Granada. Tel: 958 28 60 64 Fax: (958) 24 31 34

Spanish courses for foreign students: (1) Centro de Lenguas Modernas, Palacio de Santa Cruz, Placeta del Hospicio Viejo s/n, Realejo, 18071 Granada. Tel: 958 22 07 90 Fax: 958 22 08 44
(2) Centro Mediterráneo, Rector López Argueta s/n, 18071 Granada. Tel: (958) 24 29 22 Fax: (958) 24 29 24

Courses in languages

For languages undergraduates: The Arts Faculty provides traditional degree courses in the philologies of Arabic, Classical Languages, English, French, German, Hebrew, Italian, Portuguese, Slavonic studies and Spanish. The Faculty of Translating and Interpreting offers these and other languages, including Chinese and Russian, as part of a four-year degree in translating and interpreting. This centre has long been involved in joint language programmes with other European universities, including the UK, offering dual or triple degree qualifications in some cases.

Spanish for foreign students: The *Centro de Lenguas Modernas* offers a well-established *Curso de Estudios Hispánicos*, including Spanish Language and Culture, which students can follow for one or two semesters (four and eight months). In addition, at different times of year, it provides intensive Spanish languages courses, of four or eight weeks' duration, taught at four different levels, including beginners. Similar (summer) courses, as well as special thematic lecture programmes, are on offer, usually in September, at the *Centro Mediterráneo*, with centres in Almuñecar, Granada, Guadix, Lanjarón and Motril, as well as Ceuta and Melilla.

3.19 Huelva

3.19.1 **Ciudad de Huelva**

Basic information

Location and status: South-western Spain, 632 km from Madrid. Capital of Province of Huelva.

Population: 141,500

Geography: Lies on western shore of peninsula formed by estuaries of Rivers Odiel and Tinto. Near Atlantic. Coastline has magnificent sunny beaches.

Climate: Mild, not too extreme in summer, though can be very sultry; temperate in winter with low rainfall.

History: Founded by the Phoenecians under the name of Onuba, then a Roman colony, whose restored aqueduct now supplies the city with water. Occupied by Moors, Huelva was recaptured for the Christians in 1257 by Alfonso X the Wise of Castile. From near here (Palos de la Frontera), Columbus set sail for America.

Main historical sites: Cathedral church of La Merced. Museum of Fine Art. La Rábida Monastery where Colmbus stayed prior to his first voyage and Palos de la Frontera where his ships were constructed.

Town: Large, sprawling and industrialised. Least attractive city in Andalucía, but has beautiful views to sea. Important fishing port.

Main areas of interest: Areas associated with Columbus (*Lugares Colombinos*). Provincial Museum – history of Río Tinto mines and artefacts.

Surrounding area: Niebla – castle and city walls (17 km). Attractive Atlantic seaside resorts of Mazagón and Punta Umbría. Coto Donaña National Park – one of largest and most original in Europe, teaming with wildlife, especially birds and water fowl.

Travel and transport: Bus station is a short walk from city centre with local and long distance services. Train station is on Avenida de Italia; there is a daily train to Madrid.

Major economic activities: A major ore-shipping port, Huelva is also a fisheries headquarters. Trades in grain, grapes, olives and cork. Industrial railways link the ore mines with the port. Petrochemical industries.

Major employers: El Pozo Alimentación, S.A., Tableros de Fibras, S.A. (TAFISA), Grupo Duro Felguera, S.A., Norcontrol.

Sources of information

Tourist Office: Oficina de Turismo, Avda de Alemania 8, 21003 Huelva. Tel: 959 25 74 03

INEM: Gonzalo de Berceo 45–47, 21005 Huelva. Tel: 959 15 11 97

Town hall: Plaza de la Constitución 1, 21003 Huelva. Tel: 959 21 01 01
Chamber of commerce: Cámara de Comercio, Industria y Navegación, Sor Ángela de la Cruz 1, 21003 Huelva. Tel: 959 24 59 00 Fax: 959 26 19 49; 24 56 99

3.19.2 **Universidad de Huelva (UHU)**

Basic information

Autonomous community: Andalucía
Province: Huelva
Town: Huelva
Status: Public (1993)
Address: Plaza de la Merced 11, 21071 Huelva. Tel: 959 28 42 37/38/39 Fax:(959 28 43 05 Web site: www.uhu.es
Main campuses: Cantero Cuadrado; El Carmen; La Merced
Satellite campus: La Rábida
Students: 13,600
Staff: 643

Teaching centres

Faculties: Business; education; experimental sciences (La Rábida); humanities; law
Higher technical schools: Higher polytechnic school (La Rábida)
University schools: Labour relations; nursing; social work

Student services

Information office: (1) Servicio de Asistencia a la Comunidad Universitaria (SACU), Cantero Cuadrado 6, 21071 Huelva. Tel: 959 22 65 50 ext 209 Fax: 959 27 12 91 Email: sacu@uhu.es; eulogio@uhu.es
(2) Área de Relaciones Internacionales, Cantero Cuadrado 6, 2701 Huelva. Tel: (959) 22 65 50 Fax: (959) 27 12 91 Email: drinter@ uhu.es
Accommodation office: Dirección General de Alumnos, Plaza de La Merced s/n, 21071 Huelva. Tel: 959 28 42 37/8/9 Fax: 959 28 43 05
Health centre: See *SACU*
Spanish courses for foreign students: Secretaría, Instituto de Idiomas, Dr Cantero Cuadrado 6, 27901 Huelva. Tel: 959 22 65 50

Courses in languages

For languages undergraduates: The Faculty of Humanities offers a degree in humanities in which students may take English and/or Spanish philology or a programme of integrated philology studies. The latter includes options in French, German, Greek and Latin philologies (NOT Spanish).

Spanish for foreign students: N/A

3.19.3 **Campus of Universidad Internacional de Andalucía (see** 3.6.2**)**

3.20 Huesca

3.20.1 Ciudad de Huesca

Basic information

Location and status: North-eastern Spain, 397 km from Madrid. Capital of Province of Huesca.

Population: 45,600

Geography: In region known as Hoya de Huesca which is dominated by Sierra de Guara to north and is watered by River Flumen. Lofty mountains in central parts of Pyrenees. Extremely beautiful valleys, fertile plains in south of region. Sparkling blue glacial lakes.

Climate: Sunny all year round. Winters are mild with heavy snow in mountain passes. Warm summers, brilliant sunshine and deep-blue skies.

History: City originated as capital of Vescitan and Iberian tribes. Then it was site of the Roman mint and known by Romans as Osca. It was later occupied by the Visigoths and Moors who for a time used it as the capital of Aragón. It was known by Moors as Washka.

Main historical sites: Cathedral, on site of pagan temple and, later, a mosque (sixteenth century). Church of San Pedro el Viejo (thirteenth century). Old Parish Church (Antigua Iglesia Parroquial). Town Hall. Episcopal palace, built in Mudéjar (Christian/Islamic) style. Colegio de Santiago houses provincial archives and Museum of Fine Arts. Church of San Miguel has only tower, out of ninety-nine that formed city's defences, left standing.

Town: Least memorable of Aragonese towns, but located in very impressive setting.

Main areas of interest: Medieval centre

Surrounding area: Loarre – castle and Romanesque church (17 km). Nueva de Sigera – monastery of Santa María de Sigena (22 km). Las Mallas rock formations.

Travel and transport: Regular bus and train services. Bus and train stations are only a couple of blocks away from each other.

Major economic activities: Little industry apart from local handicrafts and manufacture of agricultural machinery.

Major employers: Caja de Ahorras de La Inmaculada, Laboratorios Proyex, S.A.

Sources of information

Tourist Office: Oficina de Turismo, Coso Alto 23, bajos, 22002 Huesca. Tel: 974 22 57 78

INEM: Casado del Alisal 17, esq. P. León, 22005 Huesca. Tel: 974 22 80 11

Town hall: Plaza de la Catedral 1, 22002 Huesca, Tel: 974 22 04 00

Chamber of commerce: Cámara de Comercio e Industria de Huesca, Santo Ángel la Guarda 7, 22005 Huesca. Tel: 974 24 46 31 Fax: 974 22 96 44 Email: ccihuesca@camerdat.es

3.20.2 **Campus of Universidad de Zaragoza (see** 3.50.2**)**

3.21 Jaén

3.21.1 **Ciudad de Jaén**

Basic information

Location and status: Southern Spain, 335 km from Madrid. Capital of Province of Jaén.

Population: 113,200

Geography: Lies on northern side of Sierra Jabalcuz. Green and silvery olive trees.

Climate: Hot in summer but windy. Sunny and warm. Mild climate; summers are not too hot and in winter temperature hardly ever drops below freezing.

History: Originally Carthaginian town. It was later captured by the Romans who exploited its silver mines. The centre of the Moorish principality of Jayyán, it was reconquered by Fernando III of Castile and León in 1246.

Main historical sites: Renaissance-style cathedral, completed in eighteenth century. Church of San Bartolomé. Castle of Santa Catalina (mentioned in twelfth century Arab chronicles).

Town: Old part of town is characterised by winding streets. Moorish atmosphere with fascinating, artistic, corners.

Main areas of interest: Elevated castle and parador complex afford splendid views over city and surrounding countryside. Eleventh-century Arab Baths (*Baños Árabes*) – largest surviving ones in Spain. Pedestrianised old quarter of the town, north-west of cathedral.

Surrounding area: Cerrillo Saliod – Visigothic necropolis (8 km). Alcalá la Real – attractive town and castle (17 km).

Travel and transport: Ample area for parking. Regular buses and trains. Bus stop round the corner from the train station.

Major economic activities: Jaén's economy is based primarily on production of olive oil. Also some chemical and lead production. Once famous for silk.

Major employers: University, El Pozo Alimentación, S.A., Cruzcampo.

Sources of information

Tourist Office: Oficina de Turismo, Arquitecto Berges 1, 23002 Jaén. Tel: 953 22 27 37

INEM: Avda de Andalucía 36, bajo, 23006 Jaén. Tel: 953 26 11 90

Town hall: Plaza Santa María 1, 23002 Jaén. Tel: 953 21 91 00

Chamber of commerce: Cámara de Comercio e Industria de Jaén, Hurtado 29, 23006 Jaén. Tel: 953 25 32 02

3.21.2 **Universidad de Jaén (UJA)**

Basic information

Autonomous community: Andalucía

Province: Jaén

Town: Jaén

Status: Public (1993)

Address: Paraje Las Lagunillas s/n, 23071 Jaén. Tel: 953 21 21 21 Fax: 953 21 22 39 Email: rg@xauen.ujaenes Web site: www.ujaen.es

Main campus: Las Lagunillas

Satellite campuses: Linares; Ubeda

Students: 15,523

Staff: 673

Teaching centres

Faculties: Experimental sciences; humanities and education; social and legal sciences

Higher technical schools: Higher polytechnic school
University schools: Nursing; polytechnic (Linares); social work (Linares); teacher training (Úbeda)

Student services

Information office: Oficina de Atención al Estudiante (OAE), Paraje Las Lagunillas s/n, Edificio 8, 23071 Jaén. Tel: 953 21 21 92 Fax: 953 21 21 99 Email: oae@xauen.ujaen.es
Accommodation office: See *OAE*
Health centre: See *OAE*
Spanish courses for foreign students: None available as yet

Courses in languages

For languages undergraduates: The English and Spanish Departments of the Arts Faculty contribute to the degree course in English language and literature, with modules in other languages, including Arabic and French.
Spanish for foreign students: None available as yet. However, the Department of English is willing to enter into Socrates-type exchanges with UK universities and already provides a special programme of Spanish studies, including project tutorials, for some students from British universities.

3.22 La Coruña (A Coruña)

3.22.1 **Ciudad de La Coruña**

Basic information

Location and status: Far north-west corner of Spain, 595 km from Madrid. Capital of Province of La Coruña. Important port on Atlantic coast.
Population: 254,800
Geography: Lies on Estuary (*Ría*) of La Coruña, an inlet of Atlantic, separating sandy bay of Orzán from Ría da Coruña.
Climate: Typical Atlantic, temperate climate: warm summers and cool, wet winters. Often windy.
History: Under the Romans, La Coruña was known as port of Brigantium. It was held by the Moors during the eighth, ninth and tenth centuries, by the Portuguese during the fourteenth century and reconquered by the Spanish in the fifteenth century. On 26 July 1588,

the Spanish Armada sailed from La Coruña against England. The city suffered heavily when Spain lost Cuba and Puerto Rico in the Spanish–American War (1898) since it had enjoyed thriving trade with those colonies.

Main historical sites: Tower of Hercules (Roman). Romanesque church of Santiago. Church of Santa María. Walled gardens of San Carlos. Island of San Antón (east) formerly contained the fort and military prison but is now an archaeological museum. Lighthouse built AD 98–117. It is the birthplace of the Spanish novelist Emilia Pardo Bazán.

Town: One of chief ports of northern Spain. Has beach resort facilities. Characteristic feature of houses on waterfront is *miradores* or window balconies which have given it name of 'City of Glass'. Originally surrounded by city walls. Narrow flag-stoned streets and squares.

Main areas of interest: Old section (*ciudad vieja*) on peninsula between Orzán and A Coruña bays. A new section (Ciudad Nueva or La Pescadería) on mainland and a narrow isthmus. Waterfront *miradores.*

Surrounding area: Cambre – church of Santa María (12 km). Muxia – shrine of Nuestra Señora de la Barca (17 km).

Travel and transport: National bus and train services. Train station is only 2 km south-west of the heart of the town.

Major economic activities: Exports farm produce (especially potatoes and onions), and imports coal, salt and manufactured goods. Nation's second largest fishing centre and has salting and canning industries. Petroleum refining is another major industry. Tobacco and linen are also produced.

Major employers: Tobacco Factory (Santa Lucía), Shipyards (fishing vessels), El Pozo Alimentación, S.A., Gestiones Sociolaborales, S.A. (Gestolasa), Grupo Fimestic, IBM España, S.A., Investigación Total Ware, S.A. (ITOWA).

Sources of information

Tourist Office: Dársena de la Marina s/n, 15001 La Coruña. Tel: 981 22 18 22

INEM: Plaza de Rafael Dieste s/n, 15008 La Coruña. Tel: 981 29 00 88

Town hall: Plaza María Pita 1, 1500 La Coruña. Tel: 981 22 14 06

Chamber of commerce: Cámara de Comercio, Industria y Navegación, Alameda 30, 15003 La Coruña. Tel: 981 21 60 72 Fax: 981 22 52 08 Email: ccicoruna@comerdata.es

3.22.2 **Universidad de La Coruña (Universidade da Coruña/ UDC)**

Basic information

Autonomous community: Galicia
Province: La Coruña
Town: La Coruña
Status: Public (1989)
Address: Paseo da Maestranza s/n, 15001 La Coruña. Tel: 981 16 70 00 Fax: 981 16 70 11 Web site: www.udc.es
Main campuses: Elviña; Maestranza; Riazor; Zapateira
Satellite campus: Ferrol
Students: 23,426
Staff: 967

Teaching centres

Faculties: Computing; economics and business; education; humanities (Ferrol); law; philology; philosophy; science; sociology
Higher technical schools: Architecture; civil engineering; higher polytechnic school (Ferrol); higher school for the merchant marine.
University schools: Business; labour relations (+Ferrol); nursing; nursing and chiropody (Ferrol); occupational therapy; polytechnic (Ferrol); technical architecture
Institutes: European studies; geology; health sciences; physical education (national institute)

Student services

Information office: Oficina de Información, Servicio de Asesoramiento y Promoción del Estudiante (SAPE), 'Casa do Francés', A Zapateira, 15071 La Coruña. Tel: 981 13 00 00 ext 2707 Fax: 981 17 47 37 Email: sape@ares.six.udc.es
Accommodation office: See *SAPE*
Health centre: See *SAPE*
Spanish courses for foreign students: Servicio de Relaciones Internacionales, Casa de la Galería, Campus de Elviña, 15071 La Coruña. Tel: 981 16 70 00 Fax: 981 16 70 13 Email: rrii@ares.six.udc.es

Courses in languages

For languages undergraduates: The Faculty of Humanities offers degree courses in English and Galician philologies. All undergraduates at the university may participate in the conversation classes in English, French, German and Italian. The course starts in early November and lasts for approximately eight weeks (five hours per week). Students are taught in groups no larger than fifteen.

Spanish for foreign students: Contact *Servicio de Relaciones Internacionales*

3.23 La Laguna

3.23.1 **Ciudad de La Laguna**

Basic information

Location and status: Situated in Tenerife, one of Canary Islands. Most important town on island after city of Tenerife, the capital.

Population: 130,000

Geography: Lies inland in the Augere valley among magnificent countryside. Surrounded by pine forests.

Climate: The Canary Islands have a climate of their own. More mountainous areas such as Tenerife have more rainfall than others. Eternal spring throughout year. Mild humid climate. Only 7 per cent of less agreeable days per year.

History: First capital of Tenerife island, first colonised by Spanish over 500 years ago.

Main historical sites: Cathedral (sixteenth century). Church of La Concepción. Episcopal and Nava Palaces. Ancient Dragon Tree in El Seminario Garden.

Town: Second city of island of Tenerife. It retains many colonial buildings, especially along Calle Agustín. It has an air of history, with pleasant, narrow streets. Typical of town are the traditional Canary wood-framed, paned windows.

Main areas of interest: Bajamar area and Punta del Hidalgo, which are linked by El Arenal beach and form important tourist centre with lovely natural pools on the edge of the sea.

Surrounding area: Monte de las Mercedes. Monte de la Esperanza. Pico del Inglés. Bajamar.

Travel and transport: Airport of Los Rodos only 5 km away. Good local bus service.

Major economic activities: Tourism is predominant all year round.

Major employers: University, tourist industry.

Sources of information

Tourist Office: C/ Carrera 1, 38201 La Laguna. Tel: 922 60 11 00
INEM: C/ Alfredo Torres Edwards s/n, 38205 La Laguna. Tel: 922 25 38 40
Town hall: Obispo Rey Redondo 1, 38201 La Laguna (Tenerife). Tel: 922 60 11 00
Chamber of commerce: (as for Tenerife) Cámara de Comercio, Industria y Navegación de Santa Cruz de Tenerife, Plaza de la Candelaria 6, 38003 Santa Cruz de Tenerife. Tel: 922 24 53 85/85

3.23.2 **Universidad de La Laguna (ULL)**

Basic information

Autonomous community: Canarias
Island: Tenerife
Town: La Laguna
Status: Public (I792)
Address: Molinos de Agua s/n, 38207 La Laguna, Tenerife, Canary Islands Tel: 922 60 30 00 Fax: 922 25 96 28 Email: info@ull.es Web site: www.ull.es
Main campus: La Laguna
Satellite campus: Santa Cruz de Tenerife (SCT)
Students: 25,620
Staff: 1,963

Teaching centres

Faculties: Biology; chemistry; economics and business; fine art (SCT); geography and history; information science; law; mathematics; medicine; pharmacy; philology; philosophy; physics; psychology
Higher centres: Agriculture; computing; education; nautical and marine studies (SCT); technical architecture
University schools: Business; nursing (SCT); nursing and physiotherapy; social work; technical architecture
Institutes: Astropysics; bio-organics; linguistics; political and social sciences

Student services

Information office: Servicio de Orientación para Alumnado (SOPA), c/ Viana 50, 38071 La Laguna, Tenerife. Tel: 922 60 30 90/91 Fax: 922 60 32 50 Email: sopa@ull.es

Accommodation office: Servicio de Alojamiento c/ Viana 50, 38071 La Laguna. Tel: 922 31 96 07 Fax: 922 31 96 24

Health centre: See *SOPA*

Spanish courses for foreign students: Servicio de Idiomas, Avda Trinidad s/n, 38071 La Laguna. Tel: (922) 31 92 00 Fax: (922) 31 92 00

Courses in languages

For languages undergraduates: The Faculty of Arts offers degree courses in English, French and Hispanic philologies.

Spanish for foreign students: The *Servicio de Idiomas* in La Laguna provides both standard (four hours per week for twenty-nine weeks) and intensive (ten hours per week for eight weeks) courses throughout the academic year in groups no larger than fifteen. *Cursos de Español para Extranjeros*, on the Santa Cruz de Tenerife campus, offer a two-week intensive Spanish language course in July.

3.24 Las Palmas de Gran Canaria

3.24.1 **Ciudad de Las Palmas de Gran Canaria**

Basic information

Location and status: Located on north-eastern coast of Gran Canaria Island, largest city on island. Capital of Province of Las Palmas.

Population: 354,000

Geography: Situated at the mouth of a ravine. Abundant palm trees.

Climate: Mild winter climate. Climate of perpetual springtime.

History: Headquarters for Spanish conquest of Tenerife and La Palma islands. Later a major supply port for ships bound for Spanish America.

Main historical sites: Vegueta quarter. Casa Francisco. Canary Museum. Cathedral of Santa Ana. Christopher Columbus's house.

Town: A bustling seaport. Takes its name from the abundant palms there. Good tourism due to mild winter climate, excellent beaches and resort facilities. Has a colonial 'feel' to it.

Main areas of interest: Oldest houses dating from fifteenth century are found in colonial quarter (Vegueta). Pueblo Canario (a group of buildings in the old Canary style of architecture). Diocesan Museum of Sacred Art. Beach of Las Canteras.

Surrounding area: Jardín Canario. Montaña de Arucas. Excellent beaches.

Travel and transport: Airport is 20 km from city centre (bus link available). Local bus service.

Major economic activities: Port has oil-bunkering facilities. Chief exports include bananas, tomatoes and other agricultural produce. Tourism is very important economically.

Major employers: Astilleros Canarios, S.A., Bull, Deloitte and Touche, S.A., El Pozo Alimentación, S.A., Mutua Intercomarcal, Page Ibérica, S.A., Serviport Las Palmas, S.A.

Sources of information

Tourist Office: Oficina de Turismo, Parque de Santa Catalina, 35007 Las Palmas de Gran Canaria. Tel: 928 26 46 23; 22 09 47

INEM: Puerto de la Luz s/n, 35010 Las Palmas. Tel: 928 26 39 50

Town hall: León y Castillo 270, 35005 Las Palmas de Gran Canaria. Tel: 928 23 01 66

Chamber of commerce: Cámara de Comercio, Industria y Navegación de Las Palmas, León y Castillo 24, 35003 Las Palmas de Gran Canaria. Tel: 928 37 10 00 Fax: 928 36 23 50 Email: camaralp@idedned.com

3.24.2 **Universidad de Las Palmas de Gran Canaria (ULPGC)**

Basic information

Autonomous community: Canarias
Island: Gran Canaria
Town: Las Palmas de Gran Canaria
Status: Public (1989)
Address: Alfonso XIII 2, 35003 Las Palmas de Gran Canaria. Tel: 928 45 10 00 Fax: 928 45 10 22 Web site: www.ulpgc.es
Main campuses: Mantaña Cardones; Obelisco; San Cristóbal; Tafira
Satellite campus: Lanzarote
Students: 19,000
Staff: 1,200

Teaching centres

Faculties: Computing; economics and business; geography and history; legal sciences; marine sciences; sports studies; philology; translating and intrepreting; veterinary science

Higher technical schools: Architecture; industrial engineering; telecommunications

University schools: Computing; polytechnic; social work; telecommunications; tourism

Student services

Information office: Servicio de Orientación al Alumnado (SOA), Alfonso XIII 2, 35003 Las Palmas de Gran Canaria. Tel: 928 45 10 72/74 Fax: (928) 45 33 01 35003 Email: soa@soaulp.ext.ulpgc.es

Accommodation office: Contact *SOA* for information on *Bolsas de Alojamiento* (flats, bed sits, family accommodation, etc.) and on the *Servicio de Alojamiento Alternativo* (*SAA*) (lodgings with senior citizens). Accommodation may be available for long-stay students in one of the four University halls of residence (Tel: 928 35 15 68)

Health centre: See *SOA,* Relaciones Internacionales, Alfonso XIII 2 (3ª planta), 35003 Las Palmas de Gran Canaria. Tel: 928 45 89 51

Spanish courses for foreign students: Aula de Idiomas, Bravo Murillo 25, 35004 Las Palmas de Gran Canaria. Tel: 928 45 18 39 Fax: 928 38 23 17

Courses in languages

For languages undergraduates: The Faculty of Translating and Interpreting offers degree courses involving English, French and German, as well as Spanish.

Spanish for foreign students: The *Aula de Idiomas* provides a wide variety of language courses for both full-time and part-time students, including modules of thirty hours' tuition in Chinese, English, French and Italian. These courses are offered at a number of levels, including beginners. Intensive courses in Spanish are offered during the summer.

3.25 León

3.25.1 **Ciudad de León**

Basic information

Location and status: North-western Spain, 327 km from Madrid. Capital of Province of León.

Population: 147,800

Geography: Lying on south-western part of central plateau (*Meseta*) at confluence of Rivers Bernesga and Torío. Mixture of mountains, flat lands, forests and fields of wheat.

Climate: Warm summers and cold winters.

History: City developed from the camp of the Roman seventh Germina Legion. The Moors held city until 850. In the tenth century, León became capital of the Kingdom of Asturias and León. It was united with Castile in 1230 and exercised considerable political, cultural and economic influence during the Middle Ages.

Main historical sites: Cathedral of Santa María de Regla (thirteenth century, Gothic). Basilica of San Isidoro (Romanesque), with Royal Pantheon (*Panteón Real*). Renaissance-style church of San Marcos (now a national Parador). Palace of Los Guzmanes. Roman walls.

Town: City of fine historic buildings with a wealth of artistic interest, it attracts large numbers of tourists. Cosmopolitan university town.

Main areas of interest: Cathedral, with stained glass windows. Various museums. Park on the banks of River Bernesga.

Surrounding area: Gradefes – church of San Miguel de Escalada (17 km). Caves of Valporquero (3 km). Navatejera – Roman villa (19 km).

Travel and transport: Regular bus and train services to Madrid and other parts of Spain. Train and bus stations on west side of River Bernesga.

Major economic activities: Economic life of the city not revived until the nineteenth century by mining after a decline in the sixteenth century. By the mid-twentieth century, León was resurgent, with a new city and industrialisation. Other important industries are: dairy products and tourism.

Major employers: Centro de Tecnologías Informáticas, S.A (CETISA), Laboratorios Ovejero, S.A., Mutua Intercomarcal, Nutreco España, S.A., Servicemaster Pollard and Wessner, S.L., Unión Eléctrica Fenosa, S.A.

Sources of information

Tourist Office: Oficina de Turismo, Plaza de la Regla 3, 24003 León. Tel: 987 23 70 82

INEM: Ramón y Cajal 14–16, 24002 León. Tel: 987 24 95 30

COIE: Edificio Servicios Universitarios, Campus Universitario de Vegazana, 24071 León. Tel: 987 29 11 66; 29 18 58 Fax: 987 29 11 58 Email: unileon@coie.es

Town hall: Plaza de San Marcelo s/n, 24002 León. Tel: 987 89 55 00

Chamber of commerce: Cámara de Comercio e Industria de León Fajeros 1, 24002 León. Tel: 987 22 44 00 Fax: 987 22 24 51 Email: ccileon@camerdat.es

3.25.2 **Universidad de León (ULE)**

Basic information

Autonomous community: Castilla y León

Province: León

Town: León

Status: Public (1979)
Address: Avda de la Facultad 25, 24071 León. Tel: 987 29 16 00 Fax: 987 29 16 14 Email: gerbms@unileon.es Web site: www.unileon.es
Main campus: Vegazana
Satellite campuses: Ponferrada; Segovia
Students: 16,281
Staff: 624

Teaching centres

Faculties: Arts; biology; economics and business; education; law; veterinary science
Higher technical schools: Agricultural engineering
University schools: Industrial engineering and computing; labour relations; mining engineering; nursing (+Ponferrada); social work; teacher training

Student services

Information office: Unidad de Información y Registro, Avda Facultad de Veterinaria 25, 24071 León. Tel: 987 29 16 35; 29 16 03 Fax: 987 29 16 14 Email: gerbms@unileon.es
Accommodation office: See *Unidad de Información y Registro*
Health centre: See *Unidad de Información y Registro*
Spanish courses for foreign students: Cursos de Español Extensión Universitaria, Avda de la Facultad 25, 24071 León. Tel: 987 29 16 56 Email: german@isidoro.unileon.es

Courses in languages

For languages undergraduates: the Faculty of Arts offers degree courses in Spanish philology
Spanish for foreign students: Cursos de Español (*Lengua Extranjera*) offer three kinds of course: (1) intensive summer courses in Spanish language and culture at various levels during July and August (also available at the Segovia campus); (2) the *Curso Permanente*; this comprises two semester-long courses (October–January and February–June); students may opt for one or two semesters; (3) tailor-made courses in language and culture can be agreed with linked univeristies abroad; duration, content, etc. are flexible. NB Students enrolled on the last two courses may enter for the DELE; exams take place in May and September.

3.26 Lérida (Lleida)

3.26.1 **Ciudad de Lérida**

Basic information

Location and status: North-eastern Spain, 470 km north-east of Madrid. Capital of Province of Lérida (Lleida).

Population: 120,000

Geography: On River Surge near confluence with River Ebro.

Climate: Dry and warm under influence of Mediterranean.

History: Of Iberian origin, the city was taken from Pompey by Julius Caesar during the Roman civil war. It was called Ilerda by the Romans. The site of Visigothic council, Lleida was captured in 713 by the Moors but was reconquered in 1149 by Ramón Berenguer IV of Aragón.

Main historical sites: Old Byzantine–Gothic cathedral – has not been used since 1707, but has been restored and declared a National Monument. Church of Sant Llorenç. Castle of La Suda. New cathedral, San Lorenzo (fourteenth century). La Pahería palace. Fortress (Alcazaba).

Town: Pleasant university town.

Main areas of interest: Moorish castle of La Suda. Several museums.

Surrounding area: Les Avellanes – mountain pass of Collegats (17 km). Balaguer – church of Santa María (27 km).

Travel and transport: Regular bus and train, local and long distance services.

Major economic activities: Based primarily on agriculture, Lleida is well known for cattle, agricultural and fruit shows. Industrial development is slight, though glass, silk, cheeses and olive oil are quite important.

Major employers: Mutua Intercomarcal, Vall Companys.

Sources of information

Tourist Office: Oficina de Turismo, Avda Madrid 36, 25007 Lérida. Tel: 973 27 09 97

INEM: Mosén Reig 3, 25008 Lérida. Tel: 973 23 05 50

Town hall: Paeria 1, 25007 Lérida. Tel: 973 24 02 00

Chamber of commerce: Cámara de Comercio e Industria de Lleida, Anselmo Clave 2, 25007 Lérida. Tel: 973 23 61 61 Fax: 973 24 74 67 Email: camara@cambrescat.es

3.26.2 **Universidad de Lérida (Universitat de Lleida/ULLE)**

Basic information

Autonomous community: Cataluña (Catalunya)
Province: Lérida (Lleida)
Town: Lérida (Lleida)
Status: Public (1991*)
Address: Plaça de Víctor Siurana 1, 25003 Lérida. Tel: 973 70 20 00 Fax: 973 70 20 99/70 20 62 Email: rectorat@udl.es Web site: www.udl.es
Main campuses: Caparrella; Capont; Rovira Roure; Víctor Siurana
Satellite campuses: N/A
Students: 11,377
Staff: 597

Teaching centres

Faculties: Arts; education; law and economics; medicine
Higher technical schools: Agricultural engineering and forestry
University schools: Civil adminstration; labour relations; nursing; polytechnic; social work; tourism
Institute: National Institute for Physical Education of Catalonia (INEFC+)

Student services

Information office: Servei d'Extensió Universitaria, Placa de Víctor Siurana 1, 25003 Lérida. Tel: 973 70 20 00 ext 3021 Fax: 973 70 20 62 Email: seu@seu.udl.es
Accommodation office: See *Servei d'Extensió Universitaria*
Health centre: Servei de Salut, Placa de Víctor Siurana 1, 25003 Lérida. Tel: 973 70 20 21 Fax: 973 70 20 62 Email: estherBarbc@salut.udl.es
Spanish courses for foreign students: Oficina de Relacions Internacionals (ORI), Plaça de Víctor Siurana 1, 25003 Lérida. Tel: 973 70 20 17 Fax: 973 70 20 162 Email: internacional@ori.udl.es

Courses in languages

For languages undergraduates: The Arts Faculty offers degree courses in Catalan, English, French and Hispanic philologies.
Spanish for foreign students: Courses in Spanish and Catalan are offered to Socrates/Erasmus students participating in an official exchange with the University of Lleida.

* The university traces its origins to 1287 as the Studium Generale.

+ Instituto Nacional de Educación Física de Catalunya

3.27 Logroño

3.27.1 **Ciudad de Logroño**

Basic information

Location and status: North-central Spain, 336 km from Madrid. Capital of Autonomous Community of La Rioja.

Population: 128,350

Geography: On Ebro River and on historic Pilgrims' Route, Camino de Santiago.

Climate: Warm summers and quite mild winters.

History: Originating in Roman times, it owed its growth to position on pilgrim route to Santiago de Compostela, as much as to the production of wool. Muslim armies gave it its name in the eighth century.

Main historical sites: Palace of Espartero. Cathedral of Santa María la Redonda (fifteenth to seventeenth century). Church of Santa María del Palacio (eleventh century). Church of Santiago el Real (sixteenth century).

Town: Ancient walled town. Modern part boasts wide boulevards and smart shops.

Main areas of interest: Old quarter down towards river. Museum of La Rioja.

Surrounding area: Navarrete – church and covered streets (10 km). Murillo de Río Leza – parish church (20 km). Iregua Valley (50 km).

Travel and transport: There is a bypass. Bus and train stations are south of the city.

Major economic activities: Trade centre in agricultural and wine-growing district, Logroño is known for Rioja wine. Industries include food-processing, saw-milling and manufacture of furniture and textiles.

Major employers: Deloitte and Touche, S.A., Ikusi–Ángel Iglesias, S.A., Norauto, Unide S. Coop.

Sources of information

Tourist Office: Oficina de Turismo, Miguel Villanueva 10, 26001 Logroño. Tel: 941 25 54 97

INEM: Calvo Sotelo 27–29, 26003 Logroño. Tel: 941 26 31 99

Town hall: Avda de la Paz 11, 26001 Logroño. Tel: 941 24 32 22

Chamber of commerce: Cámara de Comercio e Industria de La Rioja, Portales 12, 26001 Logroño. Tel: 941 24 85 00 Fax: 941 23 99 65 Email: cámaraioja@cámararioja.com

Twin town: Dunfermline

3.27.2 **Universidad de La Rioja (URI)**

Basic information

Autonomous community: La Rioja
Province: Logroño
Town: Logroño
Status: Public (1992)
Address: Avda de la Paz 93, 26004 Logroño, La Rioja. Tel: 941 29 91 00/18 Fax: 941 29 91 46/20 Email: oui@unirioja.es Web site: www.unirioja.es
Main campuses: Luis de Ulloa; Obispo Bustamante
Satellite campuses: N/A
Students: 7,300
Staff: 335

Teaching centres

Administrative centres: Human, legal and social sciences; scientific and technical studies
Departments: Agriculture and food; artistic expression; chemistry; economics and business; electrical engineering; human and social sciences; law; mathematics and computing; mechanical engineering; modern languages; Spanish and classical philologies
University schools: Labour relations; nursing; social work

Student services

Information office: Oficina Única de Información, c/ La Cigueña, 60, 26004 Logroño. Tel: 941 29 91 00 Fax: 941 29 91 46 Email: oui@adm. unirioja.es
Accommodation office: Orientación Universitaria, Oficina Única de Información, Avda de la Paz, 26004 Logroño. Tel: 941 29 91 00 Fax: 941 29 91 46 Email: oui@adm. unirioja.es
Health centre: Consejo de Estudiantes, Avda de la Paz 93, 26004 Logroño. Tel: 941 29 92 09 Fax: (941) 29 92 09 Email: consejo.estudiantes@ adm.unirioja.es *or* contact *Oficina Única*
Spanish courses for foreign students: Oficina de Relaciones Internacionales, Avda de la Paz 93, 26004 Logroño. Tel: 941 29 91 52 Email: reyes. robledo@adm.unirioja.es

Courses in languages

For languages undergraduates: The Department of Hispanic Philology offers modules in English, French and Spanish philologies within its degree courses in Spanish philology and English philology. The Department of Modern Philology offers English, French and Spanish as components of its degree course in humanities.

Spanish for foreign students: Spanish classes are available for students studying at the university as part of exchange programmes with foreign universities, including the UK. For information, contact the *Oficina de Relaciones Internacionales.*

3.28 Madrid

3.28.1 **Ciudad de Madrid**

Basic information

Location and status: Located right in geographical centre of Spain. Capital of Spain and of Autonomous Community of Madrid.

Population: 3,853,675

Geography: High, arid, undulating plateau. In the centre of the Iberian Peninsula and is, at 2,100 feet above sea level, one of Europe's highest capital cities. Located in the heart of the Peninsula and right in the centre of the Castilian plain. Treeless, almost rainless, desolate, sun-scorched and windswept plateau. Bare and exposed upland plateau, grassless, treeless and colourless; in parts landscape almost desert-like.

Climate: Healthy climate and pleasant weather, except in winter when sharp winds blow and in July and August when heat can be oppressive, rising to thirty-nine degrees centigrade. Wettest months of year are January, March and April, although only 438 mm of rain falls per year. Usually a sunny, clear, blue sky.

History: It was the subject of a dispute between Christians and Arabs until it was conquered by Alfonso VI in the eleventh century. Philip II moved his capital there in 1561. Cervantes, Lope de Vega and Calderón all lived and wrote there. What remains today of the distant past are mainly Baroque and Neo-classical structures of the seventeenth and eighteenth centuries.

Main historical sites: Prado Museum. Royal Palace (*Palacio Real*). Convent of Las Descalzas Reales. Plaza de la Villa (seventeenth-century Madrid town hall). Main Square (*Plaza Mayor*). Church of San Nicolás. Tower of Los Lujánez (medieval). National palace (rebuilt in the mid-1700s, Neo-classical; houses one of world's greatest collections of body armour, as well as swords of *conquistadores,* Hernán Cortés and Francisco Pizarro). Madrid's first cathedral, Nuestra Señora de la Almudena. National Library (*Biblioteca Nacional*).

Town: Modern, compact bustling city with several universities. Medieval and Habsburg buildings mingle with daring modern creations. Characterised by intense cultural and artistic activity and a very lively nightlife. Very cosmopolitan, yet the centre area retains a definite Spanish character. Excellent shopping.

Main areas of interest: Royal Palace. National Palace (see above). Area round Plaza Mayor and Puerta del Sol. Art galleries, including El Prado, Thyssen–Bornemisza Museum and Queen Sofia Art Centre. Retiro Park.

Surrounding area: Casa de Campo Park. Western Park (*Parque del Oeste*). Sierra de Guadarrama. Within easy reach are numerous historic towns and other places of interest, e.g. palace of Aranjuez, Ávila, Chinchón, El Escorial, Segovia and Toledo. Near El Escorial is the Valley of the Fallen (*Valle de los Caídos*), an underground cathedral/mausoleum where Franco is buried.

Travel and transport: Subway and bus systems provide local transportation. Railways radiate in all directions, connecting Madrid to other Spanish cities on both coasts. International Barajas Airport is located thirteen kilometres from city. Dense traffic along Madrid's avenues. Underground car parks, one-way streets and fly-overs proliferate. Elaborate series of ring roads soon to be constructed.

Major economic activities: Banking, insurance and tourism. Important manufacturing city producing automobile and truck engines, electric and electronic equipment, plastics, rubbers, aircraft and optical goods. Also a major publishing centre.

Major employers: Renault, Revlon, S.A., Gillette, Gestevisión, Telecinco, S.A., L'Oréal, Hewlett Packard Española, S.A., IBM España, S.A.

Sources of information

Tourist Office: Oficina Municipal de Turismo, Plaza Mayor 3, 28012 Madrid. Tel: 91 366 54 77; 588 16 36 *or* Oficina de Turismo, Calle Princesa 1, Edificio Torre de Madrid, 28008 Madrid. Tel: 91 541 23 25

INEM: Ronda de Atocha 7, 28012 Madrid. Tel: 91 468 68 63 Fax: 91 528 81 57

Town hall: Plaza de la Villa s/n, 28005 Madrid. Tel: 91 558 10 00

Chamber of commerce: Cámara de Comercio e Industria de Madrid, Oficinas y Servicios, Plaza de la Independencia 1, 28001 Madrid. Tel: 91 538 35 00 Fax: 91 538 37 19

3.28.2 **Universidad Alfonso X El Sabio (UAX)**

Basic information

Autonomous community: Comunidad de Madrid
Province: N/A
Town: Madrid
Status: Private (1993)
Address: Avda Universidad 1, Villanueva de la Cañada, 28691 Madrid. Tel: 91 810 92 00 Fax: 91 810 91 01 Email: info@uax.es Web site: www.uax.es
Main campus: Villanueva de la Cañada
Satellite campuses: N/A
Students: 6,000
Staff: 600

Teaching centres

Faculties: Applied languages; health science; social studies
Higher technical school: Higher polytechnic school (architecture, engineering, environmental sciences and physics)
University schools: N/A

Student services

Information office: Oficina del Alumno, Avda Universidad 1, Villanueva de la Cañada, 28691 Madrid. Tel: 91 810 91 80 Fax: 91 810 91 01 Email: info@uax.es
Accommodation office: See *Oficina del Alumno*
Health centre: See *Oficina del Alumno*
Spanish courses for foreign students: Oficina de Relaciones Internacionales, Avda Universidad 1, Villanueva de la Cañada, 28691 Madrid. Tel: 91 810 91 92 Fax: 91 810 97 81 Email: iris@uax.es

Courses in languages

For languages undergraduates: The Faculty of Applied Languages offers a degree course in translating and interpreting, involving English and Spanish.
Spanish for foreign students: N/A

3.28.3 Universidad Antonio de Nebrija (UNNE) (Universitas Nebrissensis)

Basic information

Autonomous community: Comunidad de Madrid
Province: N/A
Town: Madrid
Status: Private (1995)
Address: Campus de la Dehesa de la Villa, Pirineos 55, 28040 Madrid. Tel: 91 311 66 02 Fax: 91 311 66 13 Email: webmaster@dii.unnet.es Web site: www.unnet.es
Main campuses: La Berzosa (Hoyo de Manzanares); La Dehesa de la Villa
Satellite campuses: N/A
Students: 2,356
Staff: 200

Teaching centres

Faculties: Applied languages (philology), humanities and tourism; communication sciences; computer engineering; economics and business; law and European studies
Higher technical school: Higher polytechnic school
University schools: N/A

Student services

Information office: Oficina de Información, Pirineos 55, 28040 Madrid. Tel: 91 311 66 02 Fax: 91 311 66 13
Accommodation office: Servicio de Alojamiento, Pirineos 55, 28040 Madrid. Tel: 91 311 66 02 Fax: 91 311 66 13
Health centre: See *Oficina de Información*
Spanish courses for foreign students: Centro de Estudios Hispánicos, Pirineos 55, 28040 Madrid. Tel: 91 311 66 02 Fax: 91 311 66 03 Email: cehi@dii.unnet.es

Courses in languages

For languages undergraduates: The Faculty of Applied Languages offers degree courses in English, French, German and Hispanic philologies. It also runs a degree in translating and interpreting, involving the above languages.
Spanish for foreign students: the *Centro de Estudios Hispánicos* offers intensive courses of Spanish language and culture, at seven different levels, during

June and July in classes composed of no more than sixteen students. The centre also provides a wide range of courses in specialist subjects relating to Spain, of interest to both students and teachers of Spanish.

3.28.4 **Universidad Autónoma de Madrid (UAM)**

Basic information

Autonomous community: Comunidad de Madrid
Province: N/A
Town: Madrid
Status: Public (1968)
Address: Ciudad Universitaria de Cantoblanco, Ctra de Colmenar Viejo, Km 15, 28049 Madrid. Tel: 91 397 50 00; 397 50 01 Fax: 91 397 41 23 Web site: www.uam.es
Main campuses: Arzobispo; Cantoblanco; Leganés; Morcillo
Satellite campus: Segovia
Students: 37,000
Staff: 2,000

Teaching centres

Faculties: Arts; economics and business; law; medicine; psychology; science
Higher technical school: Computing
University schools: Nursing x 5; physiotherapy; teacher training (+Segovia); tourism
Institutes: Administration and business (IADE*); economic production; materials science; molecular biology; sociology of new technologies; women's studies

Student services

Information office: Oficina de Información, Rectorado, planta baja, Campus de Cantoblanco, 28409 Madrid. Tel: 91 397 51 01/02/03 Fax: 91 397 41 23
Accommodation office: Students are recommended to acquire the detailed directory published by: Centro de Información y Asesoramiento, Dirección General de Universidades, Consejería de Educación, Comunidad de Madrid
Health centre: Servicio Médico, Pabellón B, planta baja, Campus de Cantoblanco, 28409 Madrid. Tel: 91 397 41 52; 397 41 53 Fax: 91 397 41 23 NB This is open Monday–Friday from 9.00 am to 8.30 pm.

Spanish courses for foreign students: Cursos de Español para Extranjeros, Servicio de Idiomas, Pabellón A, Campus de Cantoblanco, 28049 Madrid. Tel: 91 397 46 33 Fax: 91 397 46 20

Courses in languages

For languages undergraduates: The Faculty of Arts offers degree courses in Arabic, French and Spanish philologies.

Spanish for foreign students: The *Servicio de Idiomas* offers two types of course: (1) a full-year language course at four different levels which runs from the beginning of October to the end of May. Students may begin at any stage but beginners must commence in October; (2) an intensive four-week summer course in September.

* IADE = Instituto de Administración de Empresas

3.28.5 **Universidad Camilo José Cela (UCJC)**

Basic information

Autonomous community: Comunidad de Madrid
Province: N/A
Town: Madrid
Status: Private (1998)
Address: C/ Castillo 49, 28692 Villafranca del Castillo, Madrid. Tel: 91 815 31 31 Fax: 91 815 31 30 Web site: www.ucjc@sek.es
Main campus: Villafranca del Castillo
Satellite campuses: N/A
Students: N/K
Staff: N/K

Teaching centres

Faculties: Computing; education; information science; psychology
Higher technical school: Architecture and technology
University schools: Teacher training; technical architecture

Student services

Information office: Oficina de Información. Tel: 91 815 31 31 Fax: 91 815 31 30
Accommodation office: See *Oficina de Información*
Health centre: See *Oficina de Información*
Spanish courses for foreign students: N/A

Courses in languages

For languages undergraduates: N/A
Spanish for foreign students: N/A

3.28.6 **Universidad Carlos III de Madrid (UCAR)**

Basic information

Autonomous community: Comunidad de Madrid
Province: N/A
Town: Madrid
Status: Public (1989)
Address: C/ Madrid 126–128, 28903 Getafe, Madrid. Tel: 91 624 95 00 Fax: 91 624 97 57 Web site: www.uc3m.es
Main campuses: Colmenarejo (C); Getafe (G); Leganés (L)
Satellite campuses: N/A
Students: 11,746
Staff: 801

Teaching centres

Faculties: Humanities, communication and documentation (G); social and legal sciences (C; G)
Higher technical school: Higher polytechnic school (L)
University schools: N/A
Institutes: Advanced economic studies; human rights; international and EU studies; law and economics; territory; town planning and environment

Student services

Information office: Servicio de Orientación y Planificación Profesional (SOPP), c/ Madrid 126, 28903 Getafe, Madrid. Tel: 91 624 95 21; 624 93 08 Fax: 91 624 95 97 Email: sopp.pa@uc3m.es
Accommodation office: See *SOPP* or *Oficina de Relaciones Internacionales* (below)
Health centre: See *SOPP* or *Oficina de Relaciones Internacionales* (below)
Spanish courses for foreign students: Oficina de Relaciones Internacionales, Edificio Rectorado, Despacho 8.12B, c/ Madrid 126–128, 28903 Getafe, Madrid. Tel: 91 624 95 50 Fax: 91 624 93 39 Email: ori@pa.uc3m.es

Courses in languages

For languages undergraduates: N/A

Spanish for foreign students: UCAR offers various courses in Spanish for Socrates/Erasmus students in each semester. In addition to practical language lessons offered at two levels, classes in legal and business Spanish are also available. The university also provides intensive summer courses in Spanish language for students and teachers. Self-tuition in Spanish is also available in the language laboratories and multimedia centres at Getafe and Leganés.

3.28.7 **Universidad Complutense de Madrid (UCM)**

Basic information

Autonomous community: Comunidad de Madrid
Province: N/A
Town: Madrid
Status: Public (1508*; 1836)
Address: Pabellón de Gobierno, Ciudad Universitaria, 28040 Madrid. Tel: 91 549 02 56 Fax: 91 394 34 37 Web site: www.ucm.es
Main campuses: Ciudad Universitaria; Somosaguas
Satellite campuses: Pozuelo de Alarcón; San Lorenzo de El Escorial; Segovia
Students: 110,934
Staff: 5,312

Teaching centres

Faculties: Biology; chemistry; dentistry; economics and business; education; fine art; geography and history; information science; law; mathematics; medicine; pharmacy; philology; philosophy; physics; politics and sociology; psychology; veterinary science

Higher technical school: Computing

University schools: Business studies; librarianship; nursing; optics; physical therapy; social work; statistics; teacher training

Institutes: Business communication; criminology; development and cooperation; drug dependency; economic analysis; education science; environmental science; health studies; history of the Spanish Inquisition; human rights law; industrial and financial analysis; industrial pharmacy; international studies; languages; law of parliament; market economy; 'Menéndez Pidal' seminar; modern languages and translation; music science; Olympic sports science; 'Ortega y Gasset' institute; radio communication; 'Ramón Carande' sports science institute; 'Ramón Castroviejo' institute; religion; technological institute for knowledge

Other Centres: Analysis and evaluation; centre for contemporary Latin

American studies; higher centre for management; finance; 'Francisco de Vitoria' centre for higher education (Pozuelo); 'María Cristina' royal university college (El Escorial); 'Cardinal Cisneros' university college; 'Domingo de Soto' university college (Segovia); 'San Pablo' university college

Student services

Information office: Servicio de Información, Vicegerencia de Coordinación, Avda de Séneca 2, 28040 Madrid. Tel: 91 394 10 10 Fax: 91 394 34 97 Email: infocom@ucm.es

Accommodation office: Oficina de Relaciones Internacionales, Pabellón de Gobierno, Isaac Peral s/n, Ciudad Universitaria, 28040 Madrid. Tel: 91 394 70 26 Fax: 91 394 69 24

Health centre: See *Oficina de Relaciones Internacionales*

Spanish courses for foreign students: Cursos para Extranjeros, Facultad de Filosfía y Letras, Edificio A, Ciudad Universitaria s/n, 28040 Madrid. Tel: 91 394 53 25 Fax: 91 394 53 36

Courses in languages

For languages undergraduates: The Faculty of Arts offers five-year degree courses in a wide range of modern philologies including: Arabic, French, German, Italian, Slavonic and Spanish. Hebrew and classical languages are also offered.

Spanish for foreign students: A wide range of Spanish language and culture courses, at a variety of levels and for varying periods, are held throughout the year. Classes include: Spanish language (grammar); conversation; composition and practice; Spanish literature; history of Spain; history of Spanish art; comprehension of Spanish text; Spanish geography; history of Spanish thought. In addition regular conferences are held relating to Spanish culture.

* First founded as Universidad de Alcalá

3.28.8 **Universidad Europea (CEES) de Madrid (UEM)**

Basic information

Autonomous community: Comunidad de Madrid
Province: N/A
Town: Madrid
Status: Private (1995)

Address: C/ Tajo s/n, Urbanización 'El Bosque', 28670 Villaviciosa de Odón, Madrid. Tel: 91 616 71 42; 616 94 00 Fax: 91 616 82 56 Web site: www@uem.es
Main campus: Villaviciosa de Odón
Satellite campuses: N/A
Students: 5,215
Staff: N/K

Teaching centres

Faculties: Business adminstration and management; economics and business adminstration; environmental science; health sciences; information science; legal sciences and adminstration; philology; physical education and sport; science

Higher technical schools: Architecture; computing; industrial engineering; telecommunications

University schools: Business; chiropody and optics; management computing; nursing; physiotherapy; tourism

Student services

Information office: Oficina de Información, Campus Universitario, 28670 Villaviciosa de Odón. Tel: 91 616 71 42; 616 94 00 Fax: 91 616 82 65 Email: patricia.hernandez @rx.uem.es

Accommodation office: Residencia Leonardo da Vinci, Campus Universitario, 28670 Villavicioso de Odón. Tel: 91 616 80 00 Fax: 91 616 83 83

Health centre: See *Oficina de Información*

Spanish courses for foreign students: Departamento de Relaciones Internacionales, Campus Universitario, 28670 Villaviciosa de Odón. Tel: 91 616 71 42 Fax: 91 616 82 56

Courses in languages

For languages undergraduates: The Faculty of Languages offers a degree course in translating and interpreting, the languages offered being English, French and German.

Spanish for foreign students: the university offers nine hours per week of Spanish for foreign students, including grammar, oral practice and essay writing in the Spanish language, as well as Spanish culture.

3.28.9 **Universidad Nacional de Educación a Distancia (UNED)**

Basic information

Autonomous community: Comunidad de Madrid
Province: N/A
Town: Madrid
Status: Public (1972)
Address: Bravo Murillo 38, 28040 Madrid. Tel: 91 398 60 00/01 Fax: 91 398 60 37 Email: infouned@bm.uned.es Web site: www.uned.es
Main centre: Bravo Murillo
Other centres: Currently UNED has sixty study centres in Spain (all in cities and major towns), as well as eleven abroad, including London.
Students: 134,428
Staff: N/K

Teaching centres

Faculties: Economics and business; education; geography and history; law; philology; philosophy; political sciences and sociology; psychology; science
Higher technical school: Industrial engineering
University school: Computing

Student services

Main *Information office:*
Oficina de Atención al Público, Bravo Murillo 38, 28040 Madrid. Tel: 91 398 60 00/01 Fax: 91 398 60 37
Employment office: Centro de Orientación e Información, Bravo Murillo 38, 28015 Madrid. Tel: 91 398 75 18 Fax: 91 398 75 17 Email: coie@bm.uned.es
Spanish courses for foreign students: N/A

Courses in languages

For languages undergraduates: The Faculty of Philology provides a distance-learning degree in Spanish philology.
Spanish for foreign students: N/A

3.28.10 **Universidad Politécnica de Madrid (UPM)**

Basic information

Autonomous community: Comunidad de Madrid
Province: N/A
Town: Madrid
Status: Public (1971)
Address: Ramiro de Maeztu 7, Ciudad Universitaria, 28040 Boadilla del Monte, Madrid. Tel: 91 336 60 00 Fax: 91 336 61 73 Web site: www.upm.es
Main campuses: Complutense; Montegancedo (Boadilla del Monte); Sur (Ctra de Valencia)
Satellite campuses: N/A
Students: 48,383
Staff: 3,266

Teaching centres

Faculty: Computing
Higher technical schools: Aeronautical engineering; agricultural engineering; architecture; civil engineering; forestry engineering; industrial engineering; mining engineering; naval engineering; telecommunications
University schools: Aeronautics; computing; forestry; industrial engineering; public works engineering; technical architecture; telecommunications; topography
Institutes: Advanced industrial studies and research; architecture; automobile research; education (ICE); environmental engineering; nuclear fusion; renewable energies; solar energy

Student services

Information office: Sección de Información, UPM, Edificio B, Paseo de Juan XXIII 11, 28040 Madrid. Tel: 91 336 62 30 Email: oit@sg. upm.es
Accommodation office: Contact the *Sección de Información*
Health centre: the university has an agreement with the following hospital: Clínica Nuestra Señora de Loreto, Avda Reina Victoria 62–64, Madrid
Spanish courses for foreign students: N/A

Courses in languages

For languages undergraduates: N/A
Spanish for foreign students: N/A

3.28.11 **Universidad Pontificia de Comillas (UPCO)**

Basic information

Autonomous community: Comunidad de Madrid
Province: N/A
Town: Madrid
Status: Private (1892*)
Address: Alberto Aguilera 23, 28015 Madrid. Tel: 91 542 28 00 Fax: 91 559 65 69 Email: webmaster@cal.upco.es Web site: www. upco.es:
Main campuses: Alberto Aguilera; Cantoblanco
Satellite campuses: N/A
Students: 16,820
Staff: 1,161

Teaching centres

Faculties: Arts; canon law; economics and business (ICADE**); law (ICADE**); theology
Higher technical schools: Computer science; electrical engineering; electronic engineering; industrial engineering (ICAI***); mechanical engineering
University schools: Nursing *and* physiotherapy; social work; technical industrial engineering (ICAI***)

Student services

Information office: Oficina de Información y Acogida del Estudiante (OIA), Sede ICAI–ICADE, Alberto Aguilera 21, 28015 Madrid. Tel: 91 542 28 00 Fax: 91 559 65 69 Email: insegil@oia.upco.es
Accommodation office: See *OIA*
Spanish courses for foreign students: See *OIA*

Courses in languages

For languages undergraduates: The Arts Faculty provides a degree course in translating and interpreting; the languages offered are: English, French, German, Italian and Japanese.
Spanish for foreign students: The university offers courses in Spanish to students on Socrates/Erasmus programmes. These are offered at intermediate level and above.

* The right to confer degrees was granted in 1904; in 1960 the university moved from Santander to Madrid.
** ICADE = Instituto Católico de Administración de Empresas
*** ICAI = Instituto Católico de Artes e Industrias

3.28.12 **Universidad Rey Juan Carlos I (URJC)**

Basic information

Autonomous community: Comunidad de Madrid
Province: N/A
Town: Madrid
Status: Public (1996)
Address: Independencia 12, 28931 Móstoles, Madrid. Tel: 91 665 50 60 Fax: 91 613 38 45 Email: info@.urjc.es Web site: www.urjc.es
Main campus: Alcorcón (A); Fuenlabrada (F)*; Móstoles (M); Vicálvaro (V)
Satellite campuses: N/A
Students: 3,381
Staff: 358

Teaching centres

Faculties: Health sciences (A); legal and social sciences (V)
Higher technical school: Experimental sciences and technology (M)
University schools: N/A

Student services

Information office: Servicio de Información al Alumnado, Independencia 12, 28931 Móstoles, Madrid. Tel: 91 665 50 60 Fax: 91 613 38 45 Email: info@urjc.es Madrid
Accommodation office: See *Servicio de Información*
Health centre: See *Servicio de Información*
Spanish courses for foreign students: Vicerrectorado de Relaciones Internacionales, c/ Independencia 12, 28931 Móstoles, Madrid.
Tel: 91 665 51 32 Fax: 91 665 50 93 Email: m.catala@rect.urjc.es

Courses in languages

For languages undergraduates: N/A
Spanish for foreign students: See *Vicerrectorado de Relaciones Internacionales*

* This is a new campus where eventually communication studies and technological courses will be offered.

3.28.13 **Universidad San Pablo–CEU (CEU)**

Basic information

Autonomous community: Comunidad de Madrid
Province: N/A
Town: Madrid
Status: Private (1993*)
Address: Isaac Peral 58, 28040 Madrid. Tel: 91 533 09 55 Fax: 91 533 08 47 Email: webmaster @ceu.es Web site: www.ceu.es
Main campuses: Moncloa; Montepríncipe (both in Madrid)
Satellite campuses: Barcelona; Elche; Sevilla; Valencia; Valladolid
Students: 8,100
Staff: 636

Teaching centres

Faculties: Economics and business; experimental and technical sciences; humanities; legal sciences and administration
Other centres: Architecture**; medicine***

Student services

Information office: Servicio de Información Académica, Vicerrectorado de Alumnos, Julián Romea 18, 28003 Madrid. Tel: 91 536 27 27 Fax: 91 536 06 60 Email: informa@ceu.es
Accommodation office: See *Vicerectorado de Alumnos* (*Servicio de Información Académica*)
Health centre: See *Vicerrectorado de Alumnos*
Spanish courses for foreign students: Relaciones Internacionales, Julián Romea 18, 28003 Madrid. Tel: 91 534 00 08 Fax: 91 553 30 33 Email: international.office @ceu.es

Courses in languages

For languages undergraduates: Modules in English, French and Spanish Language are offered as either core subjects or options within the degree in humanities.
Spanish courses for foreign students: Contact *Relaciones Internacionales*

* In fact it has been providing university level education since 1932.
** Awards degrees of the Universidad Politécnica de Madrid (UPM)
*** Awards degrees of the Universidad de Alcalá de Henares (UAH)

3.29 Málaga

3.29.1 **Ciudad de Málaga**

Basic information

Location and status: On southern Mediterranean coast, 548 km south of Madrid. Capital of Province of Málaga and of Costa del Sol.

Population: 556,000

Geography: Situated on River Guadalmedina in wide coastal plain and surrounded by high sierras to west, north and east. Sub-tropical vegetation.

Climate: Mediterranean: hot, dry summers and mild winters; some rain from November to February. More than 300 days' sun per year.

History: It was settled by Phoenicians, Greeks, Romans and Moors; was the capital of one of the *taifa* kingdoms. It was reconquered from Arabs in 1487 during the campaign of Ferdinand and Isabella to liberate the Moorish Kingdom of Granada. Spain's first iron and steel works were established there in the early nineteenth century.

Main historical sites: Roman Theatre. Alcazaba – Moorish fortress built on Phoenician foundations in fourteenth century. Cathedral, built between the sixteenth and eighteenth century. Medieval heart of city. Numerous renaissance and baroque religious buildings and palaces.

Town: Málaga is the largest city in Spain that is not a regional capital. Has little industry today but has major port. It is basically an administrative and commercial centre; also an important tourist city. Both city and university among the fastest growing in Spain. A major retail centre.

Main areas of interest: Panoramic views of city from top of Gibralfaro castle; overlooks port, El Parque (main avenue and gardens) and historic centre. Museo de Artes y Costumbres Populares. Botanic gardens of La Concepción and El Retiro. Birth place of Picasso. Larios shopping centre.

Surrounding area: Nearly 200 km of coastline from Estepona in west to Nerja in east, with numerous tourist resorts. Countless white villages in interior plus historic towns of Antequera and Ronda. Magnificent mountain scenery. Fertile orange/lemon groves of Guadalhorce.

Travel and transport: Málaga airport is only eight miles west of the city centre; connected by regular bus and rapid train service. Buses run from the station to all parts of the province and trains connect Málaga with Madrid (via Córdoba) and Granada. The excellent road network limits the journey to Granada to 1.5 hours and Seville to three hours. Many internal flights.

Major economic activities: Commerce, shipping, administration, tourism, wine production, olive growing, beer-brewing, oil-refining, telecommunications and finance. Málaga is location of expanding regional technology park, the Parque Tecnológico de Andalucía.

Major employers: University, Port of Málaga, Pryca and Continente, Corte Inglés, Deloitte and Touche, El Pozo Alimentación, Fujitsu.

Sources of information

Tourist Office: Oficina Municipal de Turismo, Avda de Cervantes 1, 29016 Málaga. Tel: 95 260 44 10 Fax: 95 221 41 20

INEM: Avda de Andalucía 27, 29007 Málaga. Tel: 95 232 00 50; 213 40 43

Town hall: Ayuntamiento de Málaga, Avda de Cervantes 4, 29016 Málaga. Tel: 95 213 52 00

Chamber of commerce: Cámara Oficial de Comercio, Industria y Navegación de Málaga, c/ Cortina del Muelle 23, 29015 Málaga. Tel: 95 221 16 73; 222 98 64

3.29.2 **Universidad de Málaga (UMA)**

Basic information

Autonomous community: Andalucía

Province: Málaga

Town: Málaga

Status: Public (1972)

Address: Campus de El Ejido, Plaza de El Ejido s/n, 29013 Málaga. Tel: 95 213 11 14 Fax: 95 213 11 15 Web site: www.uma.es

Main campuses: El Ejido; Teatinos (both in Málaga)

Satellite campuses: Antequera; Ronda

Students: 33,000

Staff: 1,600

Teaching centres

Faculties: Arts; computing; education; economics and business; information science; law; medicine; psychology

Higher technical schools: Electronic engineering; telecommunications

University schools: Business studies; health sciences; labour relations; nursing (+Ronda); polytechnic; social work; teacher training (+Antequera)

Student services

Information office: Aulario General, Campus de Teatinos, 29071 Málaga. Tel: 95 213 14 72 Fax: 95 213 23 12

Accommodation office: Oficina de Alojamiento, DG de Servicios Sociales, 29013 Málaga. Tel: 95 213 14 54 Fax: 95 213 25 33

Health centre: DG de Asuntos Sociales, Campus de El Ejido, 29071 Málaga. Tel: 95 213 13 54 Fax: 95 213 14 54

Spanish courses for foreign students: Cursos de Español para Extranjeros, Avda de Andalucía 2, 29007 Málaga. Tel: 95 227 82 11 Fax: 95 227 97 12 Email: cursoext@uma.es

Courses in languages

For languages undergraduates: The language departments of the Arts Faculty (*Letras*) offer: Arabic, English, French, Geman and Spanish as major modules within standard five-year degree courses in language and literature with options in linguistics etc. Students may take one or two languages. The translating and interpreting division offers the same languages as part of a four-year degree course in translating and interpreting. Students work through two or three languages, including Spanish.

Spanish for foreign students: Cursos para Extranjeros offers both a full-time course for students who wish to study for a whole year (*Diploma de Estudios Hispánicos*), which also includes aspects of Spanish culture, and short intensive languages courses (*Cursos Intensivos*), of two, three or four weeks' duration all year round, from beginners to advanced level. A summer language course (*Curso de Verano*), taught at four different levels, is available in July, August and September, both in Málaga and Ronda. All teaching is in small groups, usually no larger than fifteen.

3.30 Mondragón (Arrasate)

3.30.1 **Ciudad de Mondragón**

Basic information

Location and status: Small Basque town, located in extreme south-west of Province of Guipúzcoa (Gipuzkoa), 395 km from Madrid, 40 km inland from the Cantabrian coast (Atlantic Ocean), 33 km from Vitoria, 55 km from Bilbao and 80km from San Sebastián.

Population: 25,000

Geography: Mondragón's urban centre lies in valley at confluence of Rivers Deba and Aramayona. Surrounded by greenery and mountainous terrain. Forms part of region known as 'Alto Deba', together with Bergara, Oñati and other small towns.

Climate: Characteristically wet and temperate due to its mountain landscape.

History: First evidence of man's existence in Mondragón dates back to prehistoric times. In the deposit of *Leze Txiki* a human leg bone (dating back 40,000 years) was found. In the Middle Ages it was officially founded by King Alfonso X in 1260. In the fifteenth century it was marked by clan wars which provoked the catastrophic fire of 1448. Around the turn of that century the town began its important industrial activity of steelmaking, reaching its height in the sixteenth century with the manufacture of weapons. Its famed iron industry collapsed during the eighteenth and nineteenth centuries. In 1879 Prime Minister Cánovas was assassinated here. New industrialisation took place during the beginning of the twentieth century. In 1943 a group of co-operatives here became the first Spanish companies to operate industrial self-management by workers. This still applies today and explains why unemployment here is lower than in the rest of Spain.

Main historical sites: Palace of Monterrón. Gothic parish church of San Juan de Bautista (eighteenth–nineteenth centuries). Town Hall. Baroque church of San Francisco (sixteenth century). Santa Agueda spa (nineteenth century).

Town: Small urban centre around two local rivers and older medieval part.

Main areas of interest: Mountains and surrounding countryside. Old, medieval parts of town. June 24–26: Festival of St John. First Friday in October – Festival of *Maritxu Kajoi* in honour of pub-crawlers. December 22: St Thomas's Fair of agricultural produce.

Surrounding area: Coast (40 km); Olandiano hillside; Vitoria (33 km).

Travel and transport: Bus services to major towns and cities of the Basque Country.

Major economic activities: Metallurgy, machinery, home appliances and locksmiths' products.

Major employers: Lagun Aro Insurance, FCC Fremap, Grupo Eroski, Fagor Group.

Sources of information

Tourist Office: (Based in nearby town of Oñati) Oficina Municipal de Turismo, Plaza Fueros 1, 20560 Oñati. Tel: 943 78 34 53

(Regional tourist office) Arrasate Pasealekua 5-B, 20500 Mondragón Tel: 943 79 33 99 Fax: 943 77 08 54

INEM: Avda Navarra 4, 20500 Mondragón. Tel: 943 79 71 45 Fax: 943 79 07 06

Town hall: Ayuntamiento Herriko Plaza s/n, 20500 Mondragón. Tel: 943 77 09 00; 79 09 00 Fax: 943 79 80 56

Chamber of commerce: N/A. Enquire at Regional Tourist Office or at San Sebastián Chamber of Commerce.

3.30.2 **Universidad de Mondragón (Mondragón Unibertsitatea/MU)**

Basic information

Autonomous community: País Vasco (Euskadi)

Province: Vizcaya (Bizcaia)

Town: Mondragón

Status: Private (1997*)

Address: Loramendi 4, 20500 Mondragón, Gipuzkoa. Tel: 943 79 47 00 Fax: 943 79 15 36 Email: info@muni.es Web site: www.muni.es

Main campus: Loramendi (Mondragón)

Satellite campuses: Eskoriatza; Oñati

Students: 2,661

Staff: N/K

Teaching centres

Faculties: Business and economics (Oñati); humanities and education (Eskoriatza)

Higher technical school: Higher polytechnic school (automation and electronics; industrial organisation; technical industrial engineering x 4)

University schools: N/A

Student services

Information office: Oficina de Información, Mondragón Unibertsitatea, Loramendi 4, 20500 Mondragón, Bizcaia. Tel: 943 79 47 00 Fax: 943 79 15 36 Email: info@muni.es

Accommodation office: See *Oficina de Información*

Health centre: See *Oficina de Información*

Spanish courses for foreign students: N/A

Courses in languages

For languages undergraduates: The Faculty of Humanities and Education offers a degree course in humanities with special modules in a modern languages (mainly English and Basque).

Spanish for foreign students: N/A

* The Universidad de Mondragón claims descent from the old Universidad de Oñati founded in 1542.

3.31 Murcia

3.31.1 **Ciudad de Murcia**

Basic information

Location and status: South-eastern Spain, 395 km from Madrid. Capital of Automous Region of Murcia.

Population: 358,250

Geography: Lies at confluence of Rivers Segura and Guadlentín (Sangonera) in fertile, irrigated area known as *la huerta*. In heart of rich fertile plain at forty-three metres above sea level. Unlike the rest of the region, where terrain is dry and rugged, the soil here is irrigated by the River Segura and the land has been widely and fruitfully cultivated.

Climate: Torrid summers and very mild winters. Sub-arid with little more than 300 mm of annual rainfall.

History: Settled before the Roman occupation of southern Spain in the third century BC. It was occupied in 825 by Umayyad emir of Córdoba, Abd ar-Rahman II, who made it a provincial capital. After the fall of Córdoba in 1031, the city came under the control of Almería and then Valencia, until in 1036 its ruler declared the Kingdom of Murcia independent.

Main historical sites: The Gothic-style, fourteenth century cathedral of Santa María and Salzillo Museum. Church of San Bartolomé.

Town: Expanding city combining attractive historic centre with modern commercial area. Surprisingly cosmopolitan in parts.

Main areas of interest: Pedestrianised historic centre, including cathedral.

Surrounding area: The villages dotted around in *la huerta*. Palace of Marqueses de Espinardo (2 km). Patron Saint's church of La Fuensanta (8 km). Nature Reserve of Sierra Espuña. In addition, there are several small towns and villages with a strong Moorish flavour.

Travel and transport: Regular local and long distance bus and train services. Talgo (fast train) service to Madrid.

Major economic activities: Communications and agricultural-trade centre for surrounding areas along River Segura. Flour is processed. Silk industry. Manufactures woollen, linen and cotton goods, saltpetre, leather, aluminium products, furniture and hats.

Major employers: Estudios y Proyectos, S.L,. Bull, Empresa Municipal de Aguas y Saneamientos de Murcia, S.A. (EMUASA), Estrella de Levante, Fábrica de Cerveza, S.A., Gestiones Sociolaborales, S.A. (Gestolasa), Hatmix, S.A.

Sources of information

Tourist Office: Oficina de Turismo, Tomás Muestre s/n, Murcia. Tel: 968 21 61 15

INEM: Nueva de San Antón 27, 30009 Murcia. Tel: 968 28 15 34

Town hall: Glorieta de España 1, 30004 Murcia. Tel: 968 22 19 33

Chamber of commerce: Cámara de Comercio, Industria y Navegación de Murcia, Plaza de San Bartolomé 3, 30004 Murcia. Tel: 968 22 94 00 Fax: 968 22 94 25

3.31.2 **Universidad Católica 'San Antonio' de Murcia**

Basic information

Autonomous community: Región de Murcia

Province: N/A

Town: Murcia

Status: Private (1997)

Address: Avda de los Jerónimos 135, 30107 Guadalupe, Murcia. Tel: 968 27 88 01 Fax: 968 30 70 66 Email: rectorado@ucam.edu Web site: ucam.edu

Main campus: Guadalupe (Murcia)

Satellite campuses: N/A

Students: N/K

Staff: N/K

Teaching centres

Faculties: Health sciences, physical activity and sport; legal and business sciences; social sciences and communication

Higher technical schools: Higher school of organisation and management of quality

University school: Polytechnic

Professional specialisation schools: Applied technology; art and heritage restoration; business; legal practice; osteopathy; social health management; sports injuries; sports medicine

Student services

Information office: Oficina de Información, Avda de los Jerónimos s/n, 30107 Guadalupe, Murcia. Tel: 968 27 88 01 Fax: 968 30 70 66 Email: info@ucam.edu

Accommodation office: See *Oficina de Información*

Health centre: See *Oficina de Información*

Spanish courses for foreign students: Unidad Central de Idiomas, Avda de los Jerónimos s/n, 20107 Guadalupe, Murcia. Tel: 968 27 88 19 Email ucidiomas@ucam.edu

Courses in languages

For languages undergraduates: N/A

Spanish for foreign students: Contact *Unidad Central de Idiomas* for information.

3.31.3 **Universidad de Murcia (UMU)**

Basic information

Autonomous community: Región de Murcia

Province: N/A

Town: Murcia

Status: Public (1915)

Address: Avda Teniente Flomesta 5, Edificio Convalecencia, 30071 Murcia. Tel: 968 36 30 00 Fax: 968 36 36 03 Email: umsiu@fcu.um.es Web site: www.um.es

Main campuses: Espinardo; La Merced (both in Murcia)

Satellite campuses: Águilas (Universidad del Mar)*

Students: 36,368

Staff: 1,748

Teaching centres

Faculties: Arts; biology; business and economics; chemistry; computing; documentation sciences; education; law; mathematics; medicine; philosophy; psychology; veterinary science

Higher technical schools: N/A

University schools: Business studies; labour relations; nursing; social work; tourism

Institutes: Education (ICE); water and the environment (INUAMA)**

Student services

Information office: Servicio de Información al Estudiante (SIE), Campus de la Merced, 30001 Murcia. Tel: 968 36 30 16/17 Fax: 968 36 30 17 Email: sie@fcu.um.es

Accommodation office: See *Servicio de Información (SIE)* or Servicio de Relaciones Internacionales (SRI), Campus de Espinardo, 30100 Murcia. Tel: 968 36 40 70 Fax: 968 36 41 30

Health centre: See *Unidad de Información al Estudiabnte (SIE)* or *Servicio de Relaciones Internacionales (SRI)*

Spanish courses for foreign students: Cursos Intensivos de Español, Granero 4, 30071 Murcia. Tel: 968 21 05 66

Courses in languages

For languages undergraduates: The Faculty of Arts offers degree courses in English, French and Spanish philologies.

Spanish for foreign students: Cursos Intensivos de Español offer courses at all levels to all persons of 16 or over.

* The Universidad del Mar (University of the Sea) organises lecture courses in specialist areas during July and September.

** INUAMA = Instituto Universitario del Agua y del Medio Ambiente

3.32 Orense (Ourense)

3.32.1 **Ciudad de Orense**

Basic information

Location and status: Capital of Province of Orense in Galicia (only land-locked province in region), 521 km from Madrid, 175 km from La Coruña, 102 km from Pontevedra, 106 km from Vigo and 76 km from the Portuguese border.

Population: 111,000

Geography: North-western Spain on the eastern bank of River Miño, south south-east of La Coruña.

Climate: Mild and humid climate with warm summers and cool, wet winters.

History: The derivation of its name is still a matter of debate: either from its hot springs, known to Romans as *Aquae Originis* or *Urentae* (now used mainly for domestic supply); Germanic *Wurm See* (Warm Sea); or Latin *Auria* (gold). It was already an episcopal city in the fourth century (*Sedes Aurensis*). Occupied by Suevi tribes in the sixth and seventh centuries, the town was destroyed by Moors in 716 and rebuilt by Alfonso III of Asturias around 877. Magnificent seven-arched Roman bridge spans the River Miño, rebuilt by Bishop Lorenzo in 1230. The Gothic Cathedral was founded in 572 and rebuilt in the thirteenth century. The large Jewish population was expelled in 1492. Essentially an ecclesiastical town, it declined over centuries until the arrival of the railway in 1882 put it on the map. A new bridge (*Puente Nuevo*) was built in 1910–18. The rail link to Zamora and two new stations were built in 1952 and 1957.

Main historical sites: Plaza Mayor (Main Square). Cathedral of San Martiño (twelfth–thirteenth centuries). Church of La Trinidad Churches of Santa María Madre and San Francisco (latter thirteenth century). Roman Bridge (reconstructed in thirteenth century). Palacio Episcopal. Plazuela de la Magdalena. Archaeological and Fine Arts Museums. San Lázaro park.

Town: Three areas: the medieval (centre), the area of nineteenth century expansion and modern perimeter suburbs. Attractive, bustling centre; the old town disappears around dilapidated areas near Rúa Dois de Mayo.

Main areas of interest: Arcaded Plaza Mayor and old medieval centre. Charming squares and alleys around cathedral. Roman bridge. Thermal, mineral water fountains on Plaza das Burgas.

Surrounding area: Bande (25 km): church of Santa Comba and San Torcuato. Celanova (25 km): Plaza Mayor. Allariz (20 km). Ribadavia (Jewish quarter and wine museum).

Travel and transport: Bus and rail stations are a half-hour walk from the centre on the other side of the river. Regular services to surrounding towns. At least one bus a day to Portugal. Five trains daily to Madrid (8 hours).

Major economic activities: Sawmills, flour mills, iron foundries and light industry.

Major employers: Banco Pastor, Mutua Intercomarcal, Gestiones Socio-laborales, Unión Eléctrica Fenosa, university.

Sources of information

Tourist Office: Curros Enríquez 1, 32003 Orense. Tel: 988 37 20 20; 36 60 64

INEM: C/ Concejo, 4, bajo, 32003 Orense. Tel: 988 37 18 00 and Parque de San Lazáro 14-4°, 32003 Orense. Tel: 988 23 11 51

Town hall: Plaza Mayor 1, 32005 Orense. Tel: 988 38 81 75

Chamber of commerce: Cámara de Comercio e Industria, Avenida de la Habana 30, 32003 Orense. Tel: 988 23 21 14 Fax: 988 23 30 88 Email: cciourense@camerdata.es

3.32.2 **Campus of Universidad de Vigo (see** 3.48.2)

3.33 Oviedo

3.33.1 **Ciudad de Oviedo**

Basic information

Location and status: Northern Spain, 444 km from Madrid. Capital of Autonomous Community (Principality) of Asturias.

Population: 202,500

Geography: Lies on hill surrounded by mountains and fertile plain. Stretches along small section of coastline. Abundance of rainfall helps to make Asturias a true natural paradise as far as flora is concerned.

Climate: Coastal Atlantic climate, with warm summers and cool winters. Abundant rainfall.

History: Founded as a monastery by Fruela I in 757, it became the capital of Kingdom of Asturias in 810. One of few Spanish towns not to be conquered by Moors in the early Middle Ages.

Main historical sites: Renaissance palaces. La Foncalada fountain (fourteenth century). Cathedral (on site of original monastery). Cámara Santa. Los Ángeles. Eighteenth-century city walls. Convent of San Vicente (1493), now a provincial museum.

Town: Walled medieval city, with modern commercial centre.

Main areas of interest: Cathedral and old historic centre.

Surrounding area: Monte Naranco (2 km). Shrine of Covadonga. Churches of Santa María del Naranco and San Miguel de Lillo.

Travel and transport: Asturias airport is 43 km north-west of Oviedo. Many national flights all year round and occasionally to an international capital city. Linking bus service from airport to town. Regular bus services, local, national and international. Regular train services, local and some national.

Major economic activities: City's economy relies heavily on mining (coal and iron). Also food processing and light manufacturing.

Major employers: Bull, El Pozo Alimentación, S.A., Mutua Intercomarcal, Revlon, S.A., Banco Pastor, S.A.

Sources of information

Tourist Office: Oficina de Turismo, Plaza de Alfonso II el Castro 6, 33003 Oviedo. Tel: 98 521 33 85

INEM: General Elorza 2, 33001 Oviedo. Tel: 98 520 19 54

COIE: Principado 3, 33007 Oviedo Tel: 98 520 45 95; 98 510 40 20

Town hall: Plaza de la Constitución s/n, 33009 Oviedo. Tel: 98 521 98 75

Chamber of commerce: Cámara de Comercio, Industria y Navegación, Quintana 32, 33009 Oviedo. Tel: 98 522 33 09 Fax: 98 520 72 00 Email: ccinoviedo@camerdata.es

3.33.2 **Universidad de Oviedo (UOV)**

Basic information

Autonomous community: Principado de Asturias

Province: N/A

Town: Oviedo

Status: Public (1579)

Address: San Francisco 3, 33003 Oviedo. Tel: 98 510 40 58 Fax: 98 522 71 26 Email: vrelint@sci.cpd.uniovi.es Web site: www.uniovi.es

Main campuses: Cristo; Llamaquique; Milán

Satellite campuses: Gijón; Mieres

Students: 41,070

Staff: 1,739

Teaching centres

Faculties: Biology; chemistry; economics and business; education; geography and history; geology; law; medicine; philology; philosophy; psychology; science

Higher technical schools: Industrial engineering and computing (Gijón); mining engineering

University schools: Business (+Gijón); computer engineering (+Gijón); education; industrial engineering Gijón); labour relations (+Gijón); mining and topography (Mieres); nursing (Gijón) nursing and physiotherapy; social work (Gijón); tourism (+Gijón)

Student services

Information office: Centro de Orientación e Información al Estudiante, Principado 3, 33007 Oviedo. Tel: 98 510 40 20 Fax: 98 510 40 33 Email: coie@rectorado.uniovi.es

Accommodation office: Servicio de Relaciones Internacionale 3-2°, Principado 3, bajo, 33007 Oviedo. Tel: 98 510 40 30 Fax: 98 520 36 86

Health centre: Servicio de Seguridad e Higiene en el Trabajo, c/ Catedrático Jimeno s/n, 33007 Oviedo. Tel: 98 524 25 81; 524 47 12 Fax: 98 523 21 35

Spanish courses for foreign students: Servicio de Relaciones Internacionales, Principado 3, bajo, 33007 Oviedo. Tel: 98 510 49 01 Fax: 98 520 36 86

Courses in languages

For languages undergraduates: The Faculty of Philology offers degree courses in French, English and Spanish philologies.

Spanish for foreign students: The *Servicio de Relaciones Internacionales* offers courses throughout the year in Spanish language.

3.34 Palma de Mallorca

3.34.1 **Ciudad de Palma de Mallorca**

Basic information

Location and status: North-west Mediterranean sea. Capital of Autonomous Community of Balearic Islands.

Population: 323,200

Geography: Lies on south-western coast of island of Majorca in centre of ten-mile wide Palma bay.

Climate: Mild, classically Mediterranean climate, hot summers and mild winters. Annual average temperature is twenty degrees centigrade. High humidity. Three hundred days of sunshine a year.

History: Little is known of Palma before 123 BC when Romans conquered Majorca. Attacked by vandals in the fifth century, it became part of Byzantine Empire a century later. In the eighth century, it fell to Arabs and in 1229 was conquered by Jaume I of Aragón. When he died, it became independent again. In 1469 it became part of the Spanish monarchy on the marriage of Ferdinand II of Aragón and Isabella I of Castile.

Main historical sites: Gothic cathedral. Lonja (former exchange, now museum). Town Hall. Castle of Bellver (fourteenth century). Palace of La Almudaina. Old Quarter (*Barrio Viejo*). Italian designed sea-walls. Arab baths.

Town: Agreeable town with many attractive features.

Main areas of interest: Cathedral, castle and *Barrio Viejo*. Also port area and beaches.

Surrounding area: Beaches of Can Pastilla.

Travel and transport: Linked to mainland by frequent air and steamer services. In the Balearic Isles, only Majorca has a rail service. Daily plane and ferry-services cross to the mainland. Good road network: three motorways head out of Palma.

Major economic activities: Palma is important Mediterranean port. Tourism and manufacture of furniture, footwear and fabrics are the most important factors in city's economy. Also significant are: embroidery, pottery, artistic glasswork and ironwork, palmetto and raffia basketwork and olive wood carving.

Major employers: Instituto Oftalmológico de Alicante, S.L., Logic Control, S.A., Sema Group SAE, Banco Pastor.

Sources of information

Tourist Office: Oficina de Turismo, Jaime II 10, 07001 Palma de Mallorca. Tel: 971 71 22 16

INEM: Mateo Enrique Lladó 21, 07002 Palma de Mallorca. Tel: 971 72 86 25

Town hall: Plaza Corte 1, 07001 Palma de Mallorca. Tel: 971 72 77 44

Chamber of commerce: Cámara de Comercio, Industria y Navegación, Estudio General 7, 07001 Palma de Mallorca. Tel: 971 72 78 51 Fax: 971 732 63 02

3.34.2 **Universidad de las Islas Baleares (Universitat de les Illes Balears/UIB)**

Basic information

Autonomous community: Islas Baleares (Illes Balears)

Island: Mallorca

Town: Palma de Mallorca

Status: Public (1978)

Address: Campus Universitari, Ctra de Valldemossa, Km 7.5, 07001 Palma de Mallorca. Tel: 971 17 30 00 Fax: 971 17 28 52 Email: uibinfo@clust. uib.es Web site: www.uib.es

Main campus: Palma de Mallorca

Satellite campuses: Eivissa (Ibiza); Menorca

Teaching centres

Faculties: Arts; economics and business; education; law; science
Higher technical schools: Computer management; computer systems
University schools: Business; information systems; nursing; polytechnic; social work; teacher training; tourism

Student services

Information office: Oficina d'Informació, Edifici Ramón Llull, Campus Universitari, 07071 Palma de Mallorca. Tel: 971 17 29 39 Fax: 971 17 34 73 Email: uibinfo@cps.uib.es
Accommodation office: Servei d'Alumnes, Edifici Son Lledó, Campus Universitari, 07071 Palma de Mallorca. Tel: 971 17 34 07/08 Fax: 971 17 28 52
Health centre: Servei de Salut, Edifici Cas Jai, Campus Universitari, 07071 Palma de Mallorca. Tel: 971 17 34 61 Fax: 971 17 27 28
Spanish courses for foreign students: Servei d' Idiomes, Aulari, Campus Universitari, 07071 Palma de Mallorca. Tel: 971 17 28 24 Fax: 971 17 34 73

Courses in languages

For languages undergraduates: The Arts Faculty offers degree courses in Catalan and Spanish philologies.
Languages for foreign students: The *Servei d'Idiomes* provides courses thoughout the year for both Spanish and foreign students in Arabic, English, French, German, Hebrew, Italian and Russian (NB NOT Spanish).

3.35 Pamplona

3.35.1 **Ciudad de Pamplona**

Basic information

Location and status: North-eastern Spain, 385 km from Madrid. Capital of Autonomous Community of Navarra.
Population: 181,775
Geography: Lies on western bank of the River Agra in fertile district of La Cuenca. Rich variety of countryside and scenery.
Climate: Mild climate. In some areas, on fertile plain, drier and more extreme.

History: According to tradition, it was founded in 75 BC by Julius Caesar's rival Pompey as a military settlement during the campaign to quash the revolt against Rome. It was almost derelict after the Moorish and Frankish invasions and the final dismantling of defences by the Frankish King Charlemagne in 778. It was made the capital of the Kingdom of Navarre in 1000–35. The citadel built by Philip II of Spain in 1571 made Pamplona the most strongly fortified town of the north. After the first Carlist war (1833–40), Pamplona ceased to be the capital of the Kingdom of Navarre but became the capital of the new province of Navarre.

Main historical sites: Fourteenth–fifteenth century French Gothic cathedral, with Romanesque and Neo-classical touches. Sepulchre of Carlos III el Noble and Leonor de Castilla. House of Accounts (Royal treasury, *c.* 1364).

Town: Modern town with older centre.

Main areas of interest: Ciudadela area and parks. Renowned for week-long bull-running fiesta, *el encierro*, in early July.

Surrounding area: Cizur Mayor – church of San Andrés (9 km).

Travel and transport: Regular national buses except on Sunday. Train station is awkwardly situated to the north of the town.

Major economic activities: Pamplona is a flourishing agricultural centre. Wineskin, sandal, rope, pottery making. Manufacture of kitchenware, liquor, paper, chemicals and milling of flour and sugar. Important for communications between France and Spain.

Major employers: Universities, Bull, Hoteles Tryp, S.A., KPMG, Peat Marwick, S.A., Human Management Systems.

Sources of information

Tourist Office: Oficina de Turismo, Duque de Ahumada 3, 31002 Pamplona. Tel: 948 22 07 41

INEM: Errotazar 9, 31014 Pamplona. Tel: 948 13 28 50

Town hall: Plaza Consistorial s/n, 31001 Pamplona. Tel: 948 10 01 00

Chamber of commerce: Cámara de Comercio y Industria de Navarra, Yanguas y Miranda 27, 31002, Pamplona. Tel: 948 29 02 01 Fax: 948 24 28 94; 23 19 75 Email: navacom@encomit.es

3.35.2 **Universidad de Navarra (UN)**

Basic information

Autonomous community: Navarra
Province: N/A
Town: Pamplona
Status: Private (1952)
Address: Campus Universitario, 3180 Pamplona. Tel: 948 42 56 00 Fax: 948 12 36 50 Email: info@unav.es Web site: www.unav.es
Main campus: Campus Universitario (Pamplona)
Satellite campuses: Barcelona (IESE)*; Madrid (IESE)*; San Sebastián (ISSA)**
Students: 17,700
Students: 2,342

Teaching centres

Faculties: Arts; canon law; communication; economics and business; law; medicine; pharmacy; science; theology
Higher technical schools: Architecture; industrial engineering (San Sebastián)
University schools: Nursing; technical engineering

Student services

Information office: Servicio de Información al Estudiante (SIE), Edificio Central, Campus Universitario, 31080 Pamplona. Tel: 948 42 56 14 Fax: 948 42 56 19 Email: rfermuni@central.unav.es
Accommodation office: See *SIE* or contact Servicio de Asistencia Universitaria (SAU), Edificio Central, 31080 Pamplona. Tel: 948 42 56 00 Fax: 948 42 56 19 Email: jayala@unav.es
Health centre: The university has its own hospital, the *Clínica Universitaria* (attached to the faculty of medicine). Queries regarding the operation of the *Seguro Escolar* in the university can be directed to: Oficina del Seguro Escolar, Avda de Conde Oliveto 7, 31003 Pamplona. Tel: 948 42 72 00 Fax: 948 15 09 96
Spanish courses for foreign students: Instituto de Lengua y Civilización Españolas (ILCE), 31080 Pamplona. Tel: 948 25 27 00 Fax: 948 17 36 50

Courses in languages

For languages undergraduates: The Arts Faculty offers a degree course in Hispanic philology.
Spanish for foreign students: ILCE (see above) offers a variety of intensive

courses in Spanish language *and* culture at different levels during July; courses last two weeks.

* IESE = Instituto de Estudios Superiores de la Empresa

** ISSA = Instituto Superior de Secretariado y Administración

3.35.3 **Universidad Pública de Navarra (UPNA)**

Basic information

Autonomous community: Navarra
Province: N/A
Town: Pamplona
Status: Public (1987)
Address: Campus de Arrosadía s/n, 31006 Pamplona. Tel: 948 16 90 01 Fax: 948 10 90 05 Email: rector@upna.es Web site: www.upna. es
Main campus: Arrosadía
Satellite campuses: N/A
Students: 11,000
Staff: 670

Teaching centres

Faculties: Economics and business; humanities and social sciences
Higher technical schools: Agricultural engineering; industrial engineering and telecommunications
University school: Health studies

Student services

Information office: Negociado de Acceso, Campus de Arrosadia s/n, 31006 Pamplona. Tel: 948 16 96 48/38 Fax: 948 16 96 14 Email: alfreso@ upna.es
Accommodation office: Oficina de Relaciones Internacionales (ORI), Campus de Arrosadia s/n, 31006 Pamplona. Tel: 948 16 96 43/54 Fax: 948 16 96 41 Email: relext@upna.es
Health centre: See *Negociado de Acceso* or *ORI*
Spanish courses for foreign students: Centro Superior de Idiomas, Edificio El Sario, Ctra Sadar s/n, 31005 Pamplona. Tel: 948 16 97 90/91 Fax: 948 16 97 92

Courses in languages

For languages undergraduates: N/A

Spanish for foreign students: The *Centro Superior de Idiomas* offers intensive Spanish language and culture courses all year round for foreign students.

3.36 Pontevedra

3.36.1 **Ciudad de Pontevedra**

Basic information

Location and status: North-western Spain, 599 km from Madrid. Capital of Province of Pontevedra.

Population: 75,200

Geography: Lies on River Lérez at entry to estuary of Pontevedra, an Atlantic inlet.

Climate: Subtropical climate, mild temperatures and abundance of rainfall.

History: Likely to be of Roman origin. Known as Ad Duos Pontes – Two Bridges. The city's port and shipyards were important in the Middle Ages. It is possible that Christopher Columbus's ship, the Santa María, was built there. In 1719 it was sacked by British.

Main historical sites: Basilica of Santa María la Mayor (fourteenth century, a National Monument). Church of Virgen Peregrina. Ruins of Santo Domingo (now archaeological museum). San Francisco (fourteenth-century Gothic convent, also National Monument).

Town: Classic medieval centre.

Main aeas of interest: Ancient town centre, provincial museum and various churches (see above).

Surrounding area: Soutomaior castle (11 km). Trada – Pazo de Oca (country mansion).

Travel and transport: Bus station is a couple of kilometres south-east of centre. National services. Train station is next to bus station with regular local and national connections.

Major economic activities: Important port. Manufacturing of cloth, hats, leather, pottery, fertilisers, timber and cellulose. Active trade in wine, grain and fruit. Tourism.

Major employers: DIK MGI – Courtier, S.A., Hoteles Tryp, S.A., Tableros de Fibras, S.A. (TAFISA), Unión Eléctrica Fenosa, S.A.

Sources of information

Tourist Office: Oficina de Turismo, General Mola 2, 36001 Pontevedra. Tel: 986 85 08 14

INEM: Herreros 22–24, 36002 Pontevedra. Tel: 986 85821800
Town hall: Plaza de España 1 36002 Pontevedra. Tel: 986 84 66 11
Chamber of commerce: Cámara de Comercio, Industria y Navegación de Pontevedra, Jardines de Vicenti 4-2°, 36001 Pontevedra. Tel: 986 85 14 88 Fax: 986 86 26 43 Email: ccinpontevedra@comerdata.es

3.36.2 **Campus of Universidad de Vigo (see** 3.48.2**)**

3.37 Salamanca

3.37.1 **Ciudad de Salamanca**

Basic information

Location and status: Western Spain, 205 km from Madrid. Capital of Province of Salamanca.
Population: 186,350
Geography: Lies on elevation of 2,552 feet above sea level on north bank of River Tormes.
Climate: Often dry and sunny but subject to violent extremes. Hot summers and cold winters.
History: Important Iberian settlement. It was ravaged by the Carthaginian general Hannibal in 217 BC. A Roman town grew up there. It became a bishopric in the seventh century, although during Moorish rule the bishop lived in Oviedo. From the eighth to the eleventh century, the city was an area of warfare between Christians and Moors. The Christians took the city 1087–1102.
Main historical sites: Old and new cathedrals (former twelfth century, Romanesque). Tower of Gallo. Roman bridge (five of whose arches are Roman). Main Square (*Plaza Mayor*). University. College of Anaya (neo-classical). Several fine buildings in typical 'plateresque' style.
Town: Contains oldest university in Spain and one of oldest in Europe (see 3.37.3). One of Spain's greatest historical and artistic cities. Central Salamanca retains numerous fine old buildings, weathered to a beautiful golden brown.
Main areas of interest: Whole of historic centre, including cathedrals and university. Of particular interest are the cloisters known as Patio de las Escuelas Menores. Roman bridge.
Surrounding area: Ledesma – historic town with Roman baths (25 km).
Travel and transport: There is a bypass. Bus station is north-west of the

town centre. Plenty of regular local and national services. Regular local services and one train a day leaves for Lisbon at 4.55 am.

Major economic activities: Military airfield is 19 km east at Matacán. City serves as agricultural trade centre, but tourism is economic mainstay.

Major employers: Universities, tourist industry.

Sources of information

Tourist Office: Oficina de Turismo, Gran Vía 41, 37001 Salamanca. Tel: 923 24 37 30

INEM: Avda Hilario Goyenechea 2-41, 37008 Salamanca. Tel: 923 26 68 42 Fax: 923 12 02 27

Town hall: Plaza Mayor 1, 37002 Salamanca. Tel: 923 21 96 00

Chamber of commerce: Cámara de Comercio e Industria de Salamanca, Plaza de Sexmeros 2, 37001 Salamanca. Tel: 923 21 17 97 Fax: 923 28 01 46 Email: ef_comercio@helcom.es

3.37.2 **Universidad Pontificia de Salamanca (UPSA)**

Basic information

Autonomous community: Castilla y León

Province: Salamanca

Town: Salamanca

Status: Private (1940)

Address: Compañía 1, Apartado 451, 37002 Salamanca. Tel: 923 21 22 60 Fax: 923 26 24 56 Web site: www.upsa.es

Main campus: Calle Compañía (Salamanca)

Satellite campuses: Madrid, plus over 30 associated centres located all over Spain

Students: 8,500

Staff: 351

Teaching centres

Faculties: Computing (Madrid); education; human and social sciences; insurance and business sciences (Madrid); information science; politics and sociology (Madrid); theology; trilingual biblical philology

Higher technical school: N/A

University schools: Computing (Madrid); nursing (+Madrid); physiotherapy; teacher training (Luis Vives College)

Student services

Information office: Servicio de Atención al Alumno, Compañía 5, 37002 Salamanca. Tel: 923 21 89 04 Fax: 923 21 24 52
Accommodation office: See *Servicio de Atención al Alumno*
Health centre: See *Servicio de Atención al Alumno*
Spanish courses for foreign students: Cursos de Lengua y Cultura, Compañía 5, Apartado 541, 37080 Salamanca. Tel: 923 21 83 16 Fax: 923 26 25 46

Courses in languages

For languages undergraduates: N/A
Spanish for foreign students: Cursos de Lengua y Cultura offer one-month long courses all the year round for persons over the age of fourteen. Four hours of tuition per day. (Accommodation can be obtained in hotels, *pensiones*, in flats or with families.)

3.37.3 **Universidad de Salamanca (USA)**

Basic information

Autonomous community: Castilla y León
Province: Salamanca
Town: Salamanca
Status: Public (1218)
Address: Patio de Escuelas 1, 37008 Salamanca. Tel: 923 29 44 00 Fax: 923 29 45 02 Web site: www.usal.es
Main campuses: Patio de Escuelas; Unamuno
Satellite campuses: Ávila; Béjar; Zamora
Students: 32,338
Staff: 2,171

Teaching centres

Faculties: Agricultural and environmental sciences; biology; chemistry; economics and business; education; fine art; geography and history; law; medicine; pharmacy; philology; philosophy; psychology; science; social sciences; translating and documentation
Higher technical school: Industrial engineering (Béjar)
University schools: Agriculture; education (Ávila); endustrial engineering (Béjar); labour relations (Zamora); nursing (Ávila; Zamora); nursing and physiotherapy; polytechnic (Ávila and Zamora); teacher training (Ávila; Zamora); topographical engineering (Ávila)
Institutes: Education (ICE); integration into the community (disabled);

Latin American and Portuguese studies; molecular biology and cell cancer; neurosciences

Other centres: Biochemical microbiology; cultural design; linguistic research; multimedia technology; university history

Student services

Information office: Servicio de Orientación al Universitario (SOU), Facultad de Derecho, 1ª planta, 37007 Salamanca. Tel: 923 29 46 48 Fax: 923 29 47 17 Email: sou@gugu.usal.es Campus Unamuno Web site: www.usales/sou

Accommodation office: Servicios Generales, Fonseca 4, 37002 Salamanca. Tel: 923 29 45 70

Health centre: Hospital Universitario, Paseo de San Vicente 58, 37002 Salamanca. Tel: 923 29 11 00

Spanish courses for foreign students: Cursos de Internacionales, Patio de Escuelas s/n, 37008 Salamanca. Tel: 923 29 44 18 Fax: 923 29 45 04 Email: internat@cursos.usal.es Web site: www.usal. es/curespus

Courses in languages

For languages undergraduates: The Faculty of Arts offers degree courses in Arabic, English, French, German, Italian, Portuguese and Spanish philology. Optional languages also available are: Basque, Catalan, Galician, Greek and Slavonic studies. The Faculty of Translating and Documentation offers a degree in translating and interpreting, involving English and Spanish, as well as a range of other modern languages.

Spanish for foreign students: Cursos Internacionales run the following courses: (1) the *Programa Individualizado de Lengua Española* (*PILE*) is a highly flexible course aimed at undergraduate and post-graduate foreign students who need a rapid immersion course; classes can be arranged on an individual basis or in groups of two or four; normally students receive five hours of tuition per day (twenty-five hours per week); (2) the *Diploma de Estudios Hispánicos* (*DEH*) is an advanced course in Spanish Language and Culture which runs for a full academic year (October–June) and is organised on a termly basis; students receive three hours of tuition per day (fifteeen hours per week); the DEH examination takes place in June; (3) short courses (twelve hours) in Spanish guitar, dance, songs, cinema and bullfighting are offered in July and August under the *Cursos Culturales Complementarios* programme. Accommodation can be arranged with families in Salamanca at any time of year. Courses are also run at a variety of levels during the summer at the university campus in Ávila (see 3.4).

3.38 San Sebastián (Donostia)

3.38.1 **Ciudad de San Sebastián**

Basic information

Location and status: Capital of Basque Province of Guipúzcoa, situated on northern, Cantabrian coast of Spain, near French frontier, 488 km from Madrid, 100 km from Bilbao and 115km from Vitoria.

Population: 180,000

Geography: Fashionable seaside resort at mouth of River Urumea on the Bay of Biscay. City forms half-moon around bay and beach of La Concha. Surrounded by low green hills.

Climate: Warm summers and mild winters, but with high rainfall in winter.

History: First mentioned in document of 1014, it was granted privileges by Alfonso el Sabio of Navarre between 1160 and 1190. It was the Kingdom of Navarre's principal outlet to sea. By the sixteenth century, it had become a prosperous trade centre, specialising in the export of Castilian wool and other products to France, the Low Countries and England. In 1813 the town was virtually razed to ground after the Anglo-Portuguese troops took it from the French during the Peninsular War. It was formerly the summer residence of the Spanish Royal Court. It became a smart resort town in the late nineteenth century and has been popular with the Spanish aristocracy ever since.

Main historical sites: Plaza de la Constitución. San Vicente (sixteenth-century Gothic church). Santa María del Coro (eighteenth century church). Convent and Museum of San Telmo (tombstones, artefacts and masterpieces by Spanish artists). Cathedral of El Buen Pastor (nineteenth-century Neo-gothic). Palaces of Miramar and La Diputación.

Town: Principal Basque family resort and seaside town. Picturesque old town and harbour occupy the isthmus between the mainland and Monte Urgull. The well-planned, modern town extends across both banks of the River Urumea and to broad, beautiful beaches on La Concha bay. The old quarter houses most of the chief sights and hundreds of bars and restaurants and has plenty of character. It has preserved a rare cosmopolitan and distinguished air.

Main areas of interest: Old part of town (*Zona Romántica*). Monte Urgull and Monte Igueldo (walk or by funicular offering panoramic views of city and site of ruined castle of Santa Cruz de la Mota). Beautiful La Concha bay and beach, as well as other two beaches Ondarreta and Zurriola. Plaza de toros (bull-ring). Aquarium. Naval Museum. Sunday market. Festivals: sport (summer); regatta (September); jazz (July); International Film Festival (September); and Fiesta de San Sebastián (20 January).

Surrounding area: Pasajes de San Juan – picturesque fishing village (5 km). Tolosa – Carnival in February (23 km). Choir festival in October. Ordizia – market town and Monte Txindoki (32 km).

Travel and transport: City's airport is 22 km out of town. Offers regular flights to Madrid and occasional charters to UK cities. Main RENFE train station is across Río Urumea on line linking Paris to Madrid. Six services daily to Madrid (6–8 hours). Daily trains to other Spanish cities. The bus station is basically a car park between Plaza del Pío XII and the river, some twenty minutes walk from the centre. Buses to Bilbao, Barcelona, Vitoria, Zaragoza, Lourdes and other French towns.

Major economic activities: Fishing, tourism, metallurgical products, beer brewing and production of cement.

Major employers: University, Cruzcampo, Tormo and Asociados, Ikusi, Lloyd's Register of Shipping, Ingeniería IDOM Internacional.

Sources of information

Tourist Office: Calle de la Reina Regente s/n, 20006 San Sebastián. Tel: 943 48 11 66 or more information at: Oficina de Información Túristica del Gobierno Vasco, Paseo de los Fueros 1, 20004 San Sebastián. Tel: 943 42 62 82

INEM: Oquendo 18, 20004 San Sebastián. Tel: 943 42 45 46 Fax: 943 4256 63

Town hall: Urdaneta 13, 20006 San Sebastián. Tel: 943 48 14 35 Fax: 943 48 14 36

Chamber of commerce: Cámara de Comercio e Industria, c/ Ramón María Lili 6, 20002 San Sebastián. Tel: 943 27 21 00 Fax: 943 29 31 05 email: inet@camaragipuzkoa.com; dse@camaraguipuzcoa.com

Twin town: Plymouth

3.38.2 **Campus of Universidad de Deusto (see** 3.8.2**)**

3.38.3 **Campus of Universidad del País Vasco (see** 3.8.3**)**

3.39 Santander

3.39.1 **Ciudad de Santander**

Basic information

Location and status: Northern Spain, 393 km from Madrid. Capital of Autonomous Community of Cantabria.

Population: 194,900

Geography: Situated on northern shore of Cape Mayor, rocky peninsula extending eastward and sheltering Santander bay. High mountains, broad valleys and cliff lined coast. Rough terrain.

Climate: Mild climate, marine air is humid and temperatures never drop below round four degrees centigrade, nor rise above thirty degrees. Annual mean temperature is fifteen degrees.

History: The city's excellent harbour was possibly the site of a Roman colony. The centre of the lower town was rebuilt after fire spread by a windstorm in 1941.

Main historical sites: Palace of La Magdalena. Museum and Library of Menéndez Pelayo. Gothic cathedral. Provincial museum (with large collection of prehistoric artefacts from locality).

Town: Combines the charm of a summer resort from the turn of the century with a range of rich cultural offerings, which is constantly being renewed. A largely modern town.

Main areas of interest: La Magdalena palace. Fabulous beaches, including El Sardinero.

Surrounding area: Castañeda – Collegiate Church of Santa María (22 km). Muriedas – Ethnographic Musuem of Cantabria (10 km). Historic village of Santillana del Mar; prehistoric cave paintings of Altamira.

Travel and transport: Terminus of car ferry from Plymouth. Airport about 5 km east of town at Parayas. Regular national flights. Regular national bus services. Regular national train services from two stations.

Major economic activities: Economy is based on fishing, iron refining and activities connected with the port (shipbuilding). Variety of manufactured goods. Tourism also very important in summer.

Major employers: Universities, Deloitte & Touche, S.A., El Pozo Alimentación, S.A., Norcontrol, S.A., Profit Gestión Informática, S.A.

Sources of information

Tourist Office: Oficina de Turismo, Plaza Porticada 1, 39001 Santander. Tel: 942 31 07 08; 31 07 56

INEM: Isaac Peral 39, 39008 Santander. Tel: 942 23 46 02 Fax: 942 23 23 64

Town hall: Plaza del Generalísimo s/n, 39002 Santander. Tel: 942 21 27 00

Chamber of commerce: Cámara de Comercio, Industria y Navegación de Cantabria, Plaza de Velarde 5, 39001 Santander. Tel: 942 31 80 00 Fax: 942 31 43 10 Email: ccincantabria@camaracant.esju

3.39.2 **Universidad de Cantabria (UCN)**

Basic information

Autonomous community: Cantabria
Province: N/A
Town: Santander
Status: Public (1972)*
Address: Avda de los Castros s/n, 39005 Santander. Tel: 942 20 10 01 Fax: 942 20 10 70 Web site: www.unican.es
Main campuses: Las Llamas; Los Castros (both in Santander)
Satellite campus: Torrelavega
Students: 15,000
Staff: 965

Teaching centres

Faculties: Arts; economics and business; humanities; law; medicine; science

Higher technical schools: Civil engineering; industrial enginering and telecommunications; nautical studies

University schools: Labour relations (Torrelavega); mining engineering (Torrelavega); nursing; teacher training

Institutes: Education (ICE); physics

Student services

Information office: Relaciones Internacionales, Pabellón de Gobierno, Avda de los Castros s/n, 39005 Santander. Tel: 942 20 10 38/51 Fax: 942 20 10 78 Email: castrog@gestion.unican.es

Accommodation office: See *Relaciones Internacionales* or contact Oficina de Información y Servicios para el Alumno, Pabellón de Gobierno, 39005 Santander. Tel: 942 20 17 06

Health centre: See *Relaciones Internacionales*

Spanish courses for foreign students: Cursos de Español para Extranjeros,

CIUC, Edificio Filología, Avda de los Castros s/n, 39005 Santander. Tel: 942 22 42 94 Fax: 942 22 42 94 Email: ciuc@gestion. unican.es

Courses in languages

For languages undergraduates: The School of Teacher Training includes a foreign language module in its three-year diploma course.

Spanish for foreign students: Throughout the academic year, *Cursos de Español para Extranjeros* offer the following: (1) four- and five-week intensive language courses at beginners, intermediate and advanced levels, with three hours of tuition per day in groups of no more than fifteen students; (2) parallel classes in contemporary Spanish history, literature, society, business Spanish, geography and Spain today. Preparation for the DELE is also available. Accommodation and full board can be arranged with a Spanish family.

* First founded in 1972 as Universidad de Santander.

3.39.3 **Universidad Internacional de Menéndez Pelayo (UIMP)**

Basic information

Autonomous community: Cantabria
Province: N/A
Town: Santander
Status: Public (1932)
Address: Avenida de los Castros s/n, Las Llamas, 39005 Santander. Tel: 942 36 00 55; 36 01 59 Fax: 942 28 08 16 Web site: www.uimp.es
Main campuses: Palacio de la Magdalena; Las Llamas (both in Santander)
Satellite campuses: Barcelona; Irún; Madrid

Student services

Information office: Secretaría de Alumnos, Universidad Internacional de Menéndez Pelayo, Palacio de la Magdalena, 39005 Santander. Tel: 942 20 08 10 Fax: 942 28 08 16

Accommodation office: On the standard application form available from the *Secretaría de Alumnos*, students can request that accommodation be reserved for them either in one of the two halls of residence, one on each campus, or with families in the city of Santander.

Health centre: Students with health or other problems should contact the *Oficina de Atención al Estudiante* located within the *Secretaría de Alumnos.*

Spanish courses for foreign students: Secretaría de Cursos para Extranjeros,

Menéndez Pelayo, Avda de los Castros s/n, 39005 Santander. Tel: 942 36 00 55; 36 01 59 Fax: 942 28 08 16

Courses for foreign students

UIMP runs intensive four-week Spanish language courses in July, August and September at seven different levels from beginners to advanced. Classes range from ninety-two to 115 hours (higher levels) and there are a maximum of eighteen students per class. Students must be at least seventeen years old. In addition, students may attend courses in Spanish culture, including: Spanish economy, geography, history (golden age), history of art, contemporary politics and society and cinema. The *Diploma de Estudios Hispánicos* (*DEH*) is awarded to students who pass examinations in Spanish language, literature, history and history of art. Excursions to local places of historical and cultural interest also form a (voluntary) part of the programme. Students may also attend the series of lectures in a wide range of disciplines organised during the summer by the university and given by invited specialists from Spain and abroad.

3.40 Santiago de Compostela

3.40.1 **Ciudad de Santiago de Compostela**

Basic information

Location and status: North-western Spain, 613 km from Madrid, in province of La Coruña. Spain's most famous cathedral city and pilgrimage centre.

Population: 105,900

Geography: Stands on top of hill encircled by River Sar and its tributary, Sarela.

Climate: Splendid weather in summer. Quite mild winters.

History: In AD 813 a tomb discovered near Padrón was said to be that of the Apostle Saint James the Great (Santiago), martyred in Jerusalem in AD 44. His bones had been taken to Spain where, according to legend, he had evangelised. Over the tomb, Alfonso II built an earthen church which Alfonso III later replaced with stone. In the Middle Ages the town that grew up around it became the most important Christian place of pilgrimage after Jerusalem and Rome. The whole town except the tomb itself was destroyed in 997 by military commander of the Moorish Caliphate of Córdoba.

Main historical sites: Romanesque cathedral, completed in 1211. Hospice of Los Reyes Católicos. Collegiate Church of Santa María del Sar (Romanesque). Monastery of San Pelayo. Churches of Santa María Salomé and Santa María la Real del Sar.

Town: World Heritage Site. Beautiful old town, with a predominantly medieval air.

Main areas of interest: Whole of old historic centre, including cathedral, with abundance of other medieval buildings.

Surrounding area: Monastery of Santa María de Conxo. City within easy reach of lush green countryside and attractive long estuaries (*rías*).

Travel and transport: Lavacolla airport is 11 km south-east of city – regular national and international flights. Main bus terminus for Galicia. National and international sevices. Regular national trains. Public bus systems run around old town, though Santiago is walkable.

Major economic activities: Agriculture, industries of silverwork, jetwork and wood engraving. Also important are: brewing and distillation of spirits, foundaries and manufacture of linen, paper, furniture, soap and matches.

Major employers: University, tourist industry, Auditores Asociados de Galicia, S.A., Ingeniería IDOM Internacional, S.A., Level Telecom, S.L., Banco Pastor, S.A.

Sources of information

Tourist Office: Oficina de Turismo, Ruadel Villar 43, 15705 Santiago de Compostela. Tel: 981 58 40 81

INEM: Doctor Maceira 18, bajo, 15706 Santiago de Compostela. Tel: 981 52 26 85

COIE: COIE de la Universidad de Santiago de Compostela, Pabellón Estudiantil, Campus Universitario, 15706 Santiago de Compostela. Tel: 981 54 43 40 Fax: 981 59 51 17

Town hall: Plaza de Obradoiro s/n, 15705 Santiago de Compostela. Tel: 981 54 23 42

Chamber of commerce: Cámara de Comercio, Industria y Navegación de Santiago de Compostela, San Pedro de Mezonzo 44, 15701 Santiago de Compostela. Tel: 981 59 68 00 Fax: 981 59 03 22 Email: ccinsantiago @comerdata.es

3.40.2 **Universidad de Santiago de Compostela (USC)**

Basic information

Autonomous community: Galicia
Province: La Coruña (A Coruña)
Town: Santiago de Compostela
Status: Public (1495)
Address: Colexio de San Xerome, Praza do Obradoiro s/n, 15705 Santiago de Compostela. Tel: 981 58 38 00 Fax: 981 58 85 22 Email: rector @usc.es Web site: www.usc.es
Main campuses: Norte; Sur (both in Santiago)
Satellite campus: Lugo
Students: 35,000
Staff: 1,536

Teaching centres

Faculties: Biology; chemistry; economics and business; geography and history; humanities (Lugo); information science; law; mathematics; medicine and dentistry; pharmacy; philology; philosophy and education; physics; political and social sciences; psychology; science (Lugo); veterinary science (Lugo)
Higher techncial school: Higher polytechnic school
University schools: Business (Lugo); labour relations (+Lugo); nursing (+Lugo); optics and optometry; social work; teacher training (Lugo)

Student services

Information office: Centro de Orientación e Información al Estudiante (COIE), Pabellón Estudiantil, Campus Sur, Plaza do Seminario Estudies Galegos, 15705 Santiago de Compostela. Tel: 981 10 10 22 Fax: 981 59 51 17 Email: coisec@usc.es
Accommodation office: Oficina de Relaciones Internacionales, Pabellón Estudiantil, Campus Sur, Plaza do Seminario Estudies Galegos 15075 Santiago de Compostela. Tel: 981 58 49 89 Email: elveloso@use.es
Health centre: See *COIE*
Spanish courses for foreign students: Oficina de Cursos Internacionales, Facultad de Ciencias Políticas, Campus Universitario, 15705 Santiago de Compostela. Tel: 981 59 70 35 Fax: 981 59 70 36 Email: cspanish @usc.es

Courses in languages

For languages undergraduates: The Faculty of Philology offers degree courses in the following philologies: English, French, Galician, German, Hispanic, Italian and Portuguese.

Spanish for foreign students: Cursos Internacionales offer summer four-week courses in Spanish language at all levels during July, August and September. Language courses are supplemented by talks and conferences, combined with practical sessions, on Spanish literature, society, cinema, art. etc. The office can provide a list of available accommodation on request.

3.41 Segovia

3.41.1 **Ciudad de Segovia**

Basic information

Location and status: Located in north-central Spain, 87 km from Madrid. Capital of Province of Segovia in Autonomous Community of Castilla y León. Located 67 km from Ávila, 110 km from Valladolid and 199 km from Burgos.

Population: 56,000

Geography: 1,000 metres above sea level, most spectacularly sited city in Spain. Set high on rocky spur and surrounded by Rivers Eresma and Clamores.

Climate: Continental. Hot summers and long, cold winters with low annual rainfall.

History: Was an Iberian settlement from about 700 BC and the Celtic settlement of Segobriga when captured by the Romans around 80 BC. It was occupied by the Moors at beginning of the eighth century, from whom Alfonso VI recaptured it in 1079. Thereafter, the city enjoyed prosperity and a position of some importance in medieval Castile, serving as the royal residence during reign of Alfonso X (El Sabio) (*c.* 1284), a base for the *Cortes* (parliament) and as site of the Spanish mint from 1586 until 1730. In the late Middle Ages, it was the centre of flourishing textile industry, which declined and was replaced by agriculture. An outbreak of plague at the end of the sixteenth century ushered in a long period of decadence, but the city's fortunes revived with the railway building era of the nineteenth century. Its modern prosperity has continued since the 1960s with tourism and the introduction of some light industry.

Main historical sites: Roman aqueduct (El Puente) – finest example of its epoch, first century, and over 700 metres long. El Alcázar (fortified Moorish Palace with fairytale towers). Gothic cathedral (sixteenth century). San Esteban church (with superb tower). Churches of San Martín, San Justo, La Trinidad, San Lorenzo, San Andrés and San Millán (all Romanesque and from twelfth century). Church of Vera Cruz (thirteenth century, former church of Knights Templar). Casa de los Picos (sixteenth century). Plaza Mayor and Plaza Juan Bravo. San Juan de la Cruz (walled monastery). Synagogue (now serves as convent church of Corpus Christi). Palace of Los Dávila. Convento de los Carmelitas Descalzas (Burial site of San Juan de la Cruz). Monastery of El Parral.

Town: Ridge-top city, which to some resembles a man-of-war ploughing through the sea of Castile around it. Particularly renowned for the magnificent aqueduct, this relatively small city typifies Golden Age Castile. The old town is strung out along a ridge, rising in the east and peaking in the towers of the Alcázar to the west.

Main areas of interest: Old quarters around the Plaza Mayor. Medieval churches and squares. Museo de Holografía. Casa-Museo de Antonio Machado (one-time residence of pre-eminent Spanish poet). Casa del Sol (Museum of Segovia). Fiestas de San Juan y San Pedro (24–29 June).

Surrounding area: El Terminillo – spectacular panoramic views of city (2 km). La Granja – Bourbon summer palace and gardens (10 km). Riofrío – palace and museum (10 km). Santa María la Real de la Nieva (25 km). Collado Hermoso – monastery (20 km). Pedraza de la Sierra and Turégano – castles (35 km). Cuéllar – castle/palace (60 km).

Travel and transport: Well-connected by road and rail, although train station, like bus station, is some distance out of town. Nine trains and up to sixteen buses run daily to Madrid. Regular buses also link Segovia with La Granja, Salamanca, Valladolid and Cuéllar.

Major economic activities: Rubber, pottery, flour, biscuits, fertilizers, chemical products and cement.

Major employers: Alimentos Refrigerados, Ulma Group, Grupo General de Aguas, Banco de Santander Central Hispano (BSCH), Argentaria.

Sources of information

Tourist Office: Plaza del Azoguejo 1, 40001 Segovia. Tel: 921 44 03 02 *or* Oficina de Turismo Plaza Mayor 10, 40001 Segovia. Tel: 921 46 03 34

INEM: Avenida de Fernández Ladreda 31-2°, 40002 Segovia. Tel: 921 42 53 45 Fax: 921 43 79 71 *or* General Santiago 6, 40005 Segovia. Tel: 921 42 52 61

Town hall: Ayuntamiento Plaza Mayor 1, 40001 Segovia. Tel: 921 41 98 00 Fax: 921 41 98 40 Email: aytosego@ctv.es

Chamber of commerce: Cámara de Comercio e Industria de Segovia, Fernán García 1-1°, 40001 Segovia. Tel: 921 43 23 00/11 Fax: 921 43 05 63 Email: raznar@camerdata.es

3.41.2 **Campus of Universidad Complutense de Madrid (see** 3.28.7**)**

3.41.3 **Universidad SEK de Segovia (USEK)**

Basic information

Autonomous community: Castilla y León

Province: Segovia

Town: Segovia

Status: Private (1997)

Address: Convento de Santa Cruz la Real, Cardenal Zúñiga 12, 40003 Segovia. Tel: 921 44 47 27 Fax: 921 44 55 93 Email: usek@sgv.servicom.es Web site: www.usek.es

Main campus: Santa Cruz la Real (Segovia)

Linked SEK universities: Quito (Ecuador); Santiago (Chile). Linked colleges in Spain: La Coruña; Valencia. Linked colleges abroad: Asunción (Paraguay); Budapest (Hungary); Buenos Aires (Argentina); Guayaquil (Ecuador); Reading (UK).

Students: 890

Staff: 145

Teaching centres

Faculties: Biology; cultural heritage studies; information science; psychology

Higher technical school: Centre for Integrated Architectural Studies

University schools: N/A

Student services

Information office: Departamento de Relaciones Internacionales, Campus de Santa Cruz la Real, Cardenal Zúñiga 12, 40003 Segovia. Tel: 921 44 24 10 Fax: 921 44 55 93 Email: carmina@rrii.sek.edu

Accommodation office: See *Departamento de Relaciones Internacionales*

Health centre: See *Departamento de Relaciones Internacionales*
Spanish courses for foreign students: Cursos de Español, Cardenal Zúñiga s/n, 40003 Segovia. Tel/Fax/Email: as for *Departamento de Relaciones Internacionales*

Courses in languages

For SEK and foreign undergraduates: Throughout the academic year the *Departamento de Lenguas Aplicadas* organises courses in various languages, including English, French and German to suit the academic and professional needs of students.
Spanish for foreign students: During the summer, the university organises Spanish Courses (*Cursos de Español*) for foreign students. These take place in July and August and are offered at two levels, intermediate and advanced. Students may follow a two-week course of fifty hours or a four-week course of a hundred hours of language tuition. Language classes take place between 9.00 am and 4.00 pm, after which courses in different aspects of Spanish culture, as well as excursions, are available.

3.42 Sevilla

3.42.1 **Ciudad de Sevilla**

Basic information

Location and status: Southern Spain, 585 km from Madrid. Capital of Autonomous Community of Andalucía and of Province of Sevilla. Spain's fourth largest city.
Population: 708,705
Geography: Lies on left (east) bank of River Guadalquivir.
Climate: Excessively hot in summer. Temperatures of over forty degrees centigrade in shade in July and August are not unknown. Very mild winters.
History: Originally an Iberian town. Under Romans, it flourished from the second century BC onwards and was the administrative centre of the province. In 711 the town fell to the Muslims and became a leading cultural and commercial centre. After the Muslim possession of Seville was ended in 1248 by the Spanish Christians under Fernando III, substantial Moorish and Jewish minorities were driven into exile and the local economy fell into ruin. The Spanish discovery

of the Americas brought new prosperity to the city and Seville became the centre for exploration and exploitation of the Americas through the House of Trade (*Casa de Contratación*). It was the richest and most populous city in Spain in the sixteenth century. Seville's economy declined during the seventeenth century. In the eighteenth century, Spain's Bourbon rulers managed to stimulate a limited economic revival in the city, but in the nineteenth century the French invasion, revolutions and civil war halted such development. During the twentieth century the port was enlarged and the city revived as an important industrial and commercial centre.

Main historical sites: Gothic cathedral (housing Columbus's tomb) – largest in Spain and one of largest in world. La Giralda tower. Royal Castle (*Reales Alcáceres*). Museum of Fine Art and Archeology. The Tower of Gold (*Torre del Oro*). La Casa Lonja (houses several million documents relating to history and administration of Spain's empire in Americas). Tobacco factory (now part of university). City museum. City's oldest working ceramics factory of Santa Ana in Triana. La Casa del Pilato – an elegant mansion house with classical gardens, which once belonged to the Medinaceli family.

Town: Inland city (and port) in low lying position, with an unmistakably Moorish atmosphere which combines well with the bustle of an important political, administrative and cultural centre. The city oozes self-confidence.

Main areas of interest: Historic centre, with cathedral and nearby old commercial area including Calle Sierpes. Barrio de Santa Cruz, old Jewish quarter, is fascinating area of narrow, winding streets and corners, festooned with flowers. Elegant María Luisa Park. Promenades along the River Guadalquivir.

Surrounding area: Santiponce – ruins of Itálica (8 km). Bollullos de las Hermanas – church of La Magdalena (8 km).

Travel and transport: New railway station (Santa Justa) for high speed train (AVE) from Madrid. Airport less than 15 km from city centre – internal flights to many parts of Spain, plus some international flights.

Major economic activities: Exports wines, fruit, olives, cork and minerals. Industries include the manufacture of tobacco, armaments, porcelain, and agricultural machinery. Also important are shipbuilding and the manufacture of textiles from locally grown cotton. Tourism is a vital economic mainstay.

Major employers: Universities, Dopp Consultores, El Pozo Alimentación, S.A., Estudio de Informática, S.L., Renault, Grupo Ayllón, Grupo Lettera, S.L., Hewlitt Packard Española, S.A., IBM España, S.A.

Sources of information

Tourist Office: Oficina de Turismo, Avda de la Constitución 21, 41004 Sevilla. Tel: 95 422 14 04

INEM: Avda de San Juán de la Cruz s/n, 41006 Sevilla. Tel: 95 464 96 00

Town hall: C/ Sol 10, 41001 Sevilla. Tel: 95 459 06 00

Chamber of commerce: Cámara de Comercio, Industria y Navegación de de Sevilla, Plaza de la Contratación 8, 41004 Sevilla Tel: 95 421 10 05 Fax: 95 422 56 19 Email: ccinsevilla@camerdata.es

3.42.2 **Universidad Pablo de Olavide (UPO)**

Basic information

Autonomous community: Andalucía

Province: Sevilla

Town: Sevilla

Status: Public (1997)

Address: Ctra de Utrera, Km 1, 41013 Sevilla. Tel: 95 434 92 00 Fax: 95 434 92 04 Email: polavide@upo.es Web site: www.upo.es

Main campus: Ctra de Utrera (Sevilla)

Satellite campuses: N/A

Students: 3,611

Staff: N/K

Teaching centres

Faculties: Economics and business; experimental sciences; humanities; law

Higher technical schools: N/A

University school: Social work

Student services

Information office: Oficina de Información, Unidad de Alumnos, Campus Universitario, Ctra de Utrera, Km 1, 41013 Sevilla. Tel: 95 434 92 48 Fax: 95 434 92 49

Accommodation office: See *Oficina de Información*

Health centre: See *Oficina de Información*

Spanish courses for foreign students: N/A

Courses in languages

For languages undergraduates: Modules in a European foreign language (mainly English), including both language and literature studies, as

well as Spanish language, form part of the degree course in humanities.
Spanish for foreign students: N/A

3.42.3 **Universidad de Sevilla (USE)**

Basic information

Autonomous community: Andalucía
Province: Sevilla
Town: Sevilla
Status: Public (1505)
Address: San Fernando 4, 41004 Sevilla. Tel: 95 455 11 36 Fax: 95 421 28 03 Email: extension11@extension.us.es Web site: www.cpd.us.es
Main campuses: Macarena; Ramón y Cajal; Reina Mercedes; San Fernando
Satellite campus: Osuna
Students: 75,948
Staff: 3,010

Teaching centres

Faculties: Arts; chemistry; computing and statistics; dentistry; economics and business; education; fine art; geography and history; information science; law; mathematics; medicine; pharmacy; philology; philosophy; physics; psychology
Higher technical schools: Architecture; industrial engineering
University schools: Business studies (+Osuna); health Sciences; labour relations (+Osuna); polytechnic; social work; teacher training; technical agricultural engineering x 2; technical architecture

Student services

Information office: Servicio de Asistencia a la Comunidad Universitaria (SACU), Pabellón de Uruguay, Avda de Chile s/n, 41013 Sevilla. Tel: 95 448 60 10/09 Fax: 95 448 60 20 Email: sacuinfo@us.es
Accommodation office: Oficina de Alojamiento, SACU, Pabellón de Uruguay, Avda de Chile s/n, 41013 Sevilla. Tel: 95 448 60 14 Fax: 95 448 60 20 Email: sacuinfo@us.es
Health centre: See *SACU*
Spanish courses for foreign students: Instituto de Idiomas, Universidad de Sevilla, Avda Reina Mercedes s/n, 41004 Sevilla. Tel: 95 455 11 55 Fax: 95 455 14 50

Courses in languages

For languages undergraduates: The Faculty of Philology offers degree courses in English, French, German, Hispanic and Italian philologies.

Spanish for foreign students: The *Instituto de Idiomas* offers two semester-long courses in Spanish language starting in October and February. These are both offered at elementary, intermediate, higher intermediate (*avanzado*) and advanced (*superior*) level. At each level, there are three hours of classes per week. Accommodation can be arranged through SACU.

3.43 Tarragona (Tarragones)

3.43.1 **Ciudad de Tarragona**

Basic information

Location and status: North-eastern Spain, 555 km from Madrid. Capital of Province of Tarragona.

Population: 114,500

Geography: Lies at mouth of Francolí River, on hill (500 feet) rising abruptly from Mediterranean Sea. Fertile plain. Coastal area consists of succession of fine, sandy beaches and calm blue water. Inland area is enhanced by intense brightness of sunlight. Carob trees, vineyards, hazel, almond and olive trees give an air of grace and beauty.

Climate: During the summer the temperature ranges from twenty-three to twenty-five degrees centigrade, but constant sea breezes help maintain cool atmosphere. Winters are mild. Fairly low rainfall throughout year. An extraordinarily large number of bright, sunny days during all seasons of year.

History: Captured from the Iberians in 218 BC by the Romans who improved the harbours and walls, transforming it into the earliest Roman stronghold in Spain. The flax trade and other industries made it one of the richest seaports in the Roman Empire. The city was razed by the Moors in 714 and remained unimportant until early in the twelfth century when it was recaptured by the Christians. After 1119, Tarragona resumed a new life as an important city of the Spanish Kingdom of Aragón.

Main historical sites: Cathedral (twelfth-thirteenth centuries, Romanesque/Gothic). Amphitheatre, theatre, forum and palace of Augustus. Roman walls. Arqueological Museum.

Town: Seat of archbishop, town and port has both historic/architectural and commercial interest.

Main areas of interest: All the historic centre, especially Roman remains. Nearby beaches and coastline.

Surrounding area: Aiguamurcia – Monastery of Santes Creus (8 km). Impressive remains of Greek colony of Emporion (today's Ampurias) are not far away.

Travel and transport: Regular national bus services. Around forty regional and long distance trains a day run to and from Barcelona Sants. In summer a fast ferry service runs to and from Palma de Mallorca.

Major economic activities: Flourishing seaport, important agricultural market, centre of active tourist trade. Industrial development is slight but includes petroleum refinery that was, when it began production in 1976, among the most modern in Europe.

Major employers: Contratas y Obras Empresa Constructora, S.A., El Pozo Alimentación, S.A., Grupo Fimestic, Mutua Intercomarcal, Revlon, S.A., Petroleum Factory.

Sources of information

Tourist Office: Oficina de Turismo Fortuny 4, bajo, 43001 Tarragona. Tel: 977 20 18 59

INEM: San Antonio María Claret 19, 43002 Tarragona. Tel: 977 24 47 75 Fax: 977 24 51 80

Town hall: Plaza de de la Font 1, 43003 Tarragona. Tel: 977 29 61 00

Chamber of commerce: Cámara de Comercio, Industria y Navegación de Tarragona, Avda Pau Casals 17, 43003 Tarragona. Tel: 977 21 89 77 Fax: 977 24 09 00 Email: cambrat@tinet.jut.es

Twin town: Stafford

3.43.2 **Universidad Rovira i Virgili (URV)**

Basic information

Autonomous community: Cataluña (Catalunya)

Province: Tarragona

Town: Tarragona

Status: Public (1991*)

Address: C/ De l'Escorxador s/n, 43003 Tarragona. Tel: 977 55 80 00 Fax: 977 55 80 22 Email: sg@orgov.urv.es Web site: www.urv.es

Main campus: Escorxador

Satellite campuses: El Vendrell; Reus; Tortosa

Students: 10,309

Staff: 743

Teaching centres

Faculties: Arts; chemistry; economics and business (Reus); education and psychology; medicine and health sciences (Reus); social and legal sciences

Higher technical schools: Chemical enginering; engineering

University schools: Nursing (+Tortosa); oenology; social work

Student services

Information office: Servei d'Estudiants, c/ De l'Escorxador s/n, 43003 Tarragona. Tel: 977 55 80 00/29 Fax: 977 55 80 22

Accommodation office: See *Servei d'Estudiants*

Health centre: See *Servei d'Estudiants*

Spanish courses for foreign students: N/A

Courses in languages

For languages undergraduates: The Faculty of Arts offers degree couses in Catalán, English and Hispanic philologies.

Spanish for foreign students: N/A

* When founded, URV in fact recreated the old sixteenth-century Universitat de Tarragona.

3.44 Toledo

3.44.1 **Ciudad de Toledo**

Basic information

Location and status: South-central Spain, 70 km from Madrid. Capital of Autonomous Community of Castilla-La Mancha and of Province of Toledo.

Population: 65,100

Geography: Top of rugged promontory girded by River Tagus. Mountain ranges with white-leafed rock roses and aromatic plants. Vineyards, fields of wheat, cotton and tobacco.

Climate: Cold winters, hot summers and plentiful sunlight, sparse rainfall, though temperatures excessively rigorous during either of the seasonal extremes.

History: Conquered by Romans in 193 BC. It was the residence of the Visigothic court in the sixth century. During the Moorish period it was the home of an important Mozarab community (Arabic-speaking

Christians). Taken by King Alfonso VI in 1085, it became the most important political and social centre of Castile. It was the scene of the fusion of Christian, Arab, and Jewish cultures, an example of which is the School of Translators. The city's importance declined after Philip II made Madrid his capital in 1561.

Main historical sites: Cathedral (completed in 1492, most Hispanic of Gothic cathedrals). Church of San Juan de los Reyes (Isabelline style). Synagogue of Santa María la Blanca. Tránsito Synagogue. Castle of San Servando. Puerta Vieja de Bisagra (tenth century – gateway in city walls, traditionally used by Alfonso VI in 1085). Sixteenth-century Hospital de Santa Cruz is now used as Provincial Museum of Archaeology and Fine Arts. Town Hall. Numerous Baroque churches. Fortress of El Alcázar, rebuilt after Civil War.

Town: Toledo is considered most representative of Spanish culture, the whole urban area having been declared a National Monument.

Main areas of interest: Whole of city, especially historic centre.

Surrounding area: Illescas – Grecos (35 km). Puebla de Montalbán – church of Nuestra Señora de Melque (28 km). Whole area of La Mancha (famous for windmills and wine-growing) is worth exploring.

Travel and transport: A good network of secondary roads. Recommended that tourists park outside the old quarter, although it is possible to drive along some of the main streets. Most transport from Toledo is local and regional.

Major economic activities: Steel, particularly swords, has long been famous. Important National Arms Factory and workshops for damask and engraving which produce metalwork decorated in Mudéjar tradition. Another typical product is marzipan.

Major employers: Nuteco España, S.A., Superdiplo, S.A., ACS Proyectos, Obras y Construcciones, S.A., Tourist industry.

Sources of information

Tourist Office: Puerta de Visagra s/n, 45003 Toledo. Tel: 925 22 08 43

INEM: La Mancha 3, 45003 Toledo. Tel: 925 22 22 76

Town hall: Plaza Consistorio 1, 45071 Toledo. Tel: 925 26 97 00

Chamber of commerce: Cámara de Comercio e Industria de Toledo, Plaza de San Vicente 3, 45001 Toledo. Tel: 925 22 38 17 Fax: 925 21 47 27

3.44.2 **Campus of Universidad de Castilla-La Mancha (see** 3.14.2)

3.45 Valencia

3.45.1 **Ciudad de Valencia**

Basic information

Location and status: Eastern Spain, 352 km from Madrid. Capital of Autonomous Community of Valencia and of Province of Valencia. Spain's third largest city.

Population: 763,300

Geography: Lies on Mediterranean coast at mouth of River Turia (Guadlaviar). Surrounded by broad, fertile irrigated area, devoted to cultivation of vegetables and citrus fruits.

Climate: An annual mean temperature above seventeen degrees centigrade. Relatively humid. Over 2,600 hours of sunshine a year and little rainfall. Hot summers and mild winters.

History: Was a prosperous Roman colony. It was taken by the Visigoths in AD 413 and in 714 by the Moors. In 1021 it became the seat of a newly-established independent Moorish kingdom of Valencia. From 1089 until the final capitulation of city in 1094, the kingdom was fought for by the Spanish soldier–hero El Cid, who eventually secured it from the Moorish Almoravids. It remained under his rule until his death in 1099. The Moors recovered the city and kingdom in 1102. In 1479, with all other countries of the Aragonese crown, the kingdom was united with Castile under monarchs Ferdinand and Isabella. It was a loyalist capital for most of the Civil War (1936–39).

Main historical sites: Cathedral (completed 1482; its three doorways are respectively Romanesque, Baroque and Gothic). Convent of Santo Domingo. National Ceramic Museum. Fine Art Museum. Palace of La Diputación. Museums of art and ceramics.

Town: Originally walled town, but walls were taken down in the nineteenth century and only two gateways remain. City with the longest tradition of fairs in the country.

Main areas of interest: Old historic centre, including cathedral. Botanical gardens. Annual fiesta of Las Fallas involving the construction of enormous papier-maché sculptures, eventally burned in an orgy of fire and fiestas (culminates on 19 March).

Surrounding area: Playa de Saler (25 km). Albufera Lagoon. Monastery of Nuestra Señora de Puig.

Travel and transport: Regular air service connects national flights from the Manises Airport 15 km from city centre. Bus station is two km northwest of centre – national and international services. Regular national train services. National ferry services.

Major economic activities: Exports agricultural produce, rice, oranges, lemons, onions, wine and manufactured items including, furniture, glazed tiles and ceramics, fans, textiles and iron products.

Major employers: Baxter, S.A., Ediciones Jardin, S.L., El Pozo Alimentación, S.A., Estudio de Informática, S.L., Grupo Ayllón, Hewlitt Packard Española, S.A., IBM España, S.A.

Sources of information

Tourist Office: Oficina de Turismo, Calle de la Paz 46, 46003 Valencia. Tel: 96 352 28 97 (Tourist Line: 352 40 00)

INEM: Alfambra 4, 46009 Valencia. Tel: 96 647 89 09

COIE: COIE de la Universidad Politécnica de Valencia, Campus del Camí de Vera s/n, 46022 Valencia. Tel: 96 387 70 10 Fax: 96 387 79 10

Town hall: Plaza Ayuntamiento 1, 46002 Valencia. Tel: 96 352 54 78

Chamber of commerce: Cámara de Comercio, Industria y Navegación de Valencia, Poeta Querol 15, 46002 Valencia. Tel: 96 351 13 01 Fax: 96 351 63 49 Email: cocimu@camarau.es

3.45.2 **Universidad Politécnica de Valencia (UPVA)**

Basic information

Autonomous community: Comunidad Valenciana

Province: Valencia

Town: Valencia

Status: Public (1971)

Address: Camí de Vera s/n, 40022 Valencia. Tel: 96 387 70 04 Fax: 96 387 79 45 Email: agrales@upvnet.upv.es Web site: www.upv.es

Main campus: Camí de Vera

Satellite campuses: Alcoy; Almusases; Gandía; Montcada; Orihuela

Students: 31,035

Staff: 1,612

Teaching centres

Faculties: Business studies; computing; fine art; information science*

Higher technical schools: Agriculture; architecture; civil engineering; geodetics, cartography and topography; industrial engineering; telecommunications

University schools: Computing; Ford España (Almusases); Gandía; higher polytechnic school (Alcoy); technical agriculture; technical architecture; technical industrial engineering

Student services

Information office: (1) Área d'Informació, Camí de Vera s/n, 46022 Valencia. Tel: 96 387 90 00 Fax: 96 387 09 09 Email: areainf@upvnet.upv.es *or* (2) Servicio del Alumnado, Edificio del Rectorado, Camí de Vera s/n, 46022 Valencia. Tel: 96 387 74 01 Fax: 96 387 79 04 Email: sealu1@upvnet.upv.es

Accommodation office: Área de Programas Internacionales, Camí de Vera s/n, 46022 Valencia. Tel: 96 387 70 02 Email: api@upvnet.es

Health centre: Gabinete Médico, Camino de Vera s/n, 46022 Valencia. Tel: 96 387 74 07 Email: snl@upvnet.upv.es

Spanish courses for foreign students: Departamento de Idiomas, Camí de Vera s/n, 46022 Valencia. Tel: 96 387 75 30 Fax: 96 387 75 39 Email: depidm@upvnet.uov.es

Courses in languages

For languages undergraduates: See *Departamento de Idiomas*

Spanish for foreign students: See *Departamento de Idiomas*

* UPVA awards degrees for this associate school of the Universidad San Pablo-CEU (see 3.28.13).

3.45.3 **Universidad de Valencia – Estudi General (UV)**

Basic information

Autonomous community: Comunidad Valenciana

Province: Valencia

Town: Valencia

Status: Public (1500)

Address: Edificio Alameda, Antiga Senda de Senent 11, 46023 Valencia. Tel: 96 386 41 00 Fax: 96 386 42 24 Web site: www.uv.es

Main campuses: Blasco Ibáñez; Tarrongers (both in Valencia)

Satellite campuses: Burjasot; Catarroja; Cheste; Godella; Montcada

Students: 63,293

Staff: 3,010

Teaching centres

Faculties: Arts and education; biology (Burjasot); chemistry (Burjasot); economics and business; geography and history; law; mathematics (Burjasot); medicine; dentistry; pharmacy (Burjasot); philology; physics (Burjasot); psychology

Higher technical schools: N/A

University schools: Business studies (+Catarroja); labour relations; nursing x 3; physical education (Cheste); physiotherapy; social work; teacher training (+Godella)

Other centres: Institute of education (ICE) (Cheste); university centre for legal studies of San Pablo – CEU* (Montcada)

Student services

Information office: Servei d'Estudiants, Antiga Senda del Senent 11, 46071 Valencia. Tel: 96 386 48 02 Fax: 96 386 41 17 Email: servei.estudiants@uv.es

Accommodation office: See *Servei d'Estudiants*

Health centre: See *Servei d'Estudiants*

Spanish courses for foreign students: Gabinete de Extranjeros, Antiga Senda del Senent 11, 46071 Valencia. Tel: 96 386 41 80 Fax: 96 386 42 24

Courses in languages

For languages undergraduates: The Faculty of Arts offers degree courses in Catalan, English, French, German, Hispanic and Italian philologies.

Spanish for foreign students: The *Gabinete de Extranjeros* offers Spanish language courses for Socrates/Erasmus students at beginners and intermediate levels. Courses start at the beginning of each semester.

3.46 Valladolid

3.46.1 **Ciudad de Valladolid**

Basic information

Location and status: Located in north-western Spain on *meseta*, 193 km from Madrid. Capital of Province of Valladolid and of Autonomous Community of Castilla y León. Located 115 km from Salamanca and 122 km from Burgos.

Population: 350,000

Geography: At 700m above sea level, the city lies at confluence of Rivers Esgueva and Pisuerga, south-west of Burgos. Largest city in region.

Climate: Hot summers and long, cold winters with low annual rainfall.

History: Of uncertain origin, the first recorded mention of Valladolid (Moorish Belad Ulid) appears to be in a letter of 1074 from Alfonso VI to Count Pedro Ansúrez granting him lordship of the town. The Catholic Monarchs Isabella of Castile and Ferdinand of Aragon were married here in 1469. Columbus died here, alone and forgotten, in 1506, while Philip II was born in the palace of Los Pimentel in 1527. It grew into a city of considerable importance and was *de facto* capital of imperial Spain and a flourishing centre of Renaissance art and culture. The city suffered severely during the Peninsular War (1808–14), when many of its ancient buildings were destroyed by the French. The unfinished cathedral was begun in 1585 by Juan de Herrera and consecrated in 1688. Valladolid's university (founded 1292) is one of the oldest in Spain.

Main historical sites: Cathedral. Colleges of San Gregorio and Santa Cruz (both Plateresque, fifteenth century). University. Palace of Capitanía General. Churches of San Pablo, Santa María la Antigua and Las Angustias.

Town: Town's historical greatness has, in many respects, been overtaken by rapid and unattractive developments of modern city and its reliance on heavy industry. Old town around cathedral, university and Plaza Mayor has atmosphere and lots of interesting architecture and churches, but also has its seedy areas. True Castilian is said to be spoken in Valladolid.

Main areas of interest: Campo Grande (city park). Old quarter around cathedral, Plaza Mayor and university. Home of Cervantes. Museo Nacional de Escultura (National Sculpture Museum) (finest collection in Spain). Museo Oriental. Museo Arqueológico. Casa Museo de Colón (Christopher Columbus's house). Semana Santa (Holy Week) (some of the most extravagant and solemn processions in Spain). International Film Week (October)

Surrounding area: Simancas – castle housing national archives (11 km). Wamba – Visigothic church (20 km). Fuensaldaña – castle houses regional parliament (8 km) Montealegre (21 km). Cabezón – monastery (21 km). Sardón de Duero – monastery (17 km). Peñafiel – very impressive castle (60 km).

Travel and transport: Travel crossroads. Airport (12 km): one flight a day to Paris and another to Barcelona, with occasional charter flights. Train and bus stations on southern edge of city with regular (eight trains) links to Madrid and other major towns and cities like Bilbao, Salamanca, Zaragoza and Segovia.

Major economic activities: Heavy industry, wine industry, food processing, textiles, engineering, commerce, forestry and agriculture.

Major employers: Renault, Telebar, KPMG Peat Marwick, TAFISA, Hoteles Tryp, Deloitte and Touche, Grupo Fimestic, Pisuerga Tinto de Valladolid, ACS Proyectos, Obras y Construcciones Software de

Base, Hermanos Domínguez, Arranz K-Tuin Sistemas Informáticas, Blockbuster Video, CETISA.

Sources of information

Tourist Office: C/ Santiago 21, 47001 Valladolid. Tel: 983 35 18 01
INEM: Plaza de Poniente 1, 47003 Valladolid Tel: 983 34 12 13
COIE: COIE de la Universidad de Valladolid, Avda Real de Burgos s/n, Casa del Estudiante, 47013 Valladolid. Tel: 983 42 30 00 Fax: 983 42 32 51
Town hall: Plaza Mayor 1, 47001 Valladolid. Tel: 983 42 61 00
Chamber of commerce: Cámara de Comercio e Industria de Valladolid, Avda de Ramón Pradera s/n, 47009 Valladolid. Tel: 983 37 04 00 Fax: 983 37 06 60 Email: camara.va@dvnet.es

3.46.2 **Universidad de Valladolid (UVA)**

Basic information

Autonomous community: Castilla y León
Province: Valladolid
Town: Valladolid
Status: Public (1292)
Address: Palacio de Santa Cruz, Plaza de Santa Cruz 8, 47002 Valladolid. Tel: 983 42 30 00 Fax: 983 42 32 34 Web site: www.uva.es
Main campus: Plaza de Santa Cruz
Satellite campuses: Palencia; Soria
Students: 47,000
Staff: N/K

Teaching centres

Faculties: Arts; economics and business; education; law; medicine; science
Higher technical schools: Architecture; industrial engineering; telecommunications
University schools: Agriculture; (+Soria); business; education (+Palencia +Soria); labour relations (Palencia +Soria); nursing (+Palencia +Soria); physiotherapy (Soria); polytechnic; social work; teacher training

Student services

Information office: Centro de Orientación e Información al Estudiante, (COIE) Casa del Estudiante, C/ Real de Burgos s/n, 47100 Valladolid. Tel: 983 42 30 00 exts 4064/4335 Fax: 983 42 30 76 Email: coie @cde.uva.es

Accommodation office: Servicio de Relaciones Internacionales, Plaza de Santa Cruz 8, 47100 Valladolid. Tel: 983 42 32 83; 42 37 19 Fax: 983 42 32 66 Email: relint.@uva.es

Health centre: See *COIE* or *Servicio de Relaciones Internacionales*

Spanish courses for foreign students: Cursos de Extranjeros, Facultad de Filosofia y Letras, 47002 Valladolid. Tel: 983 42 30 00 Fax: 983 42 32 34; 42 32 51

Courses in languages

For languages undergraduates: The Faculty of Arts offers degree courses in English, French, German and Hispanic philologies. The University College (*Colegio Universitario*) in Soria offers a degree course in translating and interpreting.

Spanish for foreign students: Cursos para Extranjeros offer courses in Spanish language and culture during July. Accommodation can be arranged with families in the city.

3.47 Vich (Vic)

3.47.1 **Ciudad de Vich**

Basic information

Location and status: Located in Province of Barcelona in north-eastern Spain, between Pyrenees and Mediterranean coast. 673 km from Madrid and 93 km from Barcelona.

Population: 30,000

Geography: Handsomely sited, small town situated on Vic plain. Lies on River Meder. It is an important commercial centre.

Climate: Continental climate with hot summers and warm winters.

History: First inhabited by Ausetanos, an ancient Iberian tribe, and was called *Ausa.* It was taken by the Romans in the second century and took the name *Vicus Ausonensis* (*Ausona*) in the fifth century. The cathedral was founded in 1040 and rebuilt in the eighteenth century. In 826, this and the rest of city were destroyed by Arab invaders who then rebuilt it in 885. A powerful, self-governing city and market centre in the Middle Ages, it aided Jaume I of Aragón in his conquest of Valencia (1235–38). The French, under General Joseph Souham, defeated the Spanish at Vic in 1810. The rail link to Barcelona was built in 1875.

Main historical sites: Cathedral of San Pedro (Sant Pere) (eighteenth century). Roman temple (second century). Town hall. Santa Creu hospital (fourteenth century). Gothic Plaza Mayor.

Town: Interesting historical architecture and pleasant location. Market town atmosphere.

Main areas of interest: Archaeological Museum. Market (Tuesdays and Saturdays, selling renowned local sausages and wide range of produce). Wall paintings of Josep María Sert (inside cathedral). Episcopal museum (Catalan paintings and Roman sculpture). Old part around Plaza Mayor.

Surrounding area: Embalse de Sau reservoir (14 km). Parador de Turismo de Vic (14 km). Montseny National Park. Santa Eugenia de Berga church (3 km). Monastery of Sant Pere de Casserres (19 km).

Travel and transport: Train station on Barcelona–Puigcerdà line. Regular bus and train services to Barcelona.

Major economic activities: Agriculture (including dairy and meat processing), textiles, tannery, timber and metallurgy.

Major employers: FCC, Fremap Grupo General de Aguas, Vall Companys, university.

Sources of information

Tourist Office: Plaza Mayor 1, 08500 Vic. Tel: 938 88 20 91 Fax: 938 8826 37 Email: alemanyvdm@ajvic.es

INEM: Ramón Sala i Saçala s/n, 08500 Vic. Tel: 938 89 27 67

Town hall: Plaza Mayor 1, 08500 Vic. Tel: 938 86 21 00 Fax: 938 86 29 21

Chamber of commerce: As for Barcelona.

3.47.2 **Universidad de Vich (UVIC)**

Basic information

Autonomous community: Cataluña (Catalunya)

Province: Barcelona

Town: Vich (Vic)

Status: Private (1997)

Address: Sagrada Familia 7, 08500 Vich, Barcelona. Tel: 938 86 12 22 Fax: 938 89 10 63 Email: info.@uvic.es Web site: www.uvic.es

Main campuses: Miramarges; Palau Bojons

Satellite campuses: N/A

Students: 2,209

Staff: N/K

Teaching centres

Faculties: Education; human sciences, translation and documentation; legal and economic sciences
Higher technical school: Higher polytechnic school
University school: Health sciences

Student services

Information office: Servei de Premsa, Sagrada Famila 7, 08500 Vich, Barcelona. Tel: 938 86 12 22 Fax: 938 89 10 63 Email: rosam.sanjaume@uvic.es
Accommodation office: Servei d'Estudiants, Sagrada Familia 7, 08500 Vich, Barcelona. Tel: 938 86 12 22 Fax: 938 89 10 63
Health centre: See *Servei d'Estudiants*
Spanish courses for foreign students: Oficina de Relacions Internacionals, Sagrada Familia 7, 08500 Vich, Barcelona. Tel: 938 81 61 69; 886 12 22 Fax: 938 89 10 63

Courses in languages

For languages undergraduates: The Faculty of Human Sciences, Translation and Documentation offers a diploma in translating and interpreting, librarianship and documentation, including the use of English and Spanish.
Languages for foreign students: As part of its Summer University (*Universidad de Verano*) programme, the university organises courses in the Catalan language for foreign students.

3.48 Vigo

3.48.1 **Ciudad de Vigo**

Basic information

Location and status: North-western Spain, 606 km from Madrid, in Province of Pontevedra.
Population: 290,500
Geography: Lies along south-eastern shore of Vigo inlet of Atlantic Ocean.
Climate: Warm summers and cool winters. Abundant rain.
History: Was attacked by English admiral Sir Francis Drake in 1585 and 1589. In 1702, a British–Dutch fleet under Sir George Rooke and James Butler, Duke of Ormonde, destroyed the Franco-Spanish fleet

in the bay. The writer Laurie Lee disembarked here before walking across the whole of Spain in the 1930s.

Main historical sites: Gothic church of Santiago. Medieval chapel of Casa de Caridad. Church of Santo Cristo de la Victoria (Neo-classical). Castro castle (seventeenth century).

Town: Port town with important shipyards and naval station. Spain's chief fishing port.

Main areas of interest: Cobbled streets around Calle Real. Seafront.

Surrounding area: Church of Coruxo. Inland is lush and green; several attractive estuaries (*rías*) are within easy reach.

Travel and transport: Frequent ferries. Bypass. Bus stations well south of town – regular regional services, as well as some national services. Decent local bus service. Air services to national destinations. In summer there are sometimes charter flights to UK. Airport is about 10 km east of town. Regular local and national train services.

Major economic activities: Fishing is important. Town's industry is well developed: manufactures leather, lumber, flour, paper, sugar, brandy and machinery.

Major employers: Avalón Informática, S.L., DIK MGI – Coutier, S.A., El Pozo Alimentación, S.A., Mutua Intercomarcal, Pascual Silve, S.A., Serra Group SAE, Artel Ingenieros, S.L., Fishing industry.

Sources of information

Tourist Office: Oficina de Turismo Las Avenidas s/n, 36201 Vigo. Tel: 986 43 05 77

INEM: Urzaiz 128A, 36205 Vigo Tel: 986 27 91 12

Town hall: Plaza do Rey s/n, 36202 Vigo, Pontevedra. Tel: 986 81 01 00

Chamber of commerce: Cámara de Comercio, Industria y Navegación de Vigo, Velázquez Moreno 22, 36202 Vigo. Tel: 986 43 25 33 Fax: 986 43 56 59 Email: ccinvigo@comerdata.es

3.48.2 **Universidad de Vigo (UVI)**

Basic information

Autonomous community: Galicia

Province: Pontevedra

Town: Vigo

Status: Public (1989)

Address: C/ Oporto 1, 36201 Vigo, Pontevedra. Tel: 986 81 36 36 Fax: 986 81 35 54 Email: webmaster@uvigo.es Web site: www.uvigo.es

Main campus: Oporto (Vigo)

Satellite campuses: Orense; Pontevedra
Students: 30,000
Staff: 1,200

Teaching centres

Faculties: Economics and business (+Orense); education (Pontevedra); fine art (Pontevedra); humanities (Orense); law (Orense); philology and translation; science (+Orense); social sciences (Pontevedra)
Higher technical schools: Computing engineering (Orense); industrial engineering and mining; telecommunications
University schools: Business; computing (Orense); forestry (Pontevedra); labour relations; nursing x 2 (+Ourense +Pontevedra); physiotherapy (Pontevedra); teacher training (+Ourense); technical industrial engineering

Student services

Information office: Servicio de Información, Orientación y Promoción do Estudiante (SIOPE), c/ Oporto 1, 36201 Vigo, Pontevedra. Tel: 986 81 37 55; 81 36 30 Fax: 986 81 35 54 Email: siope@sig.uvigo.es
Accommodation office: See *SIOPE*
Health centre: See *SIOPE*
Spanish courses for foreign students: N/A

Courses in languages

For languages undergraduates: The Faculty of Philology and Translating offers degree courses in English and Hispanic philologies, as well as a full degree course in translating and interpreting involving the same languages.
Spanish for foreign students: N/A

3.49 Vitoria (Gasteiz)

3.49.1 **Ciudad de Vitoria**

Basic information

Location and status: Capital not only of southern Basque province of Álava but of entire Basque Country (País Vasco/Euskadi). Located 351 km from Madrid, 65 km from Bilbao and 118 km from San Sebastián.
Population: 214,000

Geography: Lies just north of Montes de Vitoria on River Zadorra and south-west of San Sebastián. Crowns slight rise in the heart of the fertile plain.

Climate: Mixture of Atlantic and Mediterranean. Temperate with warm summers and mild winters and far less rainfall than coastal area.

History: Originally the old Basque village of Gasteiz, was formally founded as *Victoriacum* by the Visigothic king Leovigild to celebrate victory over the Basques in 581. It was granted a charter in 1181 by Sancho VI (El Sabio) of Navarre. In 1200 Alfonso VIII of Castile captured the city and incorporated it into his kingdom. Later, as the centre of a flourishing wool and iron trade, it became a prosperous town. It expanded in the eighteenth century. Vitoria Basin was the scene, in 1813, of a decisive battle of the Peninsular War, when Wellington defeated Bonaparte. There was a tremendous growth of industry in the twentieth century. The city was named the capital of Euskadi in 1979.

Main historical sites: Old quarter. Both new (twentieth century) and old (fourteenth century) cathedrals. Plaza de España. Church of San Miguel (and fourteenth-century stone image of *Virgen Blanca*). Church of San Pedro (Gothic). Church of San Vicente (fifteenth century). Escoriaza-Esquivel palace (sixteenth century). El Portalón (sixteenth-century trading house).

Town: Ancient part of town stands on hill centred around old cathedral (Santa María). New cathedral (María Inmaculada) is in the lower, more modern part of city. University students have made it one of northern Spain's 'in' cities and the old town is full of noisy bars and excellent restaurants.

Main areas of interest: Museo de Arqueología (archaeology). Museo de Bellas Artes (fine arts). Museo de Ciencias Naturales (natural sciences). Museo de Naipes (playing card museum). Museo de Armería (museum of armour and weapons). Fiestas of La Virgen Blanca in August (4–9). Jazz festival in July.

Surrounding area: Beautiful surrounding countryside. Santuario de Estíbaliz – Roman way (10 km). Basílica de San Prudencio (3 km). Mendoza – farming village with castle (15 km). Pantanos de Zadorra: large scenic reservoir. South of Vitoria – wine-growing region of Rioja Alavesa. Trespuentes bridge and Roman settlement of Oppidum de Iruña (25 km).

Travel and transport: Bus station is a two-minute walk from the old town. Six buses daily to Madrid. Regular services to Bilbao, Pamplona, Durango and Logroño. Train station quite central, with six trains a day to Madrid. Trains to other towns, including San Sebastián. By road, N-I highway linking Madrid to San Sebastián passes by Vitoria.

Major economic activities: Furniture, bicycles, agricultural machinery and playing cards.

Major employers: Iberfluid Instruments, Ibérica Aga, Ingeniería IDOM, Internacional Moragues, Acebes and Scade (Abogados and Management), SMC España, AAF Internacional.

Sources of information

Tourist Office: Parque de la Florida, 01001 Vitoria. Tel: 945 13 13 21

INEM: Pintor Clemente Arraiz 7 01008 Vitoria Tel: 945 22 60 62 *or* Jesús Apellániz 11, 01071 Vitoria. Tel: 945 22 74 00 Fax: 945 24 69 75

Town hall: Plaza Nueva, bajo, 01001 Vitoria. Tel. 945 16 13 30

Chamber of commerce: Cámara de Comercio e Industria, c/ Eduardo Dato 38, 01005 Vitoria. Tel: 945 14 18 00 Fax: 945 14 31 56 Email: general @cameradata.com

3.49.2 **Campus of Universidad del País Vasco (see** 3.8.3**)**

3.50 Zaragoza

3.50.1 **Ciudad de Zaragoza**

Basic information

Location and status: North-eastern Spain, 325 km from Madrid. Capital of Autonomous Community of Aragón and of Province of Zaragoza.

Population: 607,000

Geography: Lies on south bank of River Ebro. Urban development continues to spread on both sides of the river.

Climate: Basically continental, with hot, dry summers and cool winters. Little rain.

History: Toward the end of the first century BC, it was taken by the Romans who made it a colony under Emperor Augustus. The chief commercial and military station in the Ebro valley, it was one of the first towns in Spain to be christianised. The city was taken by the Moors *c.* 714. In 778 it was besieged by the Frankish King Charlemagne, who had to withdraw because of a Saxon rebellion in his domain. After being captured by Almoravids in 1110, the city was taken by King Alfonso I of Aragón in 1118 and thereafter enjoyed over three centuries of prosperity as the capital of Aragón. In the Peninsular War (1808–14) it was famed for heroism of its citizens under General José de Palafox during a protracted siege by the French, who finally took the city.

Main historical sites: Pilar Basilica. Aljafería (eleventh-century Arab palace/castle). La Lonja. Roman walls (second century). Cathedrals (fourteenth century Baroque): La Seo and El Salvador (latter Gothic with some traces of earlier Romanesque church built on site of first mosque in Spain). Palace of Counts of Luna (where Court of Justice sits). Palace of Condes de Sástago y Argillo.

Town: Seat of archbishop. City that looks to future but never turns its back on its glorious past. Bustling and modern with plenty of historic interest.

Main areas of interest: Whole of the historic centre, including Aljafería and cathedrals.

Surrounding area: Pedrola – palace and churches (49 km).

Travel and transport: Bus links with airport. Regular national flights and occasional international flights. Regular national bus service. Regular national train service.

Major economic activities: Industrial centre. Industries have expanded with supply of hydroelectric power from dams in Aragonese Pyrenees and of oil from pipeline from Rota (near Cádiz). Busy railway junction and trade centre for agricultural products of the surrounding fertile river basin.

Major employers: Bull, El Pozo Alimentación, S.A., Electroacústica, General Ibérica, S.A., Grupo Fimestic, Hispano Carracera, S.A., Nutreco España, S.A.

Sources of information

Tourist Office: Oficina de Turismo, Glorieta Pio XII s/n, 50003 Zarragoza. Tel: 976 39 35 37

INEM: Mariano Turmo 24, 50015 Zaragoza. Tel: 976 73 03 52

Town hall: Plaza del Pilar s/n, 50071 Zaragoza. Tel: 976 39 84 64

Chamber of commerce: Cámara de Comercio e Industria de Zaragoza, Isabel la Católica 2, 50009 Zaragoza. Tel: 976 55 22 98 Fax: 976 35 79 45 Email: ccizaragoza@camerdata.es

3.50.2 **Universidad de Zaragoza (UZA)**

Basic information

Autonomous community: Aragón
Province: Zaragoza
Town: Zaragoza
Status: Public (1474)
Address: Campus San Francisco, Pedro Cerbuna 12, 50009 Zaragoza. Tel: 976 76 10 00 Fax: 976 76 10 09 Email: agenda@posta.unizar.es Web site: www.unizar.es
Main campus: San Francisco
Satellite campuses: Huesca; Jaca; Teruel
Students: 45,197
Staff: 2,424

Teaching centres

Faculties: Arts; economics and business; geology; humanities and social sciences (Teruel); law; medicine; science; veterinary science
Higher technica school: Higher polytechnic centre
University schools: Business (Huesca); health sciences; nursing (Huesca +Teruel); polytechnic (+Huesca +Teruel); social studies (+Huesca); teacher training (+Huesca +Teruel)
Other centres: Institute of education (ICE); institute of modern languages; institute of materials sciences of Aragón; university college of Huesca+

Student services

Information office: Centro de Información Universitaria y Reclamaciones (CIUR), c/ Pedro Cerbuna 12, 50009 Zaragoza. Tel: 976 76 10 01/02 Fax: 976 76 10 03 Email: ciu@posta.unizar.es
Accommodation office: Servicio de Alojamiento, Edificio de Servicios, Domingo Miral 4, 50009 Zaragoza. Tel: 976 76 10 47 Fax: 976 76 20 50 OR see *CIUR*
Health centre: See *CIUR*
Spanish courses for foreign students: Servicio de Difusión de Lengua y Cultura para Extranjeros, Edificio Interfacultades, 3ª planta, Pedro Cerbuna 12, 50009 Zaragoza. Tel: 976 76 10 47 Fax: 976 76 20 50

Courses in languages

For languages undergraduates: The Arts Faculty offers traditional two-cycle degree courses in English and Spanish philologies. The *Instituto de Idiomas* also provides a university-wide range of courses at different levels in practical language studies in the main European languages plus Arabic, Modern Greek and Russian.

Spanish for foreign students: The *Servicio de Difusión de Lengua y Cultura Españolas para Extranjeros* offers intensive courses in Spanish language, with additional lectures on culture, as follows: (1) a four-month course from January to May; (2) a four-month course from September to December; (3) a full-year course from September to the end of June; (4) a 3-week course in September. Summer courses, lasting a fortnight or a month, are also available in Jaca.

Appendix I

Official university qualifications in Spain

Humanidades	**Humanities**
Primero y segundo ciclos	First and second cycles
Licenciado en bellas artes	BA in fine art
Licendiado en filología alemana	BA in German philology
Licenciado en filología catalana	BA in Catalan philology
Licenciado en filología clásica	BA in Classical philology
Licenciado en filología eslava	BA in Slavonic philology
Licenciado en filología francesa	BA in French philology
Licenciado en filología gallega	BA in Galician philology
Licenciado en filología hebrea	BA in Hebrew philology
Licenciado en filología hispánica	BA in Hispanic philology
Licenciado en filología inglesa	BA in English philology
Licenciado en filología italiana	BA in Italian philology
Licenciado en filología portuguesa	BA in Portuguese philology
Licenciado en filología románica	BA in Romance philology
Licenciado en filología vasca	BA in Basque philology
Licenciado en filosofía	BA in philosophy
Licenciado en geografía	BA in geography
Licenciado en historia	BA in history
Licenciado en historia del arte	BA in history of art
Licenciado en humanidades	BA in humanities
Licenciado en traducción e interpretación	BA in translating and interpreting
Sólo segundo ciclo	Only second cycle
Licendiado en antropología social y cultural	BA in social and cultural anthropology

Licenciado en historia y ciencias de la música	BA in history and music sciences
Licenciado en linguística	BA in linguistics

Ciencias sociales y juridicas / Social and legal sciences

Primero y segundo ciclos / First and second cycles

Licenciado en administración y dirección de empresas	BA in administration and management
Licenciado en ciencias de la actividad física y del deporte	BA in physical activity and sport sciences
Licenciado en ciencias políticas y de la administración	BA in political science and administration
Licenciado en comunicación audiovisual	BA in audiovisual communication
Licenciado en derecho	BA in law
Licenciado en economía	BA in economics
Licenciado en pedagogía	BA in pedagogy
Licenciado en periodismo	BA in journalism
Licenciado en psicología	BA in psychology
Licenciado en publicidad y relaciones públicas	BA in advertising and public relations
Licenciado en sociología	BA in sociology

Primer ciclo / First cycle

Diplomado en biblioteconomía y documentación	Diploma in librarianship and documentation
Diplomado en ciencias empresariales	Diploma in business studies
Diplomado en educación social	Diploma in social education
Diplomado en gestión y administración pública	Diploma in management and public administration
Diplomado en relaciones laborales	Diploma in labour relations
Diplomado en trabajo social	Diploma in social work
Diplomado en turismo	Diploma in tourism
Maestro–especialidad de audición y lenguaje	Teaching diploma with specialist qualification in hearing and language
Maestro–especialidad de educación especial	Teaching diploma with specialist qualification in special needs
Maestro–especialidad de educación infantil	Teaching diploma with specialist qualification in nursery education
Maestro–especialidad de educación musical	Teaching diploma with specialist qualification in music education

Maestro–especialidad de educación primaria	Teaching diploma with specialist qualification in primary education
Maestro–especialidad de lengua extranjera	Teaching diploma with specialist qualification in foreign language teaching

Sólo segundo ciclo / Only second cycle

Sólo segundo ciclo	Only second cycle
Licenciado en ciencias actuariales y financieras	BA in actuarial and financial studies
Licenciado en documentación	BA in documentation
Licenciado en investigación y técnicas de mercado	BA in research and market techniques
Licenciado en psicopedagogía	BA in psychopedagogy

Ciencas de la salud / Health sciences

Primero y segundo ciclos	First and second cycles
Licenciado en farmacia	B.Sc. in pharmacy
Licenciado en medicina	B.Sc. in medicine
Licenciado en odontología	B.Sc. in dentistry
Licenciado en veterinaria	B.Sc. in veterinary science

Primer ciclo	First cycle
Diplomado en enfermería	Diploma in nursing
Diplomado en fisioterapia	Diploma in physiotherapy
Diplomado en logopedía	Diploma in speech therapy
Diplomado en podología	Diploma in chiropody
Diplomado en terapia ocupacional	Diploma in occupational therapy

Ciencias experimentales / Experimental sciences

Primero y segundo ciclos	First and second cycles
Licenciado en biología	B.Sc. in biology
Licenciado en ciencias ambientales	B.Sc. in environmental sciences
Licenciado en ciencas del mar	B.Sc. in marine sciences
Licenciado en fisica	B.Sc. in physics
Licenciado en geología	B.Sc. in geology
Licenciado en matemáticas	B.Sc. in mathematics
Licenciado en química	B.Sc. in chemistry

Primer ciclo	First cycle
Diplomado en estadística	B.Sc. in statistics
Diplomado en optica y optometría	B.Sc. in optics and optometry

Sólo segundo ciclo	Only second cycle
Licenciado en bioquímica	B.Sc. in biochemistry
Licenciado en ciencia y tecnología de los alimentos	B.Sc. in food science and technology
Licenciado en ciencias y técnicas estadísticas	B.Sc. in statistical science and techniques
Licenciado en enología	B.Sc. in oenology

Enseñanzas tecnicas / Technical courses

Primero y segundo ciclos	First and second cycles
Arquitecto	Architect
Ingeniero aeronáutico	Aeronautical engineer
Ingeniero agrónomo	Agronomic engineer
Ingeniero de caminos, canales y puertos	Civil engineer
Ingeniero de minas	Mining engineer
Ingeniero de montes	Forestry engineer
Ingeniero de telecomunicación	Telecommunications engineer
Ingeniero en informática	Computing engineer
Ingeniero industrial	Industrial engineer
Ingeniero naval y oceánico	Naval and oceanic engineer
Ingeniero químico	Chemical engineer

Primer ciclo	First cycle
Arquitecto técnico	Technical architect
Diplomado en máquinas navales	Diploma in naval machines
Diplomado en navegación marítima	Diploma in maritime navigation
Diploma en radioelectrónica naval	Diploma in naval radio electronics
Ingeniero técnico aeronáutico*	Technical engineer in aeronautics
Ingeniero técnico agrícola**	Technical agricultural engineer
Ingeniero técnico en diseño industrial	Technical engineer in industrial design
Ingeniero técnico forestal***	Technical forestry engineer
Ingeniero técnico industrial****	Technical industrial engineer
Ingeniero técnico en informática de gestión	Technical engineer in management computing

Ingeniero técnico en informática de sistemas	Technical engineer in systems computing
Ingeniero técnico de minas†	Techical mining engineer
Ingeniero técnico naval††	Technical naval engineer
Ingeniero técnico de obras públicas†††	Technical public works engineer
Ingeniero técnico de telecomunicación††††	Technical telecommunications engineer
ingeniero técnico de topografía	Technical engineer in topography (surveying)

Sólo segundo ciclo	Only second cycle
Ingeniero de materiales	Materials engineer
Ingeniero de organización industrial	Engineer in industrial organisation
Ingeniero en automática y electrónica industrial	Engineer in industrial automation and electronics
Ingeniero en electrónica	Engineer in electronics
Ingeniero en geodesia y cartografía	Engineer in geodesy and cartography
Ingeniero en máquinas navales	Engineer in naval machines
Licenciado en náutica y transporte marítimo	B.Sc. in seamanship and maritime transport
Licenciado en radioelectrónica naval	B.Sc. in naval radio electronics

Key to specialist qualifications (*Especialidades*)

* Aeroengines; aeronavigation; aeroplanes; airports; aerospace equipment materials
** Agricultural operations; horticulture, fruit-growing and gardening; agrarian food industries; mechanisation and rural constructions
*** Forestry operations; forestry industries
**** Electricity; industrial electronics; mechanics; industrial chemistry; textiles
† Mine development; electromechanical mining installations; mineralogy and metallurgy; energy, fuel and explosive resources; mining surveying and prospecting
†† Marine structures; ship propulsion and services
††† Civil construction; hydrology; urban transport and services
†††† Electronic systems; telecommuncation systems; sound and image; telematics (data transmission)

Appendix II
Useful addresses

Addresses in UK

Berlitz UK Ltd. (language school), 9–13 Grosvenor Street, London, W1A 3BZ.
Tel: 020 7915 0909 Fax: 020) 7915 0222

Bilinguagroup (language school), 3rd Floor, 25 Maddox Street, London, W1R 9LE.
Tel: 020 7493 6446 Fax: 020 7493 0168
Email: info@bilinguagroup.com Web site: www.bilinguagroup.com

British Council (HQ in UK), 10 Spring Gardens, London, SW1A 2BN,
Tel: 020 7930 8466 Fax: 020 7839 6437
Web site: www.britishcouncil.org/

British Council, Information Centre, Bridgewater House, 58 Whitworth Street, Manchester, M1 6BB.
Tel: 0161 957 7755 Fax: 0161 957 7762

Central Bureau for International Education and Training (CBIET), 10 Spring Gardens, London, SW1A 2BN.
Tel: 020 7389 4004 Fax: 020 7389 4426
Email: centralbureau@britishcouncil.org
Web site: www.britishcouncil.org/cbiet/index/htn
or Edinburgh Tel: 0131 447 8024 Fax: 0131 452 8569
or Belfast Tel: 028 9024 8220 Fax: 028 9023 7592
or Cardiff Tel: 029 2039 7353 Fax: 029 2023 7494

Centre for Information on Language Teaching and Research (CILT), 20 Bedfordbury, London, WC2N 4LB.
Tel: 020 7379 5110 Fax: 020 7379 5082
Web site: www.cilt.org.uk/

Connect Youth International, British Council, 10 Spring Gardens, London, SW1A 2BN.
Tel: 020 7389 4030 Fax: 020 7389 4033
Email: connectyouth.enquiries@britishcouncil.org

Council on International Educational Exchange (CIEE), 52 Poland Street, London,W1V 4JQ.
Tel: 020 7478 2000 Fax: 020 7734 7322
Email: infouk@ciee.org
(see also under **Addresses in Spain**)

EL Gazette and EL Prospects, Dilke House, 1 Malet Street, Bloomsbury, London, WC1E 7AJ,
Tel: 020 7255 1969 Fax: 020 7255 1972
Web site: www.elgazette.com

Euro-London Appointments, Three King's Court, 150 Fleet Street, London, EC4A 2DQ.
Tel: 020 7583 0180 Fax: 020 7583 7800
Email: city@eurolondon.com Web site: www.eurolondon.com

European Commission in London, Jean Monnet House, 9 Storey's Gate, London, SW1P 3AT.
Tel: 020 7973 1992 Fax: 020 7973 1900
Web site: www.europe.eu.int

GAP Activity Projects, Gap House, 44 Queen's Road, Reading, Berkshire, RFG1 4BB
Tel: 01734 594 914 Fax: 01734 576 634
Web site: www.gap.org.uk

Hispanic and Luso-Brazilian Council, Canning House, 2 Belgrave Square, London, W1X 8PJ.
Tel: 020 7235 2303 Fax: 020 7235 3587
Email: hlbclibrary@binternet.com

In-Lingua School of Languages, 28 Rotton Park Road, Edgebaston, Birmingham, B16 9JI.
Tel: 0121 454 0204

Instituto Cervantes, 169 Woodhouse Lane, Leeds, LS2 3AR.
Tel: 0113 246 1741 Fax: 0113 246 1023
Email: icvig@leeds.ac.uk

Instituto Cervantes, 102 Eaton Square, London, SW1 9AN.
Tel: 020 7235 0353/9 Fax. 020 7235 0329
Email: iclondre@globalnet.co.uk Web site: www.cervantes.es/

Instituto Cervantes, 326–330 Deansgate, Campfield Avenue, Manchester, M3 4FN.
Tel: (0161 661 4200 Fax: 0161 661 4203
Email (courses): cenman@cervantes.es; (cultural events): cultman@cervantes.es

Intercambio Español (student exchanges), Verbatim Language Services, Clifton House, 6 Clifton Terrace, Southsea, Hampshire, PO5 3NL.
Tel: 01705 833 121

International Association for the Exchange of Students for Technical Experience (IAESTE), Central Bureau, 10 Spring Gardens, London, SW1A 2BN.
Tel: 020 7389 4774 Fax: 020 7389 4426

International House (language school), 106 Piccadilly, London, W1V 9FL.
Tel: 020 7491 2598
Web site: www.international-house-london.ac.uk

Linguarama (language school), Oceanic House, 89 High Street, Alton, Hampshire, GU34 1LG.
Tel: 01420 80899 Fax: 01420 80856
Email: personnel@linguarama.com Web site: www.linguarama.com

Merrow Employment Agency (language recuitment specialists), 3rd Floor, 23 Bentinck Street, London, W1M 5RL.
Tel: 020 7935 5050 Fax: 020 7935 5454
Email: recruit@merrow.co.uk Web site: www.merrow.co.uk

Multilingual Services Ltd., 56 Haymarket, London, SW1Y 4RN.
Tel: 020 7930 4880 Fax: 020 7839 6756
Email: info@multilingual.co.uk Web site: www.multilingual.co.uk

Overseas Jobs Express (OJE), Premier House, Shoreham Airport, Sussex, BN43 5FF.
Tel: 01273 440 220 Fax: 01273 440 229
Web site: www.overseasjobsexpress.co.uk

Publicitas Ltd. (to advertise in Spanish newspapers), 100 Rochester Row, London, SW1P 1JP.
Tel: 020 7630 9966

Recruitment and Employment Confederation (REC), 36–38 Mortimer Street, London, W1N 7RB.
Tel: 020 7462 3260
or Tel: 0800 320 588 (jobseekers' freephone) Fax: 020 7255 2878
Email: info@rec.uk.com Web site: www.rec.uk.com

Spanish Chamber of Commerce in Britain, 5 Cavendish Square, London, W1M 0DP.
Tel: 020 7637 9061 Fax: 020 7436 7188

Spanish Consulate, 63 North Castle Street, Edinburgh, EH2 3LJ.
Tel: 0131 220 1843 Fax: 0131 226 4568

Spanish Consulate, 20 Draycott Place, London, SW3 2SB.
Tel: 020 7589 8989 Fax: 020 7581 7888

Spanish Consulate, 1A Brook House, 70 Spring Gardens, Manchester, M2 2VQ.
Tel: 0161 236 1262 Fax: 0161 228 7468

Spanish Embassy (general enquiries), 39 Chesham Place, London, SW1X 8SB.
Tel: 020 7235 5555 Fax: 020 7259 5392
Email: embespuk@mail.rae.es

Spanish Embassy (Commercial Office), 66 Chiltern Street, London, W1.
Tel: 020 7486 0101 Fax: 020 487 5586
Web site: www.mcx.es/londres

Spanish Embassy (Labour Office), 20 Peel Street, London, W8 7PD.
Tel: 020 7221 0098 Fax: 020 7229 7270
Email: spanlabo@globanet.co.uk

Spanish Embassy (Education Office), 20 Peel Street, London, W8 7PD.
Tel: 020 7227 2462 Fax: 020 7229 4965
Email: conseduca.lon@dial.pipx.com

Spanish National Tourist Office, 22–23 Manchester Square, London, W1.
Tel: 020 7486 8027 Fax: 020 7486 8034

Task Force Pro Libra, 17–18 Britton Street, London, EC1M 5TL.
Tel: 020 7251 5522 Fax: 020 7251 8318
Email: central@tfpl.com

Trinity College Dublin, College Green, Dublin 2, Republic of Ireland.
Tel: 003531 677 2941 Fax: 003531 677 2694

UK Socrates and Erasmus Council (Student exchange programmes), R&D Building, The University, Canterbury, Kent, CT2 7PD.
Tel: 01227 762 712

University of Cambridge Local Examination Syndicate (UCLES), Syndicate Buildings, 1 Hills Road, Cambridge, CB1 2EU.
Tel: 01223 553 311 Fax: 01223 460 278

Voluntary Service Overseas (VSO), 317 Putney Bridge Road, London, SW15 2PN.
Tel: 020 8780 7200 Fax: 020 8780 7300
Web site: www.vso.org.uk

Addresses in Spain

British Chamber of Commerce, Plaza de Santa Bárbara 10–1A, 28004 Madrid.
Tel: 91 341 30 81 Fax: 91 341 46 05

British Consulate (Alicante), Plaza Calvo Sotelo 1/2–1, Apartado de Correos 564, 03001 Alicante.
Tel: 96 521 61 90, 521 60 22 Fax: 96 514 05 28

British Consulate-General (Barcelona), Edificio Torre de Barcelona, Avda Diagonal, 477 - 13, 08036 Barcelona.
Tel: 93 419 90 44 (eight lines) Fax: 93 405 24 11

British Consulate-General (Bilbao), Alameda de Urquijo 2–8, 48008 Bilbao.
Tel: 94 415 76 00, 415 77 11, 415 77 22 Fax: 94 416 76 32

British Consulate (Granada), Carmen de San Cristóbal, Ctra de Murcia s/n, 18010 Granada.
Tel: 958 27 47 24 Fax: 958 22 14 60

British Consulate (Las Palmas), Edificio Cataluña, c/ Luis Morote 6, 35007 Las Palmas
Tel: 928 26 25 08 Fax: 928 26 77 74

British Consulate-General (Madrid), Centro Colón Marqués de Ensenada 16–2, 28004 Madrid.
Tel: 91 308 52 01 Fax: 91 308 08 82

British Consulate (Málaga), Edificio Duquesa, C/ Duquesa de Parcent 8, 29001 Málaga.
Tel: 95 221 75 71 Fax: 95 222 11 30

British Consulate (Balearic Islands – Palma), Plaza Mayor 3D, 07002 Palma de Mallorca.
Tel: 971 71 24 45; 71 20 85; 71 60 48 Fax: 971 71 75 20

British Consulate (Santa Cruz de Tenerife), Plaza Weyler 8–10, 38003 Santa Cruz de Tenerife.
Tel: 922 28 68 63; 28 66 53 Fax: 922 28 99 03

British Consulate (Santander), Paseo de Pereda 27, 39004 Santander.
Tel: 942 22 00 00, Fax: 942 22 29 41

British Consulate (Sevilla), Plaza Nueva 8, 41001 Sevilla.
Tel: 95 422 88 75 Fax: 95 421 03 23

British Consulate (Vigo), Plaza de Compostela 23–6 (Apartado 49), 32601 Vigo.
Tel: 986 43 71 33 Fax: 986 43 71 33

British Council (Barcelona), Paseo de Gracia 11, 08007 Barcelona.
Tel: 93 317 32 20

British Council (Madrid), Plaza Santa Bárbara 10, 28010 Madrid.
Tel: 91 337 35 00

British Embassy, C/ Fernando el Santo 16, 28010 Madrid.
Tel: 91 319 02 00 Fax: 91 310 04 23
Web site: www.ukinspain.com

Consejo de Juventud (advice for students), Ministerio de Educación, Cultura y Deporte (MEC), c/ Monte Esquinza, 42, 28019 Madrid.
Tel: 91 419 77 89

Council on International Educational Exchange (CIEE), c/ Sagasta 4–2 dcha, 28004 Madrid.
Tel: 91 532 23 10 Fax: 91 532 94 15
Email: infospain@ciee.org
(see also under **Addresses in UK**)

English Educational Services (recruitment agency), c/ Alcalá 20–2, 28014 Madrid.
Tel: 91 532 97 34; 532 47 83 Fax: 91 531 52 98

Escuela Oficial de Idiomas, c/ Jesús Maestro s/n, Madrid.
Tel: 91 533 58 05

Instituto Nacional de Empleo (INEM), Condesa de Venadito 9, 28027 Madrid.
Tel: 91 585 98 88
Web site: www.inem.es

Instituto Nacional de la Salud (INSALUD), c/ Alcalá 56, 28014 Madrid.
Tel: 91 338 00 00

Instituto Nacional de la Seguridad Social (INSS), Padre Damián 4, 28071 Madrid.
Tel: 91 564 90 35
Web site: www.seg-social.es

International House (language school), c/ Zurbano 8, Madrid.
Tel: 91 310 13 14

Ministerio de Asuntos Exteriores, Plaza de la Provincia 1, 28012 Madrid.
Tel: 91 379 97 00

Ministerio de Educación, Cultura y Deporte (MEC), Subdirección General de Títulos, Convalidaciones, y Homologaciones, Paseo del Prado 28, 28071 Madrid.
Tel: 91 420 16 93

Ministerio de Educación, Cultura y Deporte (MEC), Servicio de Información General, C/ Alcalá, 36, 28071 Madrid.
Tel: 91 701 80 00

Ministerio de Trabajo y Asuntos Sociales, Bretón de los Herreros 41, 28003 Madrid.
Tel: 91 441 15 00 Fax: 91 399 25 44

Red Española de Albergues Juveniles (youth hostels), José Ortega y Gasset 71, 28006 Madrid.
Tel: 91 347 77 00 Fax: 91 401 81 60

Relaciones Culturales Internacionales, c/ Ferraz 82, 28008 Madrid.
Tel: 91 542 71 03 Fax: 91 559 11 81

Servicio Central de Cursos Español, c/ Trafalgar 32–I°D, 28010 Madrid.
Tel: 91 593 19 49

Turismo e Intercambio de Jóvenes y Estudiantes (TIVE), c/ José Ortega y Gasset 71, 28006 Madrid.
Tel: 91 347 7700 Fax: 91 402 2194

Addresses in France

Coordinating Committee for International Voluntary Service (CCIVS), Resource Centre, UNESCO House, 1 Rue Miollis, Paris 75732.
Tel: 00 33 1 4568 4936 Fax: 00 33 1 4273 0521
Email: ccivs@unescvo.org

Appendix III
Sample forms

On the following pages are samples of forms which you may well have to fill in at some time during your stay in Spain:

(a) *Solicitud de preinscripción para iniciar estudios en los primeros ciclos en todos los centros de las universidades andaluzas*
This is a typical application form which Spanish students must complete as a first step towards gaining a place at university. While this form applies specifically to the universities of the autonomous community of Andalucía, it is typical of forms used throughout Spain. You should note, however, that this form will only apply to you if you are transferring from the UK to Spain to become a full-time student in that country. It can be obtained from the information office of any university within the autonomous community in which you wish to study. Once accepted by a university, at the beginning of the academic session you should attend the registration session for your faculty and fill in an appropriate enrolment form (*solicitud de matrícula*).

(b) *Solicitud de matrícula: alumnos Erasmus/Socrates*
This form is used by the Universidad de Málaga for students from other EU countries intending to follow a full-time course of studies at that university as part of their home university degree or diploma programme. Other universities provide similar forms for European students, as well as students from other countries. This form is filled in at registration at the start of the academic session, in the same way as similar forms for Spanish students. The form can only be filled in once you have been accepted for the course concerned and you should provide appropriate documentation (e.g. letter from your placement tutor) to prove that this is so.

(c) *Contrato de arrendamiento de fincas urbanas*
This form is a rent contract form which you should insist on filling in if you intend to rent a flat or house while you are living in Spain. It is available (cost approximately 2000 pesetas) from most *estancos* (tobacconists). The

first side, *Ejemplar para el arrendatario* (copy for the tenant), is obviously the form which you must fill in, while the *Ejemplar para el arrendador* (copy for the landlord/landlady) is self-explanatory. You must make sure that both parts of the form are filled in and that you are given a copy of both. Clearly, you should read the small print carefully before you put your signature to this very important document.

(d) *Curriculum vitae (CV) in Spanish*

If you are looking for full- or part-time employment in Spain, it is essential that before you go you should prepare a CV in Spanish. You should take several copies with you and make sure that they are of good quality. Although the format of CVs in Spain varies quite significantly, the version shown below contains most of the elements that are normally used in a standard one. Naturally it is vitally important that the document is completed on a word-processor and that due attention is paid to the quality of its presentation. To guide you in the preparation of your Spanish CV, a key to the essential vocabulary is included after the model in Spanish.

If applicable, you are also advised to take with you to Spain references from former employers. In addition, you should take copies of any degree, diploma or other certificates which you may have been awarded – plus the originals, which some employers may insist on seeing.

(a) Solicitud de preinscripción (page 1)

SOLICITUD DE PREINSCRIPCIÓN PARA INICIAR ESTUDIOS EN LOS PRIMEROS CICLOS EN TODOS LOS CENTROS DE LAS UNIVERSIDADES ANDALUZAS

ATENCIÓN: No escriba en los cuadros marcados en rojo (están reservados a la Universidad)

A) DATOS PERSONALES DEL SOLICITANTE DNI / Pasaporte : ☐

D.N.I. O PASAPORTE Nº ______ LETRA NIF: ______ SEXO (Hombre / Mujer):: ______
(Adjuntar Fotocopia del DNI o Pasaporte)
PRIMER APELLIDO: ______ SEGUNDO APELLIDO: ______
NOMBRE: ______ TELEFONO: (______) / ______
DOMICILIO, CALLE: ______ NÚMERO: ______
LOCALIDAD: ______ CÓDIGO POSTAL: ______

NACIONALIDAD : ☐ ESPAÑOLA O DE OTRO ESTADO DE LA UNIÓN EUROPEA
☐ DE ESTADOS NO MIEMBROS DE LA UNIÓN EUROPEA.
Si vd. es natural del Reino de Marruecos y desea acogerse al convenio de Cooperación Cultural de fecha 14 /10/1980, existente con su país, (B.O.E. nº 243 de 10/10/85; Art. IV), marque además una 'X' en el siguiente casillero: ☐ (en este caso vd. participará en las mismas condicionesque los españoles u otros de estados miembros de la U. E.)

☐ TENGO RECONOCIDO UN GRADO DE MINUSVALÍA IGUAL O SUPERIOR AL 65%; MENOSCABO TOTAL DEL HABLA; O PERDIDA TOTAL DE LA AUDICIÓN
(Adjuntar certificado expedido por la Delegación Provincial de Asuntos Sociales de la Junta de Andalucía u organismo competente en otras comunidades autónomas)

☐ TENGO RECONOCIDA LA CONDICIÓN DE DEPORTISTA DE ALTO NIVEL POR EL CONSEJO SUPERIOR DE DEPORTES
(Adjuntar certificado acreditativo expedido por el Consejo Superior de Deportes)

B) DATOS PREVIOS PARA LA CONSIDERACIÓN DE LA SOLICITUD
Marque con una 'X' el apartado correspondiente a la vía de acceso que cumple el solicitante y por la que efectua la preinscripción

11 ☐ HE SUPERADO LAS PRUEBAS DE ACCESO EN UNA UNIVERSIDAD ANDALUZA Y NO ESTOY EN POSESIÓN DE UN TÍTULO UNIVERSITARIO.

12 ☐ HE SUPERADO LAS PRUEBAS DE ACCESO EN LA U.N.E.D. Y RESIDO EN ANDALUCÍA, EN CEUTA O EN MELILLA Y NO ESTOY EN POSESIÓN DE UN TÍTULO UNIVERSITARIO.
(Adjuntar certificado de estar empadronado en Andalucía, en Ceuta o en Melilla, con anterioridad al 1 de enero de 1997)

21 ☐ HE SUPERADO EL CURSO DE ORIENTACIÓN UNIVERSITARIA (C.O.U.), CON ANTERIORIDAD AL CURSO ACADÉMICO 1974/75; O EL CURSO PREUNIVERSITARIO Y LAS PRUEBAS DE MADUREZ; O EL BACHILLERATO DE PLANES ANTERIORES A 1953; EN UN CENTRO UBICADO EN ANDALUCÍA, EN CEUTA O EN MELILLA Y NO ESTOY EN POSESIÓN DE UN TÍTULO UNIVERSITARIO.

31 ☐ HE SUPERADO LA FORMACIÓN PROFESIONAL DE SEGUNDO GRADO O MÓDULO PROFESIONAL DE NIVEL III, EN UN CENTRO UBICADO EN ANDALUCÍA, EN CEUTA O EN MELILLA Y NO ESTOY EN POSESIÓN DE UN TÍTULO UNIVERSITARIO.

32 ☐ HE SUPERADO UN CICLO FORMATIVO DE FORMACIÓN PROFESIONAL ESPECÍFICA DE GRADO SUPERIOR, EN UN CENTRO UBICADO EN ANDALUCÍA, EN CEUTA O EN MELILLA Y NO ESTOY EN POSESIÓN DE UN TÍTULO UNIVERSITARIO.

41 ☐ ESTOY EN POSESIÓN DE UN TÍTULO UNIVERSITARIO O EQUIVALENTE, QUE HABILITA PARA EL ACCESO A LA UNIVERSIDAD, OBTENIDO EN UN CENTRO UBICADO EN ANDALUCÍA, EN CEUTA O EN MELILLA.

51 ☐ HE SUPERADO LAS PRUEBAS DE ACCESO EN LA U.N.E.D. Y RESIDO EN EL EXTRANJERO.
(Adjuntar certificado de residencia en el extrajero, así como certificación expedida por la U.N.E.D. en el que se haga constar que la universidad elegida como primera opción es una de las ubicadas en Andalucía)

71 ☐ NO REUNO LOS REQUISITOS ANTERIORES, PERO SI LOS ACADÉMICOS EXIGIDOS EN LA PRESENTE CONVOCATORIA Y RESIDO O HE TENIDO QUE TRASLADAR MI RESIDENCIA A UNA LOCALIDAD DE ANDALUCÍA, CEUTA O MELILLA.
(Adjuntar los certificados del cambio de residencia según normativa de Distrito Único Andaluz -ver dorso del Mapa de Titulaciones que se acompaña-)

81 ☐ NO CUMPLO NINGUNO DE LOS APARTADOS ANTERIORES PERO REUNO LOS REQUISITOS ACADÉMICOS EXIGIDOS EN LA PRESENTE CONVOCATORIA Y NINGUNA DE LAS TITULACIONES QUE SOLICITO SE IMPARTEN EN LA UNIVERSIDAD (O CONJUNTO DE UNIVERSIDADES) EN LA QUE ME CORRESPONDE CURSAR ESTUDIOS.
(Adjuntar certificado expedido por la correspondiente universidad, en el que conste de forma expresa que ninguna de las titulaciones solicitadas se imparten en la misma o en otra universidad que pueda constituir, junto con ella, un 'distrito único')

91 ☐ NO HE SEÑALADO NINGUNO DE LOS APARTADOS ANTERIORES Y REUNO LOS REQUISITOS ACADÉMICOS PARA ACCEDER A LA UNIVERSIDAD.
(En este caso, su solicitud únicamente será considerada en el supuesto que queden plazas vacantes una vez finalizada la adjudicación de las mismas entre todos los solicitantes -fase de junio y septiembre- que cumplan, al menos, uno de los apartados anteriores)

LEA CON ATENCIÓN LOS SIGUIENTES EPÍGRAFES Y RELLENE EL QUE LE CORRESPONDA

A) SI VD. SEÑALÓ LOS APARTADOS 11 ó 41	indique en qué Universidad Andaluza:	______	(universidad)
B) SI VD. SEÑALÓ EL APARTADO 51	indique la Universidad Andaluza elegida:	______	(universidad)
C) SI VD. SEÑALÓ LOS APARTADOS 12, 71, 81, ó 91	indique la Provincia de Residencia:	______	(provincia)
D) SI VD. SEÑALÓ LOS APARTADOS 21, 31 ó 32	indique la Provincia del Centro:	______	(provincia)

C) A RELLENAR POR LA UNIVERSIDAD

Identificación: ______ / ____ / ______ Fecha de Entrada: ____ / ____ / ____

Codificación: ☐☐-☐☐-☐☐-(☐☐-☐☐-☐☐)
Opción Universidad Provincia

DECLARO **bajo mi responsabilidad** que todos los datos consignados son ciertos y que ésta es la ÚNICA SOLICITUD presentada para iniciar estudios en la Universidades Andaluzas.

FIRMA DEL SOLICITANTE

EXCMO. Y MGFCO. SR. RECTOR DE LA UNIVERSIDAD DE: ______
(Universidad de Entrega)

FECHA : ____ / ____ / ____

(a) Solicitud de preinscripción (page 2)

D) DATOS ACADÉMICOS DEL SOLICITANTE

Marque con una 'X' el apartado correspondiente a la situación académica por la que efectúa la preinscripción, y cumplimente el resto de datos demandados

1 HE SUPERADO LAS PRUEBAS DE ACCESO Y NO ESTOY EN POSESIÓN DE UN TÍTULO UNIVERSITARIO.
(Adjuntar fotocopia y original, para su cotejo, de la tarjeta de Selectividad)
Señale y rellene uno sólo de los 4 apartados siguientes, según le corresponda (ver las opciones en el Mapa de Titulaciones):

1.1 ☐ HABIENDO CURSADO EL COU EN EL CURSO 88/89 O POSTERIOR — Indicar la/s opción/es entre (A,B,C,D) ☐☐ ☐☐

1.2 ☐ HABIENDO CURSADO EL COU CON ANTERIORIDAD AL CURSO 88/89 — Elegir una opción entre (A,B,C,D) ☐ ☐

1.3 ☐ HABIENDO CURSADO EL BACHILLERATO R.E.M. — Indicar la modalidad entre (1,2,3,4,5,6) ☐ ☐

1.4 ☐ HABIENDO CURSADO EL BACHILLERATO L.O.G.S.E. — Indicar la/s opción/es entre (A,B,C,D,E) ☐☐ ☐☐

2 ☐ HE SUPERADO EL C.O.U. CON ANTERIORIDAD AL CURSO ACADÉMICO 1974/75; O EL CURSO PREUNIVERSITARIO Y LAS PRUEBAS DE MADUREZ; O EL BACHILLERATO POR UN PLAN ANTERIOR AL DE 1953; Y NO ESTOY EN POSESIÓN DE UN TÍTULO UNIVERSITARIO. — Elegir una opción entre (A,B,C,D) ☐ ☐
(Adjuntar fotocopia y original, para su cotejo, de las correspondientes páginas del libro de calificación escolar)

3 ☐ HE SUPERADO LA FORMACIÓN PROFESIONAL DE SEGUNDO GRADO O MÓDULO PROFESIONAL DE NIVEL III Y NO ESTOY EN POSESIÓN DE UN TÍTULO UNIVERSITARIO.
Indicar la Rama de F.P. 2º grado entre (A,B,C,D,E,F,G,H,I,J,K,L,M,N,O,P,Q,R,S,T,V,Y) ☐ ☐
(Adjuntar original y fotocopia, para su cotejo, de Certificación Académica Oficial con la nota media final y nota media de desempate, en que se haga constar que ha sido expedida conforme a la Resolución de 25/04/96 de la Dirección General de Investigación Científica y Enseñanza Superior, así como adjuntar original y fotocopia, para su cotejo, de Certificación del Expediente Académico)
(Adjuntar original y fotocopia, para su cotejo, del título obtenido o del resguardo de haber abonado los derechos de expedición)

4 ☐ HE SUPERADO UN CICLO FORMATIVO DE FORMACIÓN PROFESIONAL ESPECÍFICA DE GRADO SUPERIOR Y NO ESTOY EN POSESIÓN DE UN TÍTULO UNIVERSITARIO.
Indicar el código entre los que figuran en el 'CUADRO DE CICLOS FORMATIVOS' ☐☐ ☐☐
(Adjuntar original y fotocopia, para su cotejo, del título obtenido o del resguardo de haber abonado los derechos de expedición)

5 ☐ ESTOY EN POSESIÓN DE UN TÍTULO QUE HABILITA PARA EL ACCESO A LA UNIVERSIDAD.
(Adjuntar original y fotocopia, para su cotejo, del título obtenido o del resguardo de haber abonado los derechos de expedición)

SI VD. SEÑALÓ LOS APARTADOS 1.1, 1.2, 1.3, 1.4, 3 ó 4 ____________ ☐☐'☐☐
(Indique la calificación de acceso) ☐☐'☐☐ ☐☐'☐☐ ☐☐'☐☐

INDIQUE LA CONVOCATORIA EN QUE FINALIZÓ LOS ESTUDIOS QUE LE HABILITA EL ACCESO (F=Febrero/J=Junio/S=Septiembre) ☐/☐☐
(F/J/S) AÑO

D) A CUMPLIMENTAR OBLIGATORIAMENTE POR QUIENES ESTÉN O HAYAN ESTADO MATRICULADOS EN UNA UNIVERSIDAD ANDALUZA Y NO SON TITULADOS UNIVERSITARIOS

¿DESEA SIMULTANEAR LOS ESTUDIOS UNIVERSITARIOS QUE AÚN NO HA FINALIZADO CON LOS QUE AHORA SOLICITA? ____________ ☐ (S/N)
(Lea atentamente las instrucciones sobre 'Simultaneidad de Estudios' que figuran en el dorso del Mapa de Titulaciones)

ÚLTIMOS ESTUDIOS MATRICULADOS: Código |_|_|_|_|_|_| ¿Superó alguna asignatura? ☐ (S/N) ¿Agotó las convocatorias de alguna asignatura? ☐ (S/N)
(Escoger el código que más se aproxime en el Mapa de Titulaciones)

PENÚLTIMOS ESTUDIOS MATRICULADOS: Código |_|_|_|_|_|_| ¿Superó alguna asignatura? ☐ (S/N) ¿Agotó las convocatorias de alguna asignatura? ☐ (S/N)
(Es coger el código que más se aproxime en el Mapa de Titulaciones)

RELACIÓN DE ESTUDIOS POR ORDEN DE PREFERENCIA

Escoger los códigos (6 cifras) de la 'Relación de Titulaciones por Centros que se imparten en las Universidades Andaluzas' (Mapa de Titulaciones)

1		16		31		46		61		76		91	
2		17		32		47		62		77		92	
3		18		33		48		63		78		93	
4		19		34		49		64		79		94	
5		20		35		50		65		80		95	
6		21		36		51		66		81		96	
7		22		37		52		67		82		97	
8		23		38		53		68		83		98	
9		24		39		54		69		84		99	
10		25		40		55		70		85		100	
11		26		41		56		71		86		101	
12		27		42		57		72		87		102	
13		28		43		58		73		88		103	
14		29		44		59		74		89		104	
15		30		45		60		75		90		105	

RELLENE CON CUIDADO EL ORDEN DE PREFERENCIA DE LOS ESTUDIOS, YA QUE SERÁ VINCULANTE DURANTE TODO EL PROCESO DE PREINSCRIPCIÓN. NO SE ATENDERÁN LAS RECLAMACIONES DE CAMBIO DE ORDEN, SUPRESIÓN O AMPLIACIÓN DE ESTUDIOS.

(b) Solicitud de matrícula: alumnos Erasmus (Socrates)

SOLICITUD DE MATRICULA ALUMNOS ERASMUS

D./Dª ....con D.N.I. nº ....

y domicilio para notificaciones en C/ ....

.... Provincia .... C.P. ....

Teléfono ....

Se matricula como alumno/a Erasmus para el curso académico 00/01, de las siguientes asignaturas:

Código	Asignatura	Titulación	Turno(1)
....	....	....	....
....	....	....	....
....	....	....	....
....	....	....	....
....	....	....	....
....	....	....	....
....	....	....	....
....	....	....	....
....	....	....	....
....	....	....	....
....	....	....	....
....	....	....	....
....	....	....	....
....	....	....	....
....	....	....	....

Málaga, ... de ....de 200 ....

Firma del/la interesado/a

(1) En el caso de titulación con doble turno especificar el elegido: Mañana (M) o Tarde (T)

(2) No podrá formalizar matrícula en asignaturas que tengan limitado el número de plazas para alumnos de nuevo ingreso

(c) Contrato de arrendamiento (Ejemplar para el arrendador)

CONTRATO DE ARRENDAMIENTO
DE FINCAS URBANAS

CLASE 2ª 0003801 **EJEMPLAR PARA EL ARRENDADOR**

IDENTIFICACIÓN DE LA FINCA OBJETO DEL CONTRATO

(1) ....

Vía pública (2) ....

Localidad .... *C.P.* ....

Provincia ....

Comunidad Autónoma ....

Referencia catastral ....

Inscrita en el Registro de la Propiedad núm. ....

de ...., *al tomo* ...., *libro* ....,

folio ...., *finca núm.* ...., *inscripción* ....

IDENTIFICACIÓN DE LOS CONTRATANTES

Arrendador:

D./D.ª ...., *natural de* ....

.........., *provincia de* ....,

de .... *años, de estado civil* ...., *y*

profesión ...., *vecino en la actualidad de* .... *con D.N.I.* ....

como (3) ....

actuando en su propio nombre y derecho, o en su representación:

D./D.ª ....

con D.N.I. ...., *en virtud de* (4) ....

Arrendatario:

D./D.ª ...., *natural de* ....

.........., *provincia de* ....,

de .... *años, de estado civil* ...., *y*

profesión ...., *vecino en la actualidad de* .... *con D.N.I.* ....

actuando en su propio nombre y derecho, o en su representación:

D./D.ª ....

con D.N.I. ...., *en virtud de* (4) ....

Impuesto sobre Transmisiones Patrimoniales y Actos Jurídicos Documentados.

Título primero.—*Transmisiones Patrimoniales.*

Real Decreto Legislativo 1/1993, de 24 de septiembre (*B.O.E.* de 20 de octubre).

Artículo 12.

1.—Podrá satisfacerse la deuda tributaria mediante la utilización de efectos timbrados, según la siguiente escala:

	Pesetas
Hasta 5.000,00 pesetas	15
De 5.000,01 a 10.000 pesetas	30
De 10.000,01 a 20.000 pesetas	65
De 20.000,01 a 40.000 pesetas	130
De 40.000,01 a 80.000 pesetas	280
De 80.000,01 a 160.000 pesetas	560
De 160.000,01 a 320.000 pesetas	1.200
De 320.000,01 a 640.000 pesetas	2.400
De 640.000,01 a 1.280.000 pesetas	5.120

De 1.280.000 en adelante, 4 pesetas por cada 1.000 o fracción.

*Artículo 10.2.*e).

En los arrendamientos servirá de base la cantidad total que haya de satisfacerse por todo el período de duración del contrato; cuando no constase aquél se girará la liquidación computándose seis años, sin perjuicio de las liquidaciones adicionales que deban practicarse, caso de continuar vigente después del expresado período temporal; en los contratos de arrendamiento de fincas urbanas sujetas a prórroga forzosa se computará, mínimo, un plazo de tres años.

F.N.M.T.

Reunidos los comparecientes anteriormente indicados, contratamos el arrendamiento del inmueble urbano que ha sido identificado encabezando este contrato, por tiempo de (5) .... *y precio de* (6) .... *cada año, pagaderas por* .... *con las demás condiciones que se consignarán al dorso.*

Formalizado así este contrato y para que conste, lo firmamos por duplicado en .... *a* (7) ....

de .... *de* ....

EL ARRENDADOR, *EL ARRENDATARIO,*

(1) *Identificación del inmueble arrendado: vivienda, garaje, local de negocio, ...*
(2) *Consígnese el nombre, número de la vía, el piso, letra o puerta.*
(3) *Expresar el carácter con el que interviene el titular: propietario, usufructuario, ...*
(4) *Consígnese si se actúa en virtud de poder, representación verbal, etc.*
(5) *Determinar el plazo del arrendamiento, indicando si es por meses o por años.*
(6) *Indíquese importe y moneda empleada: pesetas, euros u otra.*
(7) *Consígnese la fecha en letra.*

NOTA: Este documento ha sido diseñado en sextos de pulgada a efectos de posibilitar su tratamiento informático.

(c) Contrato de arrendamiento (Ejemplar para el arrendatario)

CONTRATO DE ARRENDAMIENTO
DE FINCAS URBANAS

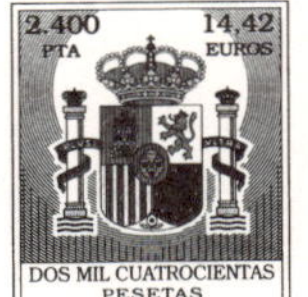

CLASE 2ª

0003801

EJEMPLAR PARA EL ARRENDATARIO

IDENTIFICACIÓN DE LA FINCA OBJETO DEL CONTRATO

(1) ....

Vía pública (2) ....

Localidad .... *C.P.* ....

Provincia ....

Comunidad Autónoma ....

Referencia catastral ....

Inscrita en el Registro de la Propiedad núm. ....

de ...., *al tomo* ...., *libro* ....,

folio ...., *finca núm.* ...., *inscripción* ....

IDENTIFICACIÓN DE LOS CONTRATANTES

Arrendador:

D./D.ª ...., *natural de* ....

.........., *provincia de* ....,

de .... *años, de estado civil* ...., *y*

profesión ...., *vecino en la actualidad de* .... *con D.N.I.* ....

como (3) ....

actuando en su propio nombre y derecho, o en su representación:

D./D.ª ....

con D.N.I. ...., *en virtud de* (4) ....

Arrendatario:

D./D.ª ...., *natural de* ....

.........., *provincia de* ....,

de .... *años, de estado civil* ...., *y*

profesión ...., *vecino en la actualidad de* .... *con D.N.I.* ....

actuando en su propio nombre y derecho, o en su representación:

D./D.ª ....

con D.N.I. ...., *en virtud de* (4) ....

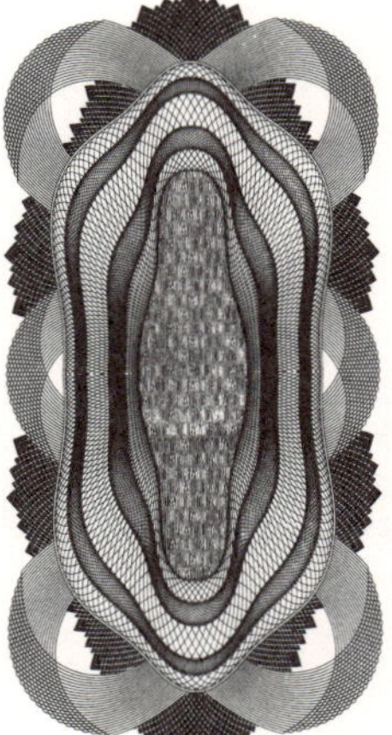

Impuesto sobre Transmisiones Patrimoniales y Actos Jurídicos Documentados.

Título primero.—*Transmisiones Patrimoniales.*

Real Decreto Legislativo 1/1993, de 24 de septiembre (*B.O.E.* de 20 de octubre).

Artículo 12.

1.—Podrá satisfacerse la deuda tributaria mediante la utilización de efectos timbrados, según la siguiente escala:

	Pesetas
Hasta 5.000,00 pesetas	15
De 5.000,01 a 10.000 pesetas	30
De 10.000,01 a 20.000 pesetas	65
De 20.000,01 a 40.000 pesetas	130
De 40.000,01 a 80.000 pesetas	280
De 80.000,01 a 160.000 pesetas	560
De 160.000,01 a 320.000 pesetas	1.200
De 320.000,01 a 640.000 pesetas	2.400
De 640.000,01 a 1.280.000 pesetas	5.120

De 1.280.000 en adelante, 4 pesetas por cada 1.000 o fracción.

Artículo 10.2.e).

En los arrendamientos servirá de base la cantidad total que haya de satisfacerse por todo el período de duración del contrato; cuando no constase aquél se girará la liquidación computándose seis años, sin perjuicio de las liquidaciones adicionales que deban practicarse, caso de continuar vigente después del expresado período temporal; en los contratos de arrendamiento de fincas urbanas sujetas a prórroga forzosa se computará, mínimo, un plazo de tres años.

Reunidos los comparecientes anteriormente indicados, contratamos el arrendamiento del inmueble urbano que ha sido identificado encabezando este contrato, por tiempo de (5) .... *y precio de* (6) .... *cada año, pagaderas por* .... *con las demás condiciones que se consignarán al dorso.*

Formalizado así este contrato y para que conste, lo firmamos por duplicado en .... *a* (7) .... *de* .... *de* ....

EL ARRENDADOR, *EL ARRENDATARIO,*

(1) *Identificación del inmueble arrendado: vivienda, garaje, local de negocio, ...*
(2) *Consígnese el nombre, número de la vía, el piso, letra o puerta.*
(3) *Expresar el carácter con el que interviene el titular: propietario, usufructuario, ...*
(4) *Consígnese si se actúa en virtud de poder, representación verbal, etc.*
(5) *Determinar el plazo del arrendamiento, indicando si es por meses o por años.*
(6) *Indíquese importe y moneda empleada: pesetas, euros u otra.*
(7) *Consígnese la fecha en letra.*

NOTA: Este documento ha sido diseñado en sextos de pulgada a efectos de posibilitar su tratamiento informático.

(d) Curriculum Vitae (CV)

A Datos Personales

Nombres y Apellidos: María Dolores Crespo Escudo
Fecha de Nacimiento: 27 de Julio de 1.973
Lugar de Nacimiento: Aranda de Duero (Burgos)
Estado Civil: Soltera
Domicilio Actual: C/ Naranjos, 25 2°C, 09001 Burgos
Teléfono: 947 64 46 77
Fax: 947 64 46 78
Email: mdcreso@maptel.es

B Datos Académicos

1991–1996: Licenciatura en Ciencias Empresariales (especialidad en Marketing) por la Universidad Autónoma de Madrid
1995 (Febrero–Julio): Universidad de Leeds, Inglaterra, Intercambio Socrates
1987–1991: BUP/COU, Instituto El Cid Campeador, Burgos

C Experiencia Profesional

Desde Marzo 2000: Directora de Ventas, *Juguetes para Hoy,* Miranda de Ebro (Burgos)
Enero 1997–Marzo 2000: Encargada de Administración, *Ropa Deportiva Castellana,* Burgos
Octubre 1996–Enero 1997: Adjunta de Administración, *Ropa Deportiva Castellana*, Burgos
Octubre–Diciembre 1996: Prácticas laborales en el Departamento de Marketing de *Continente*, Fuencarral (Madrid)

C Información Complementaria:

Idiomas: Inglés: Dominio total, lengua escrita; uso habitual en el entorno laboral
Francés: Dominio total, hablado y escrito (madre francesa)
Informática: Destreza en el uso y aprovechamiento de recursos de informática en la empresa

Key to CV *(Spanish–English)*

Datos Personales *Personal Information*
Nombres y Apellidos First names and Surnames
Fecha de Nacimiento Date of Birth
Lugar de Nacimiento Place of Birth
Estado Civil Marital Status
Domicilio Actual Current Address
Teléfono Telephone
Datos Académicos *Academic Information*
Experiencia Profesional *Work/Professional Experience*
Información Complementaria *Additional Information*
Idiomas Language skills
Informática Computing skills

Appendix IV
Provincial telephone codes

Note: The provincial area codes are required even in local telephone calls; thus calling a Madrid number within the city requires the 91 prefix.

*Province**	*Code*	*Province*	*Code*	*Province*	*Code*	*Province*	*Code*
Álava (Alaba)	945	Albacete	967	Alicante	96	Almería	950
Asturias	98	Ávila	920	Badajoz	924	Baleares (Balears)	971
	93	Burgos	947	Cáceres	927	Cádiz	956
Cantabria	942	Castellón (Castelló)	964	Ceuta	95	Ciudad Real	926
Córdoba	957	La Coruña (A Coruña)	981	Cuenca	969	Gerona (Girona)	972
Granada	958	Guadalajara	949	Guipúzcoa (Gipuzkoa)	943	Huelva	959
Huesca	974	Jaén	953	León	987	Lérida (Lleida)	973
Lugo	982	Madrid	91	Málaga	95	Melilla	95
Murcia	968	Navarra	948	Orense (Ourense)	988	Palencia	979
Las Palmas	928	Pontevedra	986	La Rioja	941	Salamanca	923
Segovia	921	Sevilla	95	Soria	975	Tarragona	977
Tenerife	922	Teruel	978	Toledo	925	Valencia	96
Valladolid	983	Vizcaya (Bizcaia)	94				

* In the case of the following six area codes, the numbers apply to autonomous communities: Asturias, Cantabria, La Rioja, Madrid, Murcia, Navarra.

Other useful numbers

Exchange	*Number*	*Exchange*	*Number*
Directory Enquiries – Provincial/A. Community 003	003	Directory Enquiries – National	009
Directory Enquiries – International	008	Emergencies (medical)	061
Time	093	Civil Guard	062
News	095	Police	092
Weather	094	Fire brigade	080
Sports News	097		

NB In order to ring the UK from Spain, callers should now ring 00 44 followed by the required STD code, minus the 0.

Appendix V
Additional web site addresses

Specific sites

Academic Associates International: *www.aaiuk.org* (work placement programmes)
British Trust for Conservation Volunteers: *www.btcv.org.uk*
Chambers of Commerce: *www.camerdata.es/*
COIE job offers site: *www.trabajos.com/ ofertas*
Department of Social Security: *www.dss.gov.uk*
El Mundo: *www.el-mundo.es*
El País: *www.elpais.es*
European Employment Services (EURES): *http: / / europa.eu.int/ jobs/ eures* and UK site: *www.employmentservice.gov.uk*
Inland Revenue: *www.inlandrevenue.gov.uk*
Lonely Planet travel guides: *www.lonelyplanet.com/*
STA Travel (Student travel): *www.statravel.co.uk*
Teaching Abroad: *www.teaching_abroad.uk.com*
TESOL (Teaching English to Speakers of Other Languages): *www.tesol.edu/*
Vacation Work Publications: *www.vacationwork.co.uk*

Recruitment agencies

www.Infoempleo.es
www.ctv.es/ people/
www.forcem.es
http: / / nuevotrabajo.abc.es/ nuevotrabajo
www.adecco.es/ empleo/ cenempl.htm
www.ozu.es/ sui/ ozu/ bolsa_fr.cgi
www.digigrup.com/ empleo
http: / / hispavista.trabajos.com/

General sites

http://dir.yahoo.com/Regional/Countries/Spain (links to information and web sites Spain)

http://tuspain.com/ (links to information and web sites for Spain)

www.red2000.com/spain/ (information about Spain)

www.tourspain.es/ (tourist information)

http://citizens.eu.int (information on living and working in Spain)

www.sispain.com (information about Spain)

www.el-castellano.com/index.html (promotes Spanish language and contains useful information and links)

www.langre.com/cvitae (Spanish site which allows you to post your CV on the Internet)

www.spanishlanguage.co.uk (Spanish language site)

Appendix VI
Glossary of terms

albergues de la juventud (*or* **albergues juveniles**) youth hostels
alumno/a student
alumno/a de nuevo ingreso freshman; new student
alumno/a visitante visiting student
arquitecto/a architect
arquitecto/a técnico/a technical architect
asignatura (academic) subject
asignaturas de libre configuración electives (university)
asignaturas obligatorias compulsory subjects (university)
asignaturas optativas options (university)
asignaturas troncales core subjects (university)
asistencia attendance
ayuntamiento town/city hall
Bachillerato Spanish A-level equivalent
beca grant; scholarship
bolsa de trabajo employment agency
cajero automático ATM; cash dispenser
cámara de comercio, industria y navegación chamber of commerce, industry and shipping
carrera diploma/degree course
carta de presentación letter of introduction
cartilla de la Seguridad Social social security card
castellano Castilian (standard Spanish)
catedrático/a professor
centro de formación profesional vocational training centre
certificado de asistencia attendance certificate
ciclo corto short cycle (first cycle only course)
ciclo largo long cycle (two cycle course)
claustro (university) senate; (school) staff
clínicas médicas private health clinics
colegio mayor hall of residence

colegio nacional state school (centre of basic education)
colegio público state school (primary education)
colegio universitario university college
colegios concertados maintained schools
comisaría de policía police station (national police)
Congreso de los Diputados Congress of Deputies
Consejería de Educación y Ciencia (Regional) Ministry of Education and Science
consejos escolares schools councils; the governors
contrato a tiempo parcial part-time contract
contrato de trabajo employment contract
contrato en prácticas training contract
convalidación validation/recognition (academic qualifications)
Consejo de Universidades Universities' Council
cotizaciones (social security) contributions
cuatrimestre semester (four month period)
curso course; academic year
curso de español para extranjeros Spanish course for foreigners
decanato dean's office
decano dean (academic)
demandante de empleo job seeker
departamento department
diplomado/a diplomate; diploma holder
diplomatura diploma; HND-type course
diputación provincial provincial council; offices of provincial council
doctorado doctorate; PhD
educación infantil nursery/pre-school education
enseñanza(s) media(s) middle-school education
enseñanza primaria primary education
enseñanza secundaria secondary education
escuela técnica superior higher technical school
escuela universitaria university school
estudiante student
euroconsejero euroadviser
facultad faculty
formación profesional vocational training
formación del profesorado teacher training
franquicias franchises
horas de consulta times of availability (academic staff)
ideario educational ethos
ingeniero/a engineer
ingeniero/a técnico/a technical engineer
inscripción enrolment; registration
instituto (university) institute; high school
intercambio exchange (usually conversation)

jornada intensiva intensive working shift
licenciado/a BA/B.Sc./licienciate/first degree holder
licenciatura BA; B.Sc.; licenciate
maestro/a primary school teacher; teaching diploma
masificación overcrowding (of class rooms)
matrícula enrolment/registration (fee)
oferta de empleo job advertisement
oficina de alojamiento accommodation office
oficina de empleo employment office
oficina de información information office
páginas amarillas yellow pages
patronato trust; board
plan de estudios curriculum; syllabus
politécnica (=universidad politécnica) polytechnic
prestaciones (social security) benefits
primer ciclo first cycle
pruebas de aptitud para el acceso a la universidad (PAAU) university entrance examination (see also **selectividad**)
rector vice-chancellor; rector (of university)
rectorado vice-chancellor's office
segundo ciclo second cycle
secretario/a secretary
secretaría secretary's office
selectividad university entrance examination (see **PAAU**)
sociedad anónima (S.A.) public limited company (plc)
sociedad anónima liberal limited liability company
sociedad limitada limited company
solicitud application
tarjeta de residencia residence card
tarjeta de selectividad university entrance qualification card
tasas académicas tuition fees
tercer ciclo third cycle
trabajo vacante job vacancy
universidad university

Appendix VII
Lists of towns and universities

Note: In list (a) the regional language version of the town is given in brackets. In list (b), where the location of a university is not obvious from its name, the town (or towns) concerned is indicated in brackets.

(a) Towns in Spain with university/ies or major university campus(es)

Alcalá de Henares
Alicante (Alacant)
Almería
Ávila
Badajoz
Baeza
Barcelona
Bilbao (Bilbo)
Burgos
Cáceres
Cádiz
Cartagena
Castellón (Castelló) de la Plana
Ciudad Real
Córdoba
Elche (Elx)
Gerona (Girona)
Granada
Huelva
Huesca
Jaén
La Coruña (A Coruña)
La Laguna
Las Palmas de Gran Canaria
León
Lérida (Lleida)
Logroño
Madrid
Málaga
Mondragón (Arrasate)
Murcia
Orense (Ourense)
Oviedo
Palma de Mallorca
Pamplona
Pontevedra
Salamanca
San Sebastián (Donostia)
Santander
Santiago de Compostela
Segovia
Sevilla
Tarragona (Tarragones)
Toledo
Valencia
Valladolid
Vich (Vic)
Vigo
Vitoria
Zaragoza

(b) All universities in Spain (with acronyms)

(i) Public universities

Alcalá de Henares (UAH)
Alicante (Alacant) (UAL)
Almería (UALM)
Autónoma de Barcelona (UAB)
Autónoma de Madrid (UAM)
Barcelona (UB)
Burgos (UBU)
Cádiz (UCA)
Cantabria (UCN) (Santander)
Carlos III de Madrid (UCAR)
Castilla-La Mancha (UCLM) (Ciudad Real and Toledo)
Complutense de Madrid (UCM)
Córdoba (UCO)
Extremadura (UEX) (Badajoz and Cáceres)
Gerona (Girona) (UDG)
Granada (UGR)
Huelva (UHU)
Internacional de Andalucía (UIA) (Baeza, Huelva and Sevilla)
Internacional de Menéndez Pelayo (UIMP) (Santander)
Islas Baleares (Illes Baleares) (UIB) (Palma de Mallorca)
Jaén (UJA)
Jaume I de Castellón (Castelló) (UJCS)
La Coruña (UDC)
La Laguna (ULL) (Tenerife)
La Rioja (URI) (Logroño)
Las Palmas de Gran Canaria (ULPGC)
León (ULE)
Lérida (Lleida) (ULLE)
Málaga (UMA)
Miguel Hernández de Elche (UMH)
Murcia (UMU)
Nacional de Educación a Distancia (UNED) (Madrid)
Oviedo (UOV)
Pablo de Olavide (UPO) (Sevilla)
País Vasco (UPV) (Bilbao, San Sebastián and Vitoria)
Politécnica de Cartagena (UPCT)
Politécnica de Catalunya (UPC) (Barcelona)
Politécnica de Madrid (UPM)
Politécnica de Valencia (UPV)
Pompeu Fabra (UPF) (Barcelona)
Pública de Navarra (UPNA) (Pamplona)
Rey Juan Carlos (URJC) (Madrid)
Rovira i Virgili (URV) (Tarragona)
Salamanca (USA)
Santiago de Compostela (USC)
Sevilla (USE)
Valencia – Estudi General (UVEG)
Valladolid (UVA)
Vigo (UVI)
Zaragoza (UZA)

(ii) Church-owned universities

Católica 'San Antonio' de Murcia (UCAM)
Católica 'Santa Tesesa de Jesús' de Ávila (UCAV)
Deusto (UD) (Bilbao)
Navarra (UN) (Pamplona)
Pontificia de Comillas (UPCO) (Madrid)
Pontificia de Salamanca (UPSA)

(iii) Other private universities

Alfonso X El Sabio (UAX) (Madrid)
Antonio de Nebrija (UNNE) (Madrid)
Camilo José Cela (UCJC) (Madrid)
Europa de Madrid – CEES (UEM)
Internacional de Cataluña (UIC) (Barcelona)
Mondragón (MU)
Oberta de Catalunya (UOC) (Barcelona)

Ramón Llull (URL) (Barcelona)
San Pablo-CEU (CEU) (Madrid)
SEK de Segovia (USEK)
Vich (UVIC)

(c) Universities listed according to autonomous community

(*Church-owned; **Other privately-owned)

Andalucía
- Almería
- Cádiz
- Córdoba
- Granada
- Huelva
- Internacional de Andalucía
- Jaén
- Málaga
- Pablo de Olavide**
- Sevilla

Aragón
- Zaragoza

Asturias
- Oviedo

Baleares
- Islas Baleares (Illes Balears)

Canarias
- La Laguna
- Las Palmas de Gran Canaria

Cantabria
- Cantabria
- Internacional de Menéndez Pelayo

Castilla y León
- Burgos
- Católica 'Santa Teresa de Jesús' de Ávila*
- León
- Pontificia de Salamanca*
- Salamanca
- SEK de Segovia**
- Valladolid

Castilla-La Mancha
- Castilla-La Mancha

Cataluña (Catalunya)
- Autónoma de Barcelona
- Barcelona
- Gerona (Girona)
- Internacional de Cataluña**
- Lérida (Lleida)
- Politécnica de Catalunya
- Pompeu Fabra
- Oberta de Catalunya**
- Ramón Llull**
- Rovira i Virgili
- Vich (Vic)**

Comunidad Valenciana
- Alicante (Alacant)
- Jaume I de Castellón (Castelló)
- Miguel Hernández de Elche
- Politécnica de Valencia
- Valencia – Estudi General

País Vasco (Euskadi)
- Deusto*
- Mondragón**
- País Vasco

Extremadura
- Extremadura

Galicia
- La Coruña (A Coruña)
- Santiago de Compostela
- Vigo

La Rioja
- La Rioja

Madrid
- Alcalá de Henares
- Alfonso X El Sabio**
- Antonio de Nebrija**
- Autónoma de Madrid

Camilo José Cela**
Carlos III de Madrid
Complutense de Madrid
Europea (CEES) de Madrid
Nacional de Educación a Distancia
Politécnica de Madrid
Pontificia de Comillas*
Rey Juan Carlos
San Pablo-CEU**

Murcia
- Católica 'San Antonio' de Murcia*
- Murcia
- Politécnica de Cartagena

Navarra
- Navarra*
- Pública de Navarra

Bibliography

Contemporary Spain

Anuario El País (annual).
Brooksbank-Jones, A. (1997), *Women in contemporary Spain*, Manchester University Press.
Edles, L. D. (1998), *Symbol and ritual in the new Spain: the transition to democracy after Franco*, Cambridge University Press.
Elms, R. (1994), *Spain: a portrait after the general*, Mandarin,
Europa World Yearbook, volume 2: Spain (annual), Europa
Gies, D. T. (ed.) (1999), *The Cambridge companion to modern Spanish culture*, Cambridge University Press.
Gillespie, R., F. Rodrigo and J. Story (1995), *Democratic Spain*, Routledge.
Graham, H. and J. Labanyi (eds) (1995), *Spanish cultural studies: an introduction: the struggle for modernity*, Oxford University Press.
Heywood, P. (1995), *The government and politics of Spain*, Macmillan.
Hooper, J. (1995), *The new Spaniards*, Penguin.
Jordan, B. and R. Morgan-Tamosunas (eds) (2000), *Contemporary Spanish cultural studies*, Arnold.
Lalaguna, J. (1990), *A traveller's history of Spain*, Windrush.
Lawlor, T. and M. Rigby (1998), *Contemporary Spain: essays and texts on politics, economics, education and employment, and society*, Longman.
Newton, M. T. (1997), *Institutions of Modern Spain*, Cambridge University Press.
Preston, P. (1986), *The triumph of democracy in Spain*, Methuen.
Rodgers, E. (ed.) (1999), *Encyclopedia of contemporary Spanish culture*, Routledge.
Ross, C. J. (1997), *Contemporary Spain: a handbook*, Arnold.
Salmon, K. (1995), *The modern Spanish economy*, Pinter.
Shields, G. J. (1994), *Spain: a selected and annotated bibliography*, 2nd edn., Clio Press.
Smith, P. J. (2000), *The moderns: time, space, and subjectivity in contemporary Spanish culture*, Oxford University Press.
Truscott, S. and M. García (1998), *A dictionary of contemporary Spain*, Hodder & Stoughton.

Travel guides

Ellingham, M. and J. Fisher (1999), *Spain: the rough guide*, 8th edn., The Rough Guides.
Fodor's 2001 Spain (2000), Fodor.
Gilmour, D. (1992), *Cities of Spain*, John Murray.
Guía Shell del viajero: España, Portugal (1998), Plaza and Janés.
Simonis, D. *et al.* (1999), *Lonely planet: Spain*, 2nd edn., Lonely Planet Books.
Spain and Portugal 2001 (2001), Michelin.

Spanish education system

Eurydice database: *www.eurydice.org* (EU database of information relating to policies and organisation of primary/secondary/tertiary education in member states).
McNair, J. and J. Beattie (1991), *Education for the new Spain*, University of Liverpool, Centre for Community and Educational Policy Studies.
World of learning (annual), Europa.

Studying in Spain

Parker, G. and A. Rouxeville (eds) (1995), *The year abroad: preparation, monitoring, evaluation*, CILT.

Living and working in Spain

Adventure holidays (annual), Vacation Work.
AGCAS (annual), *Working in Europe: first steps*, CSU.
Archer, W. H. and A. J. Raban (1995), *Working in the European Union: a guide for graduate recruiters and job-seekers*, 4th edn., Hobsons Publishing.
A year between (annual), Central Bureau for International Education and Training.
A year off ... a year on? (annual), Biblios.
Benn's Media Directory, volume 2: Europe (2000), United Business Media Information Services.
Bird, P. (2000), *Taking a year out: making the most of your gap year*, 2nd edn., Hodder & Stoughton Educational.
Campos de trabajo (2000), Instituto de la Juventud.
Casas, P. (1996), *Discovering Spain: an uncommon guide*, Alfred A. Knopf.
EL Gazette (monthly), EL.
English language teaching guide (2000), EFL.
Gap year guidebook (annual), Peridot Press.
Griffith, S. and S. Legg (1997), *The au pair and nanny's guide to working abroad*, 3rd edn., Vacation Work.

Guía de las empresas que ofrecen empleo: España y Portugal (annual), Fundación Universidad-Empresa.
Guía práctica para trabajadores extranjeros en España (annual), Ministerio de Trabajo y Asuntos Sociales (also available from Canning House Library).
Guide to languages and careers (1997), CILT.
Hampshire, D. (2000), *Living and working in Spain*, 3rd edn., Survival Books.
Hempshell, M. (1995), *How to get a job in Europe*, 3rd edn., How to Books.
International directory of voluntary work (2000), Vacation Work.
International youth hostel handbook (annual), YHA Services.
Johnson, P. (1998), *Teaching English in Spain*, In Print Publishing.
Marvin, G. (1990), *Coping with Spain*, Blackwell.
Packer, J. (1998), *Live and work in Spain and Portugal*, Vacation Work.
Richards, R. (1992), *How to live and work in Spain*, How to Books.
Roberts, E. (2000), *The directory of jobs and careers abroad*, 10th edn., Vacation Work.
Settling in Spain (annual), British Embassy.
Social security abroad (annual), Department of Social Security.
Spain: a guide to work opportunities for young people (2000), Canning House.
Summer jobs abroad (annual), Vacation Work.
Teaching English abroad (2000), 5th edn., Vacation Work.
Teaching English as a foreign language and teaching abroad (2000), AGCAS.
Teaching overseas (annual), British Council.
Volunteer work (2000), Central Bureau for Educational Visits and Exchanges.
Work and study abroad (annual), CIEE.
Willings Press Guide 2001 (2001), 127th edn., Hollis Directories.
Work your way around the world (annual), Vacation Work.
Workcamp organisers (2000), UNESCO: Co-ordinating Committee for International Voluntary Service.
Working for charities (annual), Charity Appointments.
Working holidays (annual), Central Bureau for International Education and Training (formerly Central Bureau for Educational Visits and Exchanges).
Working in ski resorts: Europe and North America (annual), Vacation Work.
Working in tourism: the UK, Europe and beyond (annual), Vacation Work.
Working with the environment (annual), Vacation Work.

Classic travellers' accounts

Borrow, G. (1985), *The Bible in Spain*, Century.
Brenan, G. (1987), *The face of Spain*, Penguin.
Brenan, G. (1981), *South from Granada*, Cambridge University Press.
Chetwode, P. (1985), *Two middle-ages ladies in Andalusia*, Century.
Ford, R. (1966), *A hand-book for travellers in Spain*..., Centaur Press.
Hopkins, A. (1993), *Spanish journeys: a portrait of Spain*, Penguin.
Lapierre, D. and L. Collins (1988), *Or I'll dress you in mourning*, Weidenfeld & Nicolson.

Lee, L. (1971), *A rose for winter: travels in Andalusia*, Penguin.
Lee, L. (1971), *As I walked out one midsummer morning*, Penguin.
Michener, J. (1983), *Iberia: Spanish travels and reflections*, Fawcett.
Morris, J. (1988), *Spain*, Barrie and Jenkins.
Pritchett, V. S. (1984), *The Spanish temper*, Hogarth.
Richardson, P. (1998), *Our Lady of the Sewers*, Abacus.
Stewart, C. (1999), *Driving over lemons: an optimist in Andalucía*, Sort of Books.
St Jorre, J. de (1990), *The insider's guide to Spain*, Moorland.

Index